AF572146

HOW TO BUY OR SELL THE CLOSELY HELD CORPORATION

LAWRENCE C. SILTON

PRENTICE HALL
Englewood Cliffs, New Jersey 07632

Prentice-Hall International, Inc., *London*
Prentice-Hall of Australia, Pty. Ltd., *Sydney*
Prentice-Hall Canada, Inc., *Toronto*
Prentice-Hall of India Private Ltd., *New Delhi*
Prentice-Hall of Japan, Inc., *Tokyo*
Prentice-Hall of Southeast Asia Pte. Ltd., *Singapore*
Editora Prentice-Hall do Brasil Ltda., *Rio de Janeiro*
Prentice-Hall Hispanoamericana, S.A., *Mexico*

Library of Congress Cataloging-in-Publication Data

Silton, Lawrence C.
How to buy or sell the closely held corporation.

Includes index.
1. Close corporations—Valuation. 2. Close corporations—Taxation—United States. 3. Close corporations—United States. I. Title.
HG4028.V3S54 1987 658.1′6 87-14433

ISBN 0-13-403064-8

Printed in the United States of America

DEDICATION

To my parents, who have played such an important role in my life.

ACKNOWLEDGMENT

I would like to acknowledge the active assistance of my wife, and the moral support of my children and our dog Frisky, who tolerated my moods during the period of writing this book and through the many changes in the tax law.

WHAT THIS BOOK WILL DO FOR YOU

Without the proper background, the sale of a business can be a frustrating, fruitless, and intimidating proposition. The process, unlike many of the other exercises that we encounter in our daily lives, is rarely repetitive. It is the unusual and fortunate individual who will sell more than one business during his business life. Accordingly, when we approach the sale of the business, we immediately encounter problems that we have not yet dealt with in our business lives. If not for the possibility of the sale, we probably would never consider the following questions:

- What is the business worth?
- Who are the potential buyers?
- Should we sell the assets or the stock?
- If we sell with a purchase money interest, what is the appropriate security?

Each of these questions must be asked and the appropriate answers received before it will be possible to successfully market the business. This book will take you from the beginning to the end of the sale. While it will not make you an expert on all facets of the sale process, it will keep you aware of each and every step and will provide you with intelligent questions to ask. It will also ensure that most of the problems that could impede the sale have been considered, and appropriate answers arrived at even before the sale process begins.

Anyone who has gone through the sale of a business realizes that it requires a strong captain at the helm of the ship; and the only person who can be the captain is the individual owner of the business. Unless he knows the problems, pitfalls, and guideposts, he will not be able to use his personnel correctly, and there will be a lot of "spinning of wheels" and "unproductive effort expended" on his behalf. Intelligent directions by the captain/owner increase the productivity of the team members and accordingly increase the chance for success. Improper or misguided directions can result in nonproductive expenditure of time and effort and can result in extremely high attorneys' and accountants' bills without the commensurate success of the sale of the business at the highest price.

While each business is unique and presents its own problems and opportunities, this book will serve as a general guide from beginning to end. It will show you

1. how to recognize when it is an appropriate time to sell. Even if you consider that it is the right time to sell, the extrinsic and intrinsic factors must be weighed before any decision is made.
2. how to analyze the strengths and weaknesses of your business.
3. how to arrive at the appropriate value of the business so that you can market it successfully. Determining the value of the business is like asking a parent about his children; self-analysis is rarely objective.
4. how to decide who should market the corporation. There are three different and distinct parties to consider: the owner, the business broker, or the business real estate broker.
5. how to disseminate the type of information that will help attract buyers who are interested and can afford to purchase. Not only must you find them, but you must approach them correctly. An improper approach can turn off even the best of sales prospects.
6. how to determine the terms of sale. As the selling shareholder, if you proceed correctly, you will get the first opportunity to present your side as to terms and conditions. The basic terms and conditions are simple. They involve the PSTT concept—Price, Security, Terms, and Taxes. Do not be intimidated.
7. how to approach the final two steps: the preparation of a signed letter of intent, followed by a comprehensive sales agreement.
8. how to differentiate between the basic terms (PSTT concept) and necessary boilerplate; and how to use the letter of intent and sales contract and what are the terms and conditions of each.

The process itself is not complicated; however, if the steps are not taken in the proper order, they can lead to failure. With the proper knowledge, the process to be followed is relatively simple and clear-cut.

While this book attacks the problem of the sale of a business from the prospective of the selling shareholder, it can be used successfully by any individual interested in buying a corporation. Many closely held corporations or individuals, from time to time, may acquire a business. In this acquisition process, they may meet with the unsophisticated seller, the unscrupulous seller, or the highly sophisticated seller. In any of these three cases, the purchaser must be aware of the various steps in the sales process, and anticipate and plan for each in order to purchase the business on acceptable terms and conditions.

Accordingly, this book can be used by anyone who owns a closely held corporation, contemplates the purchase or sale of a business, or is the attorney or accountant advising the purchaser or seller. After reading this book you will be aware that, while the sale of a business is an art and not a science, knowing the sales process will increase your chance for a successful transaction and give you the best opportunity to maximize your after-tax proceeds on the sale of the corporation with specific reference to the problems and planning opportunities created by the Tax Reform Act of 1986.

CONTENTS

SECTION 1

THE MIND-SET OF THE BUYER OR SELLER OF A SMALL CORPORATION

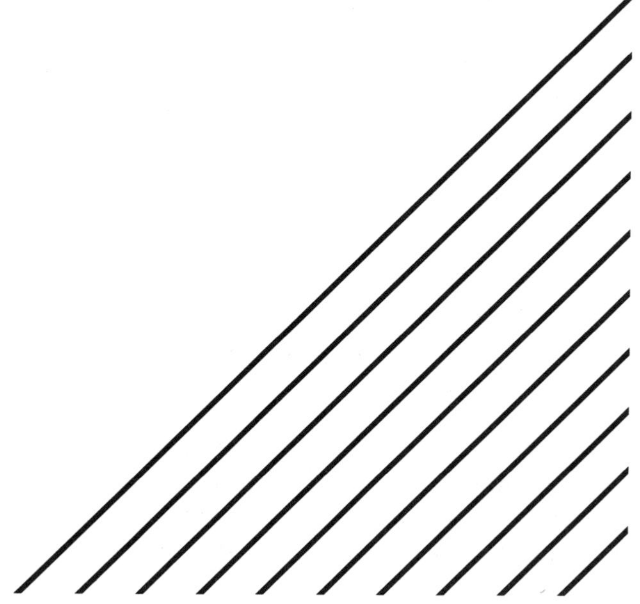

As a seller, you have within your grasp the ability to sell your corporation at any time.

Example: A client of mine coveted a particular business for many years. He was more than willing to pay the price; however, the seller was not going to sell because of his hope to "retain it in the family." It was only when the last of the owner's many children went to medical school and he suffered some physical setbacks that the business became available for purchase.

You, the seller, normally control your own destiny. It is up to you to decide

a. when to sell;

b. what the asking price should be; and

c. whether or not you should sell for cash or on terms.

You are the prime mover and if you do your homework and take the proper steps, you can successfully guide the sales process from its inception to its completion.

Five Steps to a Successful Sale

The successful sale of a business will include taking the following steps:

1. analyzing your reasons for sale—developing the proper mind-set
2. recognizing an appropriate time to sell
3. valuing your business
4. developing a marketing strategy
5. structuring the sale

While there are factors beyond the control of either party that might prevent the sale of the business, there are steps that can be taken to ensure that there is a maximum chance for success. These include making the appropriate legal and financial decisions as well as developing the proper mind-set. Before attempting any sale, be introspective and determine your exact motivations for selling. It is extremely important to be objective at all times during the sales process. Normally, the owner of a small business will be emotionally involved with his business and it is imperative that he be able to separate his subjective feelings from the need for objective decisions. A good deal of soul searching and self-analysis at the beginning will save aggravation and expense throughout the sale process.

Key Idea: Before an owner of a business should consider selling, he should analyze his own personal motivations. Some of the common reasons for a sale of a business are

1. need to expand the business but lacking the financial means to accomplish it alone
2. owners and upper management are older and no replacements have been forthcoming within the family
3. change in the business environment with the owners being unable or unwilling to change with the times
4. internal strife between the individual owners has made the successful continuation of the business difficult, if not impossible
5. the owners are tired. They find that the operation of the business that was once challenging and fun, is now drudgery.

WHEN THE BUYER CAN INITIATE THE SALES PROCESS

If there is an educated seller who knows where he was, where he is, and where he wants to be, the potential buyer will normally be the one who responds to his overtures. The purchaser is usually at a disadvantage because the parameters have already been established. For example, the initial determination as to whether the business is for sale is only in the hands of the seller. The establishment of the offering price, how it is to be paid, and what security is to be requested is usually proposed by the seller. The potential buyer can only respond to these overtures. This, however, should not be construed to mean that the buyer is solely at the mercy of forces beyond his control. At times, the buyer may be the prime mover and make an impossible sale possible.

The following are situations where the buyer may be able to initiate the sales process:

1. the buyer is an employee of the corporation
2. the buyer and seller are related and the buyer knows of one of the following personal reasons that may dictate the sale of a business:
   a. there is internal feuding.
   b. the seller is getting old.
   c. the seller is not physically well.
   d. there are other family problems that may dictate the sale, the most common of which is the need for money.
   e. The seller is concerned about the future of the business.
3. the potential buyer has worked with the seller in various civic ventures and, although they are competitors, he has a personal relationship with him

The following example will illustrate how the potential buyer takes advantage of his relationship to purchase the business.

Example: An employee of a veterinary practice, on being hired, was told by the owner of the practice that if everything worked out he would give him the opportunity to purchase the practice. There was no firm commitment, only a statement of general intent. The employee came to my office and requested help in structuring an offer to purchase. Before my client was employed, the practice had been extremely run down. My client was extremely conscientious and his productivity increased the profitability and resulting asking price of the business. Correspondingly, his ability to purchase was virtually being decreased daily. Theoretically, the business at that particular time was not even for sale. This was the first hurdle that had to be overcome. The second hurdle, and the one that proved the most difficult, was the historical method of valuing veterinary practices (one times gross fees). This valuation method was no longer indicative of the fair market value of these practices. The historical method had been developed at a time when there were fewer veterinarians and the competition was not as great.[1]

---

[1]The problem of a historical method not being indicative of the true value of a business is prevalent in many areas, not only in valuing veterinary practices. One area in which historical methods seem to be particularly inappropriate is in valuing independent insurance agencies. Independent insurance agencies have historically sold at between one and one-half and two and one-half times the net premium to the agency. The change in the industry has caused a decline in the cost of insurance (per dollar). In addition, the commission dollar has decreased because insurance companies have reduced the portion of premiums payable to the agency. These factors have completely upset the prior valuation structure.

Accordingly, the ability of the young veterinarian to purchase this practice on its face appeared hopeless. The seller really was not of a mind to sell, and even if he was interested in selling, the traditional methods of valuing the practice would have placed the purchase price beyond the reach of the young veterinarian who had little, if any, capital.

In this case, logic and morality were the keys to success. The offer submitted allocated all the net current income of the practice for the next ten years to the seller as payment of the purchase price. For this purpose, "net current income" was defined as the total gross sales less current expenses and a reasonable salary for the veterinarian. My client pledged this future income to consummate the sale. Accordingly, a price was determined and a payment structure was established. Security was at best dubious, as it amounted to a pledge of intangible assets and the personal guarantee of a veterinarian who had little net worth. However, this appealed to the seller's logic and feeling of moral responsibility. Logically, the young veterinarian had agreed to pay all that he could. The seller felt a moral responsibility to satisfy the obligation he had verbally made in order to secure the buyer as an employee.

The above example shows that while the seller is normally in control, in some cases the buyer can take advantage of his relationship with the seller to initiate and direct the sale process. Obviously the young veterinarian did not dictate the terms of the sale. However, he used his position to help structure a sale that under normal circumstances probably could not have taken place. Normally, the buyer will be able to help structure the sale only when he has an established relationship with the seller. Aside from being a relative, employee, minority shareholder, or friend of the owner, the buyer could also have an established business relationship with the seller. This would give him inside financial information as well as easy access to the confidence of the seller. When a buyer has what can be classified as an insider's knowledge, he should initiate the proceedings in such a way that he can take advantage of this relationship for his benefit.

HOW YOU CAN ANALYZE THE OTHER PARTY'S OBJECTIVES

Whether you are the seller or the potential buyer of a business, it is absolutely imperative that, during every step of the sales process, you keep not only your objectives in mind, but also try to put yourself in the other person's shoes. The reason this becomes particularly significant is that it allows you to focus on the other party's weaknesses and overcome his strengths in order to obtain your goals.

Example: Max owns XYZ Corporation, a successful distributor of widgets. The company lacks middle management and Max, who has been ill, believes that, on his death or complete disability, the company will no longer be profitable. A large portion of Max's assets are invested in XYZ Corporation as well as in the building (owned individually) that is leased to XYZ. Armed with this information, a potential purchaser can stress financial security to Max. He will point out that on his death, XYZ Corporation's value will drop about fifty percent. The current purchase can provide security to Max and his family now. This reasoning probably can secure a lower price and more favorable terms because the purchaser has focused on Max's fears and desires.

The Three All-Important Questions That Buyers and Sellers Should Ask

The questions you should ask yourself involve not only *your* needs, desires, and motivations, but also the other party's, and should include such questions as:

1. Why are you buying or selling the business? Are the owners of the business approaching retirement and have no successors been found? Are you purchasing the business to eliminate a troublesome competitor or to open up new markets? Does the purchase allow your salesman to sell additional products?
2. What alternatives are available for both you and the other party? For example, if you are the only buyer and if you do not buy, can he liquidate? If you are the buyer and he does not sell, can you establish a competing business? If so, what would the cost be and how much time would be lost?
3. What, exactly, are you buying or selling; hard assets, soft assets, income potential, new markets, or eliminating a competitor?

These considerations as well as many others must always be kept in the forefront. It is easy to lose perspective in the sales process. It is also easy to become myopic and focus only on one portion of the sale.

Why Price Is Such a Problem

The most common problem area appears to be price. Realistically, if you are the buyer, do you care that you are paying an inflated price if you can purchase the business on your terms? If you are the seller, what good is it to sell the business at an inflated price if you do not obtain proper security from the buyer to ensure payment of this purchase price? Purchase price or any other area of controversy is relative. Remember, certain businesses can be worth more to one individual than to another. Some businesses are worthless except to one person.

Eleven Reasons for Selling a Business

The following is a short list of the motivating factors that may prompt the owner to consider a sale of his business.

1. age
2. health
3. personal needs to convert "value" into "cash"
4. wish to capitalize on prior success
5. tired of "fighting the wars"
6. disappointment in his family's failure to follow in his footsteps and failure of succession of management within the family
7. not enough leisure time
8. no desire to put additional funds into business
9. management too thin to cover the operation of the business
10. need to change business operations to accommodate changes in economy and industry
11. internal feuding

Seven Reasons for Buying a Business

The following short list enumerates goals and desires of the buyer.

1. eliminate a competitor
2. provide for diversification of business (either horizontally or vertically)
3. provide a new sales network
4. provide additional products for sale by the existing sales network
5. provide for expansion into new geographic or market areas
6. provide for business opportunities for family members

7. ego reasons, some of which are almost impossible to determine, but may play an important role

"To Thine Own Self Be True"

In the sales process, you as the owner of the business are never objective. You may be too critical and see all the problems, real or imagined. More than likely, however, your vision of the business is unrealistically rosy and you do not see any of the problems.

The next chapter will examine the problem from both the business and personal sides, and help you determine when it is the correct time to attempt to sell your business. It will show how to take the first steps in the sales process.

ANALYZING YOUR COMPANY BEFORE YOU SELL

The sales process requires introspective analysis at every step. It is absolutely imperative, before you become involved in the sale process, to analyze your reasons for selling if you are the seller, or to understand the reasons that the business is being sold if you are the buyer. In all cases, it requires you to disassociate your feelings from the judgments that will be made throughout the sales process. It is one of the most difficult tasks you will face during the entire sales process.

One of the most complex problems, but not the only one, will be evaluating the business and establishing a sales price. The outside world will value your business from a viewpoint that is different from yours; the outsider's viewpoint is not influenced by your personal prejudices. It is important to understand the reasons for this lack of objectivity so that you become aware of your innate prejudices.

Businesses that are going to be sold usually have several characteristics in common:

1. They have been in the family for a long time.

2. They have been incorporated and have at one time or another been successful. There are two major categories of reasons for incorporating—tax and nontax. Virtually all businesses, especially in the service area, that have been incorporated in the last fifteen years, have been incorporated for tax reasons. (See pages 101 through 113 of *Taking Cash Out of a Closely-Held Corporation* published by Institute of Business Planning by Lawrence C. Silton.) Accordingly, while not

all successful businesses are corporations, the tax advantages usually dictate incorporation at an early stage.

3. They have provided a fairly comfortable living for the owner and have possibly supported additional family members. In addition to the material gratification that the business has given you, it has also provided you with emotional strokes. You have been in authority. Decisions have been made by you and now you are at a point where your success is being valued.

Example: I recently visited a client and found that he ran his business with Stone Age equipment. In comparison to a modern office complete with computerized word processing, sophisticated dictation and duplication equipment and systemized phone systems, he still had a dial telephone and electric typewriter. It became difficult to imagine how this business generated over $250,000 a year in net after-tax income plus a substantial salary to him. When we started to discuss a sale, I realized that this business had produced a living for several generations of this family, and would be extremely difficult to value and sell because of the owner's attachment to the business.

Accordingly, the first step was to try and disassociate his emotions and feelings from the real worth of the business. It became imperative to show him that while in the past he had been operating with minimum overhead, virtually all of the potential purchasers would require a substantially greater investment in equipment. The potential purchasers were divided into two categories—competitors, and customers who purchased the business's products. In either case, an economical acquisition would require that the premises be abandoned and consolidated with the purchaser's other business. Therefore, it would not be possible to operate with the minimum overhead as was done in the past. The $250,000 net income would have to be discounted before the appropriate earnings could be determined. It was decided to proceed with a more realistic price that could be justified by the past earnings of the business after discounting the price because of the capital expenditures that would be needed by the purchaser. The seller's mind-set from the very beginning was attuned to the problems of the buyer. He had to be educated in valuing his business from the buyer's as well as the seller's perspective.

Key Idea: It is extremely important at the outset of the sales process to change your mind set from an emotional feeling of attachment to an objective appraisal of what you have to sell.

WHEN TO SELL—TIMING IS THE KEY

The largest single factor in buying and selling a business is beyond your control; it involves luck or fate. Anyone who is attempting to buy or sell a business will tell you that timing is the key. The following example will illustrate how frustrating attempts sometimes give rise to success when the time is right.

Example: XYZ and Building Corporation manufactured products used in construction. Their merger would be a perfect match. XYZ was owned by Joe Smith and John Jones. Joe was the chief operating officer, and John, at least to the outside world, was nothing more than a silent partner. The business faced numerous obstacles from its inception. It was undercapitalized, lacked middle management, and had no unified cohesive marketing system. Building Corporation had approached Joe and John a number of times and asked to purchase the business. XYZ Company's products could easily be added to the product line of Building Corporation. Building Corporation was financially sound and, therefore, could add the financial stability that was sorely lacking at XYZ. Building Corporation had excess manufacturing capacity and a sophisticated marketing staff that could incorporate the additional product line at virtually no cost.

The problem from the beginning was not whether XYZ Company was for sale, but how Joe Smith and John Jones could ever decide what they wanted. Building Corporation approached XYZ Company three times over a period of four years. Each time, Building Corporation requested a D & B (Dunn and Bradstreet Report) for XYZ Company. Each time, the D & B came back showing that they were farther behind in making payments to their creditors. For the first three years, the overtures met with polite response, but no action. During the fourth year, Joe purchased John's stock. This proved to be the final blow. Unbeknownst to Building Corporation and the outside world, John had been the stabilizing force of the twosome. It may have appeared to the outside world that he did not contribute; however, he was the person who, behind the scenes, added stability and guidance. Without this stability, Joe was emotionally drained. Just before the fourth and successful attempt to purchase the business, a D & B again was requested and this time the corporation was in its best financial condition. This fourth attempt should also have failed; however, the added emotional strain made the time right to sell.

The above example illustrates that unless the time is right, any attempt to buy may lead to nothing more than frustration. Proper timing is dependent on two separate and distinct factors—personal reasons and proper planning considerations. These are discussed in Section 2.

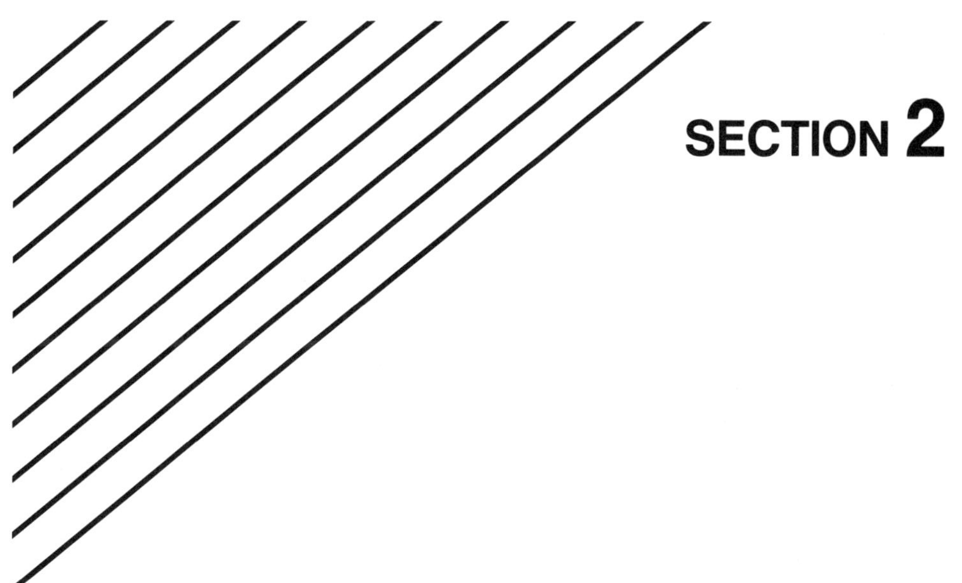

SECTION 2

HOW TO RECOGNIZE THE RIGHT TIME TO SELL A BUSINESS

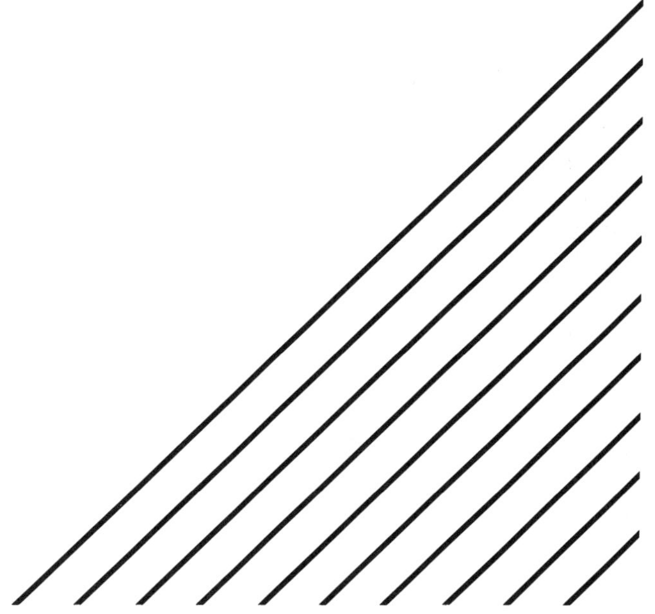

This section will help you determine when it is the correct time to attempt to sell your business. You will learn how to carefully analyze both the business and the personal factors that go into this decision. You will see how to formulate plans to take the first steps in the sales process.

HOW TO DETERMINE THE RIGHT TIME TO SELL

Businesses follow an earnings curve. The factors that affect these curves are both intrinsic and extrinsic. The growth of the business may be limited by both personal and business factors. The personal factors can include limitations on expansion because of the individual's desires not to expand the business. For example, you may have a successful business within a particular community. The natural move would be to establish a new outlet in the neighboring community. The owners may be personally satisfied with their current success without establishing an additional outlet. The age and health of the individuals may also be factors.

As far as the business factors are concerned, the marketplace itself may limit the amount of expansion. Future growth may also be limited by the productivity of the plant, the sales force, or the need for capital to expand into other products or geographical areas. A competitor may have established a business and this could adversely affect the future growth. These and many other factors will have an effect on the earnings curve. If you look at the factors that affect the curves, you may be able to compare the business that you are dealing with to one or a variation of one of these curves:

Nobody can predict with a great deal of certainty what is going to happen. Accordingly, when valuing a business (see Chapter 3 for a detailed discussion), the future earnings potential is based on the prior years' earnings. It is best to sell your business when it is near the top of the earnings curve. There are two sets of factors that will determine exactly where your business is on this curve: the intrinsic and the extrinsic.

How Do the Intrinsic Factors Affect the Earnings Curve?

In the sales process, timing is subject to intrinsic and extrinsic factors. The intrinsic factors are those that help determine when the business will attain a profit plateau internally or reach its full potential. Virtually all businesses will, if they increase in size, reach a time when they can only increase their sales and/or profits through expansion of plant, equipment, personnel, or through research and development. If you are in a service business, you may need to open up a new office before you can increase your sales. If you operate a manufacturing plant, it may be that you are at the maximum production level where expansion is impossible without additional equipment and/or a plant. It is necessary and appropriate in these cases to analyze these intrinsic factors and to determine their impact on the corporation.

Key Idea: It is important to analyze the intrinsic factors of the business to determine when it is at its maximum profitability without the need for additional expenditure of funds for expansion.

How to Determine the Extrinsic Factors and What Effect They Have on the Earnings Curve

The extrinsic factors are those that are prevalent in the industry and general economy. Some of these factors are

1. the general status of the economy. Is it booming? Is it in the doldrums? Is it declining through a recession or depression?
2. the individual segment of the economy. For example, even though the economy itself may be booming, certain segments always lag behind. Currently, a perfect example of this is the agricultural portion of our economy.
3. the geographic region may also have an effect. Recently the South has been growing rapidly and certain segments of even a

depressed economy may be doing better in the South than in the Midwest or Northeast.

Communities throughout Wisconsin are dairy and farm dependent. The extrinsic factors have an inordinate impact on those manufacturing companies supplying these industries. Because of the depressed farming economy, it has been virtually impossible to sell any of these ancillary businesses. The reason for this is obvious. The capacity of all farm suppliers is at least twice the actual current demand. Accordingly, the oversupply has reduced profitability in most cases and eliminated it in others. Notwithstanding this negative environment, several companies are particularly well situated within the agricultural manufacturing community and have remained profitable. However, even if an attempt to sell any of these businesses during these depressed times was successful, the business would realize only a fraction of its true worth.

In analyzing the appropriate factors, it is important to realize that the intrinsic and extrinsic factors are the objective economic factors that help determine the correct time to sell. The time to sell the business often will be dictated by events that are beyond your control.

Key Idea: Before determining whether or not it is the appropriate time to sell, it is important to analyze the individual business's niche in the general economy and to determine how the investing community values this segment of the economy.

Key Idea: The optimal time to sell a business is at the top of its earnings curve without the need to invest in additional plant, equipment, or personnel and to correlate these intrinsic factors with the high earnings curve prevalent in its segment of the economy. A perfect example of this would be to attempt to sell a high tech business at the peak of its intrinsic earnings curve and at a time that high tech industries are selling at inflated prices. The worst time to sell is on the downside of its earnings curve during a period when its segment of the economy is depressed. A perfect example of the worst time to sell would be to attempt to sell an agriculturally dependent business at the current time.

UNDERSTANDING WHY THE SALES OF MANY BUSINESSES ARE NOT PLANNED

In analyzing the appropriate factors, it is important to realize that the intrinsic and extrinsic factors are the objective economic factors that help determine the correct time to sell. The time to sell the business often will be dictated by events that are beyond your control.

A business may be offered for sale at a seemingly inopportune time for personal reasons. The analysis of this business's extrinsic and intrinsic factors, along with an analysis of the projected earnings curve indicate that the time is not right to sell. Obviously, when this is the case, there are other factors that dictate when the sale is to occur. It could be that the business is being offered for sale because the owner has become seriously ill and the remainder of the family no longer has interest in continuing the business. In this case, the owners should realize that in all likelihood it will not yield its true fair market value. Two other reasons that businesses are put up for sale at an inopportune time are a need for additional capital and a need for increased time commitment.

The earnings curve may have reached a plateau, and the business would need a substantial investment in additional capital to increase sales and profits. The owners may be unable or unwilling to make this additional commitment. Accordingly, the business may be sold at a time that will not yield its true fair market value. A full discussion of other factors that dictate the time of sale follows.

1. Internal Feuding Can Cause the Sale at an Inopportune Time

To be really successful, most businesses require input from the salesman, the financial person, and the plant manager. Generally, these roles are filled by three people; sometimes one person can serve in more than one capacity. When there are three separate people, one occupying each role, one or more may feel that the other members are not pulling their load. This can mean intrusion in the other person's particular segment of the business, disdain for the efforts of the other members' contributions, and other feelings that can cause friction and lead to feuding. When the owners of a business are feuding, they become more concerned about their individual problems and less attuned to the profitability of the business. A study by the *Wall Street Journal* indicates that over eighty percent of all small businesses are involved in material feuding. Accordingly, this can cause the business to be sold when other factors would indicate that the time is not right.

2. Other Factors that Can Cause a Sale at an Inopportune Time

An additional factor that sometimes poses problems concerns the differences in the owners' ages. Even if the principals are healthy, they may be more attuned to sell as they get older. Illness could also cause a business to be sold at a time that may not be appropriate.

Some people who have very successfully run businesses are not attuned to the changes in the industry. For example, if business had been operated through independent sales representatives and now requires employed salesmen, this seemingly small change in operation may not be readily acceptable to the owners. They may look for a way out.

It is amazing how many businesses are sold because the principals are just tired. Running a small business, contrary to all the favorable publicity that the entrepreneurial spirit has received, is tough work. When a business is suffering, its problems wear down the owners. If you ask them to be introspective (see Chapter 1), they may find it extremely difficult to articulate their motivation. However, if confronted, they may readily admit to the fact that they are just tired of fighting the battle.

There are always other personal reasons that will prompt a sale. These include divorce, emotional problems, and so on.

CLASSIFY AND ANTICIPATE YOUR BUSINESS' POTENTIAL

Basically the business community is divided into three separate and distinct classifications:

1. manufacturing,
2. merchandising, and
3. service.

While no two businesses are exactly the same, the business that is subject to sale will usually fall into one or more of these categories. The categories are not exclusive and many conglomerates occupy all three categories.

If the business being sold can be classified, it will be possible to analyze the valuation, sales, and security problems inherent in the specific group. For example, if you are dealing with a manufacturing corporation, you are dealing with a capital intensive business.

Selling a Manufacturing Business

In selling a manufacturing business, a value is arrived at through the tried and true historical procedure of determining adjusted book value and the appropriate price earnings ratio. Because of the current low price earnings ratios of these businesses, the actual determination of value may be substantially less than its true value and should serve only as a guideline.

Once you have arrived at this point, analyze the potential purchaser's mind-set as his alternatives are defined: to buy your business, to buy a competitor's business, to start a new business, or to do nothing and maintain the status quo.

It should be relatively simple for you to put yourself in his shoes and analyze how much it would cost for him to start a competing business. You could determine the amount of equipment, inventory, receivables, and other start-up costs needed. Assuming that all these costs were $1 million, how much more would the potential purchaser be willing to pay for a growing business with established sales but without all the initial problems? If, in addition to the above factors, you could insert into this equation the intangibles inherent in a new business (unforeseen start-up problems, hiring personnel, establishing credit, and so on), a realistic price could be determined. This price will in all likelihood be substantially greater than that determined by historical methods.

Example: XYZ is anticipating expanding its business into the Southwest from its central location in the Midwest. Its basic business is in steel and aluminum fabrication. Business has been lost because of the transportation costs from its manufacturing base in the Midwest to the customer. This has placed XYZ at a competitive disadvantage. The cost of plant and equipment have been ascertained at $1 million. With proper amortization of the debt, it has been estimated that this plant will have to generate $2.5 million in additional sales each year to break even. There is an aluminum and steel manufacturing business available for sale. Its current annual sales are $1.5 million. If the purchase price is less than $2 million, the purchase of this business will probably be contemplated rather than the establishment of a new plant.

The moral, if there is one, is that in selling manufacturing companies in today's marketplace, it may be difficult to justify the true value of the business as the value has generally declined. The return on investment is usually substantially less than that which can be obtained in service and merchandising corporations. The most common method used to value any business is a multiple of its net after-tax earnings. (See Chapter 3.) The return on invested assets of a manufacturing company is significantly less than that of a service or merchandising business.

Manufacturing businesses, because of many factors, not the least of which is their capital-intensive nature, have been selling at lower price earnings ratios than sales and merchandising businesses.

How to Determine the Price/Earnings Ratio

Example: XYZ Company is currently trading at $24. The twelve-month prior earnings have been $2 per share in after-tax income. The price earnings ratio (24 divided by 2) is 12.

Accordingly, when determining the value of a manufacturing business, the selling shareholder may be very disappointed, and may need to develop an analysis as set forth above to arrive at an acceptable price.

Some of the negative factors that gave rise to the low valuation of the manufacturing business may be a benefit at other times in the sales process. For example, it is extremely easy to obtain security in a manufacturing business. This type of business, because of its capital-intensive nature, will have a good deal of collateral with which to secure the unpaid portion of the sales price.

The difference between a manufacturing concern with its heavy investment in hard assets, which include real estate, equipment, inventory, and receivables, and the sales organization with a small amount of hard assets and substantial soft assets, which include good will, favorable contracts, and the like, is that for the first it is hard to obtain an acceptable value, yet easy to secure. For the second, it is easy to obtain an acceptable value, yet difficult to secure.

Selling a Service Company

If you are selling an insurance brokerage business, the hard assets that you may have to sell are insignificant. A major portion of the purchase price consists of the soft asset designated good will. The security problem surfaces when the prospective purchaser does not have or does not wish to pay for the agency in cash. He wishes to finance it and pay the purchase price out of the future earnings. There are few hard assets to secure this purchase price. This problem can be exemplified by the situation in which the purchaser of the insurance business becomes an alcoholic after purchasing the business. By the time the seller can reacquire control of the business after default by the purchaser, the good will has turned bad. The only real assets left may be the hard assets, which include an old desk and an obsolete computer.

Key Idea: The first step in analyzing the correct method of selling the business is to classify the business as a manufacturer, a merchandiser, or a service organization.

Key Idea: After classifying the business, try to initially determine the inherent characteristics of the business and how these will positively or negatively affect the sales process.

Key Idea: The next step in the process is to determine exactly who the potential purchasers are and what are their alternatives: for example, how many other competitive concerns exist, whether or not the business can be established from scratch, and to what use will they put this business. (Does he really need to purchase the business or is it just a whim?)

HOW TO ANALYZE YOUR BUSINESS'S POTENTIAL

Outsiders will begin their analysis of the business's potential by examining its past history. There is no doubt that the most difficult types of sales are those that involve a new business or a business whose past history is not reflective of its true potential.

Example: The owner of the business has, for personal reasons, determined that it is time to sell. An analysis of the financial statements for the past five years indicates no real earnings. When questioned, the owner rationalizes that he has expended all the development costs. The future profitability is assured and all that remains is to reap the benefits of previous efforts. He compares the current status of his business to that of a farmer who has prepared and tilled the soil, sowed and watered the crops, and is now waiting for the harvest. The business community is extremely skeptical in these particular instances; results are all that count. It is usually necessary for the owner to realize some of the success from his past efforts. His return on investment will substantially increase once some of the development costs ripen into profits.

Key Idea: When the full potential of the business cannot be determined from its prior history (it is a new business or its past earnings are not indicative because of the development costs incurred) defer the sale until the business has begun to reap some of the benefits from the prior expenditures.

Example: Publishing, Inc. is a small publisher of a magazine in a specialty market (Antique Widgets) that started in business five years ago. Buyers for such publications are always available. Many bigger publishing houses are always looking for new markets and appear more willing to purchase an existing publication (even at an inflated price) than to invest in a new business where the potential costs and problems are indeterminable. Accordingly, even in the beginning when the home subscriptions were small and the magazine was barely breaking even, there were a number of inquiries. The owners' goal was to realize enough money from the sale so that they would never have to work again. After four years in existence when the business was marginal and had only 15,000 home subscribers, they approached me with the question of whether or not they could profitably sell the business. Their argument was similar to that set forth above. Their position was that they had made all of the mistakes, expended all of the development costs and the future was assured. The price that could be realistically asked, pursuant to a historical valuation, was determined at one-third of their asking price of $1,750,000 (enough money to allow them to retire). When this price was proposed to the potential buyer (against my better judgment), he was, to say the least, turned off. However, three years later when they were generating $250,000 in net after-tax income, the same buyer reappeared and purchased the business.

Five Steps to Determine Future Growth Limits

In determining true potential, it is first necessary to look at past history and then compare the business being sold with its competitors. It is important to determine how the future growth will be limited by the marketplace; that is, your current and potential competitors. The following steps will help you determine how your future growth may be limited:

1. Determine the normal geographic sales and marketing area of a business similar to yours.
2. Determine the total number of individual purchasers of your products within that geographic and marketing area.

3. Determine the average sales of a comparable company in a market area similar to yours.
4. Determine the current and potential competitors in that area.
5. Determine any factors that may give you an edge over your competitors.

Key Idea: Compare your business at all times during the sales process with that of your competitors. It will show how you are doing in the marketplace, give rise to a true fair market value and indicate how your future growth may be limited by competition.

Key Idea: Throughout the sales process, it will be necessary to compare the business being sold with that of its competitors. As an individual, you are often judged by the company you keep. The business that you are selling will be categorized and compared to its competitors.

The prospective purchaser will want to know how you rate with your competitors. If this knowledge will not be to your advantage, you may need to alter your presentation. For example, if you are categorized as a manufacturer supplying the farm industry, and agricultural businesses are selling at tremendous discounts, it will be necessary for you to reclassify your business or to show how well you have done in comparison to others in your field. Imagination regarding the presentation can yield vast profits in the future. For example, even if you are an agricultural manufacturer, you may wish to establish an additional unit for commercial buildings, which may be booming at that time. In your sales presentation, you will not stress the fact that seventy-five percent of your sales are in the agricultural market but that your commercial division has grown from 0 to $2 million in sales in two years and the potential for future growth is great. The key is presenting your company in the most favorable vein. Each business must be reviewed and analyzed to obtain the results desired.

In Wisconsin, most full-time restaurants in the small communities are called "supper clubs." These supper clubs include those with nothing more than a bar and two or three tables used to serve food, to restaurants that can serve as many as 500 people. In Wisconsin, to determine a supper club's potential, it is necessary to look at the size of the community as well as at the sales of the best supper club in the area. For example, if we were valuing a supper club in Plover, Wisconsin, a small community of approximately 1,000 people, its maximum potential would be substantially less than a sophisticated German restaurant in downtown Milwaukee. The maximum amount of business that a Milwaukee restaurant can generate is greater because of the population base. However, when you analyze the potential of the Milwaukee restaurant, you have to insert in the equation the possibility of current and future competition. The potential of a full-line supper club going into competition with the established restaurant in Plover, Wisconsin, is negligible. On the other hand, even though you have a successful German restaurant in downtown Milwaukee, the amount of potential business that can be generated is limited by your own success.

Success in and of itself will attract competitors. We could call this the "McDonald" concept. The concept of a drive-in hamburger restaurant was so successful that it spawned numerous imitators and competitors—Burger King, Wendy's, Hardee's, and the like. Potential is a function of not only how much business there is—population base—but also how much business can be generated before you are too successful and an imitator/competitor may be established. In analyzing potential in Plover, it is probably appropriate to look at potential sales from the total population base in the community. In Milwaukee, it is appropriate to consider maximum sales of similar restaurants. In analyzing supper clubs' potential, it is important to be aware of the total community population as well as how easy it is to attract competitors.

Key Idea: The potential growth of all businesses is limited by the size of the marketplace and the ability to attract competitors.

Four Keys to Competing with an Established Business

There are four keys to the ability of others to compete with the established business.

1. Capital Investment. The greater the capital investment, the greater the risk and the less likelihood of attracting competition. The less capital investment, the less risk and the greater the probability for competition.

2. Location. If location is a major factor, it will tend to reduce the possibility of competition. In certain businesses (especially restaurants) location seems to be everything.

3. Idea or Patent. If your business potential is dependent on a patent, it gives you the exclusive right of use and your fear of duplication is minimal. This concept is exemplified by the growth of

Polaroid. On the other hand, if it is just a good idea or concept, the potential for competition is great. For example, in the fast food restaurants, McDonald's was the first, but Burger King, Hardee's, Wendy's, and the like have duplicated the idea. Therefore, it is easy to see that an idea alone may not protect you.

4. Personnel. Sometimes the success of the business is dependent on your employees, especially in service businesses. If key personnel are instrumental to the future success of your business, some of the questions you should ask are as follows:

a. What is it that they are contributing to the success of the business?

b. How easy are they to replace?

c. What happens if they leave your employ and start a competing business?

Many times the fear of having personnel leave the business and start a competing business or go to work for a competitor has prompted the employer to consider entering into an employment contract containing a covenant not-to-compete. The status of these covenants not-to-compete, at least in Wisconsin, is in doubt; however, their enforceability should be investigated and appropriate covenants should be entered into with key personnel.

Key Idea: If personnel are the key to the success of a business, employment contracts with the appropriate covenants not-to-compete should be entered into with these employees.

Key Idea: In determining the real potential of the business, you must answer the following questions:

1. What is the possibility for the growth within your own particular segment of the business?
2. What is the ability of a potential competitor to duplicate your business?

Key Idea: In considering the possibility of a competitor duplicating your business, it is important to weigh the attributes that give your business the edge and determine how easy they are to duplicate, namely:

1. capital
2. location

3. idea or patent
4. personnel

HOW THE STRUCTURE OF A COMPANY AFFECTS ITS SALEABILITY

It is necessary to consider all forms in which a business can be conducted in order to anticipate the inherent problems that may present themselves during the sales process.

The Sole Proprietorship

The sole proprietorship is the most basic form in which a business can be conducted. There is no need (except in some states that require registration under a fictitious name statute) to file documents with any state office (other than the Department of Revenue for a sales tax number). All that is required is to hang out a shingle and conduct business. If there are excess assets, these can be removed without tax ramifications. If the business needs money, the owner can transfer his personal funds to it without tax or financial implications. The assets, whether they are owned in the name of the business or by the owner, are still the owner's. This simplifies both the transfer of assets and the liquidation of the business.

The tax and nontax advantages inherent in the corporate form normally indicate incorporation at the earliest possible time. The foremost tax advantages include the ability to divide the income and thereby reduce the overall tax burden and to implement a full line of fringe benefits that are not available to the sole proprietor. It should be noted that the tax advantages of incorporating have been reduced by the Tax Reform Act of 1986. In the future, incorporation solely for tax purposes may be delayed. It should also be considered that the nontax advantage of limited liability of the corporate form often outweighs the advantages of flexibility and low cost of the sole proprietorship.

The Partnership

The partnership is nothing more than a multiple sole proprietorship. In other words, two or more people join together to operate a business and contribute time, capital, and effort to the success of the enterprise. The sale of a partnership, while not as simple as that of the sole proprietorship, is still not complex. For example, if the partnership is a manufacturing concern, it will in most cases own inventory, receivables, equipment, real estate, and the like. If the prospective purchaser wants to purchase only the operating assets and not the real estate, this will pose no substantial tax or financial problems. The sale of each asset will be realized separately and there is no taxation at the partnership level. All income (or loss) is divided among the partners. Again, for various tax and nontax reasons, most businesses with substantial worth will not be in the form of a partnership.

The C Corporation

The C Corporation is a separate entity for both tax and nontax purposes. There are three separate and distinct classifications of individuals that affect the corporate existence. Their rights and obligations have an impact on the sale.

Shareholders—The Owners of the Corporation

The first group of individuals, the shareholders, have limited day-to-day authority but have ultimate control over the business. Normally, their function is very limited and their sole responsibility on a continuing basis is to appear at the annual meeting to elect a board of directors. They will, from time to time, be called on to make some decisions that impact upon their ownership rights.

For example, their approval will usually be required by corporate law before a business can be sold or liquidated. While their rights are somewhat limited, historically they have received virtually all of the benefits from the sale. In our age of the "golden parachute" and other benefits for the employees value may have been shifted to other than the true equity owners of the corporation.

A "golden parachute" is recognized as payments in the form of cash, property, or fringe benefits to the officers, not for current or future services to be rendered, but for other considerations, including but not limited to facilitating the transfer of control after sale, facilitating the sale of the business, terminating employment peacefully, and so on.

The Overseers of the Corporation

The second group of individuals, the directors, are the overseers of the corporation. They are the ones who appoint officers, set salaries, are required to approve the sale of assets and/or the business, and provide the overall guidance that a corporation will need, both in its daily existence and during the sales process. It is easy to compare the directors' function to that of a foreman. A foreman will rarely work on the production line; yet few decisions as to who is on the production line and what products will be run are made without his approval.

The Managers of the Corporation

The third group of individuals, the officers, are usually the ones who are identified with the business. While they control its operation on a day-to-day basis, their ability to direct and control the sales process is limited. It is normally assumed that the owners of the business are the officers of the company.

In small corporations, it is not unusual for all three functions to be carried on by the same individuals. In other words, unless there are passive, silent investors, the shareholders in a small corporation serve as its officers and directors. However, in dealing with the purchase or sale of the business, it is usually a good idea to identify the principals and to analyze their individual interests in the corporation.

For example, the president who is also the chief executive officer may own an insignificant percentage of the total stock outstanding. If the corporation is sold, he will receive little, if any, direct benefits, unless specific actions are taken by the purchaser. As his position permits him to hinder the sales process, it may be necessary to buy him out through an offer to purchase that includes a "golden parachute."

If the shareholders, officers, and directors are one and the same, and if each of the shareholders owns the same percentage of stock, an offer can be structured in such a way that there is equality among all. In dealing with the purchase of a corporate business, it is imperative to understand the tax ramifications involved. The corporation as a separate taxable entity requires that any transaction between the shareholders, directors, and officers will result in a taxable event unless specifically excluded from taxation by the Internal Revenue Code. (Part 5 of Section 5 discusses the tax impact on the sale of the corporation.) The following example shows the adverse impact of the failure to consider the tax ramifications during the sales process.

Example: XYZ Company, a manufacturing corporation, with substantially appreciated personal property, sold all the equipment that it owned (depreciated book value $10,000) for $110,000 in 1986. The terms of sale were no money down, with the remainder of the purchase price payable in ten equal installments of $10,000 plus accrued interest. The remainder of the assets, including cash, inventory, and receivables, were retained by the corporation. For the purpose of simplification, it will be assumed that the cash, inventory, and receivables provided sufficient funds to pay all corporate debts. Accordingly, the only cash funds to be returned to the shareholders were from the sale of equipment. Because a corporation is not a consumer, and cannot eat, breathe, or go on vacation, the question was how to get the cash to the shareholders. The most logical way was to liquidate XYZ Company. The owner of XYZ Company, Mr. Smith, was under the impression that the sale of the equipment would qualify as an installment sale. He would only report income as it was received. The first bad news was that the law had changed under the Tax Equity and Fiscal Responsibility Act of 1982. TEFRA now requires that in the case of depreciation recapture (see page 139) all the gain must be reported in the year of sale even though no cash was received. Accordingly, the $100,000 gain would have to be reported at the corporate level in the year of sale as ordinary income. The resulting federal tax would be $25,750. The corporation incurred a greater tax liability than the cash it received. Even worse, in addition to the corporate tax, Mr. Smith will have to report gain and pay a tax on the actual cash from the sale as it is received. His net proceeds from sale (the sales price less corporate tax) of $84,250 will produce approximately another $16,850 in taxes. His net return from the sale is reduced to a mere $67,400. If the sale had occurred in 1987 or 1988 (rather than 1986), the Tax Reform Act would have reduced the after-tax proceeds to Mr. Smith.

The sum and substance of the above example is not to describe the horrendous tax problems that can occur without proper planning, nor to highlight the changes that have occurred under the 1986 Tax Reform Act, but to show that the tax ramifications may have a tremendous impact on the ability of the business to be sold. It would appear that the tax impact in the above example is so onerous that, if it had been known in advance, alternatives would have been explored or the transaction would probably not have occurred. The most obvious alternative that should have been considered was to sell the stock instead of the assets. If the appreciated property owned by the corporation had given rise to capital gain instead of ordinary income (that is, land or good will) the sale of the corporate assets could, in all likelihood, have been accomplished without the horrendous tax consequences. Therefore, the type, nature, and constitution of the assets of a corporation may dictate how it is going to be sold.

Warning: Before selling a corporate business, one should look at the types of assets that are owned by the corporation and the possible tax impact on the sale to determine whether it will be possible to sell the assets or if a stock sale is the only feasible alternative.

The S Corporation

The fourth type of business that is subject to sale is the S Corporation. The Subchapter S Corporation, or as it is now referred to, the "S Corporation," creates a different set of problems from either the partnership or C Corporation. The S Corporation is considered an incorporated partnership. Since the Subchapter S Act of 1982, there is a good deal more validity to this analogy. However, to speak of the S Corporation as an incorporated partnership is an oversimplification and may lead to tax disaster. For example, if the corporation was operated originally as a C Corporation and converted to S Corporation status, it may have both retained earnings and accumulated earnings and profits. Extreme care must be exercised in a redemption of a shareholder's interest, otherwise the shareholder may not receive the expected tax results. Notwithstanding the tax treatment, the Subchapter S Corporation is a separate and distinct entity for nontax purposes and must comply with all state corporate laws.

Virtually all businesses of any substantial value will probably be incorporated and will be treated as C Corporations for tax purposes. There is no doubt that while the sale of a corporation offers the greatest opportunity for both tax and nontax planning, it also poses the greatest problems and presents numerous tax traps for the unwary.

HOW YOUR OWNERSHIP INTEREST AFFECTS THE SALE OF THE BUSINESS

Once you have evaluated the type of business and determined its inherent tax problems, you have to consider two additional factors:

1. What percent interest do you represent?

2. Is the purchaser of the business interested in "buying" the current owners who are also employees of the business?

In selling a business, there are four different fractions of ownership interests that you can represent. The first category, simplest to represent, is 100 percent of the ownership. If you are representing the entire interest, you will have complete flexibility as to how to structure the sale. The second category and one that also allows for a great deal of planning potential is representing those individuals who own a majority interest in the business. In this instance, the minority interest may be either neutral, reluctant, or adverse to selling. The third category is the 50 percent interest and the fourth is the minority interest.

HOW THE INTEREST OWNED
AFFECTS THE SALES PROCESS

Interest Owned	Flexibility in allocation of Purchase Price among various assets.	Problems that other interests can cause.	Possibility of sale without other shareholders' approval.
100%	Complete—except for those presented by the tax law.	N/A	N/A
Majority	Must consider minority's interest as well as the tax law.	Can affect the sales process; may only be able to sell stock, not assets.	Minority can exert a negative influence on the sale. His adverse interest may discourage any purchaser from purchasing the majority interest in the business without purchasing 100%.
50%	Can't act without approval of other party.	Need others' approval unless going to sell his stock interest only.	Need acquiescence to sell assets. May still dispose of stock.

Less than 50%	Can rarely create positive situations.	Subject to the whims of the other shareholders.	Can sell stock only in special instances. Even in these instances, will probably sell for less than true value.

Each interest will pose different problems and offer planning opportunities. There are problems inherent in any sale if a corporation is not owned by just one individual.

Restrictions on the Sale of a Majority Interest

What restrictions are placed on the sale of a majority interest? When representing a majority, you must be aware that the minority will have rights conferred on them by corporate law. Many times these are in the form of derivative suits against the misuse of power by the controlling shareholders. A derivative action is a lawsuit by the shareholders for and on behalf of the corporation against officers and directors for misuse of their power when acting as officers and directors.

The following examples will illustrate the concepts set forth in this paragraph.

Example: A, the majority shareholder, president and sole director of XYZ Corporation, buys a condominium in Aspen, Colorado ostensibly to entertain customers. XYZ Corporation is a manufacturer of scuba equipment. None of its customers ski and all are located in Florida. The derivative lawsuit commenced by the other shareholders on behalf of the corporation would be for A to compensate XYZ Corporation for the costs incurred in maintaining the condominium. The question raised in the lawsuit would be "Did the corporation or president benefit from the purchase of the condominium?" If the sole benefit was for the president and no benefit was derived by the corporation, the president would have to reimburse the corporation for the cost of operation. Unfortunately, the answers to these questions are rarely as self-evident as in this example. Accordingly, the rights and remedies accorded to minority shareholders are not as defined.

Example: A owns eighty percent of XYZ Corporation and B owns twenty percent. A has determined to sell all the assets of XYZ Corporation to an unrelated party. Instead of valuing the assets at $1,000,000, he has valued them at $800,000 and allocated the additional $200,000 to a long-term employment contract and covenant not-to-compete for his sole benefit. Under many existing state laws, B would have the right to sue and obtain the "true fair market value" for his stock.

The representation of the interest of less than 100 percent of the corporate stock will have an impact on your ability to reallocate a portion of the purchase price to such items as a covenant not-to-compete payable to the seller or an employment contract. If a part of the purchase price is allocated to other than stock or assets, the shareholders who are not receiving the covenant not-to-compete or employment contract will not receive the "true fair market value" for the stock and could assert their rights against the majority shareholders as shown in the above example.

How Differences in Participating Affect a Sale

A sale of a business may be prompted by the majority or minorities' dissatisfaction with their return on investment.

Example: The minority passive shareholder requests a return on his investment in the form of dividends. The majority active shareholder prefers his return to be reflected as additional salary, which is more desirable for tax purposes. On the other hand, if the majority shareholder is the passive shareholder, he may not be receiving sufficient return on his total investment. In either event, the differing expectations of the shareholders can pose problems.

How Family Ownership Affects A Sale

In family situations, you cannot deal solely in economic reality. Many times, the payment for the majority interest will be at the same per share value as that of the purchase of the minority interest. It should be noted that the majority interest is normally valued at a premium and the minority interest is sold at a discount (see page 76). To keep peace in the family, we have to sell the shares at the same price but compensate one set of shareholders differently. The majority shareholders, if they are retained as employees, may have their salary exceed the worth of the services they will render to the business. This difference in compensation, while not stated, may be intended to reflect the inherent difference between the value of a minority and majority interest.

How to Sell a Minority Interest

Any time that you sell a business where there are active and inactive shareholders as well as majority and minority shareholders, there are inherent conflicts of interest. Even in equal situations, equality is rarely appreciated by the participants. Each party's perspective is affected by his feelings; rarely are they coexistent. On one end of the spectrum is the sale of a corporation with one shareholder. This is the easiest. On the other end, the most difficult to sell is a minority interest without the sale of an entire business.

There is no doubt that times have been changing. The Courts and the Legislature have placed greater responsibility on the majority for their actions as they affect the vested rights of the minority. Even with these protections, there is little market for a minority interest in a privately held corporation. The sole exception is when there is no single controlling shareholder and a minority interest is tied with an employment relationship. The easiest form of minority interest to sell is the one-third interest in the business with three equal owners. Even in this case, a purchaser buying one-third is at a disadvantage unless he is needed for the successful continuation of the business. Usually, the ability to sell this interest other than to the remaining partners is minimal. As with all generalizations, there are exceptions; for example, a competitor may be delighted to buy a one-third interest in the business. The leverage and insight it would give him could be used to the corporation's disadvantage.

How to Sell a Fifty-percent Interest

The fifty-percent ownership is probably the most interesting to deal with. Theoretically, he is in the same position as a minority shareholder because he cannot control his own destiny. On the other hand, because of his fifty-percent interest, he can "block" any action taken by the other individual. The ability to sell this interest, especially without complete approval or acquiescence of the other shareholder, is against the odds, but not impossible. The purchase of the interest provides more than just the ability to get a foot in the door. It is the ability to be an equal partner. Accordingly, while the minority interest becomes almost impossible to sell, the fifty-percent interest becomes an interesting product and requires imagination, which even in an adverse situation may offer a possibility for success.

Example: Mr. Older, age 70, and Mr. Younger, age 45, each own fifty percent of the outstanding stock of Widget International. Mr. Older wants to sell his stock and retire. Mr. Younger does not want to obligate himself for the future purchase. This situation becomes a standoff. While Mr. Older can sell his stock to a third party, the purchaser would face a difficult situation. Neither can take any positive action without the other. This includes but is not limited to appointing officers, setting salaries, and acquiring major assets.

There may be two ways to circumvent this problem. Mr. Younger realizes that he is not in complete control of his own destiny. Therefore, he wants to obtain control as long as he does not have to obligate himself to the future payments.

Method 1: The corporation redeems all of Mr. Older's stock for a promissory note secured by the corporate assets.

Method 2: Mr. Younger buys one percent of Mr. Older's stock. The remaining forty-nine percent is purchased by an ESOP established by the corporation.

Neither of the above methods is perfect but each provides a solution to the impasse that can be presented by two fifty-percent shareholders. A more complete discussion of the alternatives is found in Section 5.

WHAT IS THE DEFINITION OF A CLOSELY HELD CORPORATION FOR SALE PURPOSES?

This book will apply to any nonpublic corporation that would be classified as closely held. The concepts presented in this book could, however, be equally applicable to a small publicly traded corporation. Closely held corporations will, of necessity, require that only one family or a small group of families control the corporation. To the individual shareholders, their stock is not only an investment, but the key to their livelihood. When this fact is considered with the small number of executive positions within these corporations, the environment of the closely held corporation becomes defined. The nature of the investment limits the number of people who are willing to become stockholders in a closely held corporation. The most common way of taking money out of a closely held corporation is in a tax-deductible form either through salaries or fringe benefits. Because it is extremely difficult to take money out in a tax-deductible form for an inactive shareholder, and because investors wish a return on their investment, shareholders will perform services for the corporation and serve as officers and directors.

Dividends in a small corporation are usually avoided. Dividends are paid in after-tax income not deductible to the corporation. In addition, they are taxable to the individual shareholders. The corporation gets little, if any, benefit from dividends, except in some special situations. The difference in tax cost to the corporation can be illustrated as follows:

Example: A Corporation is in the thirty-four percent effective tax bracket. It has $10,000 it can distribute to its two shareholders, Mr. Jones and Mr. Smith. As compensation, the total amount can be paid to them at no tax cost to Corporation A.

Income before payment of additional bonus	$10,000
Bonus	$10,000
Additional taxable income	0

If this must be paid to Mr. Jones and Mr. Smith as dividends, only $6,600 can be distributed.

Income	$10,000
Deductible distribution	0
Additional taxable income	$10,000
Tax	($3,400)
After-tax income available for distribution	$6,600

Dividends in widely traded publicly held corporations are an important tool in their valuation and acceptance by the investing public. If substantial dividends are being paid, we can assume the corporation is not closely held.

Additional characteristics of a closely held business are that they have less than $10,000,000 in sales and fewer than 100 employees. The bigger and more successful the small closely held business becomes, the more likely it is to be incorporated. The smaller the business, the more likely it is to be a sole proprietorship or a partnership. Businesses with sizable sales and net worth are usually C corporations.

Key Idea: The closely held corporation will normally have the following characteristics:

1. a small number of shareholders own a majority interest
2. ownership and management are one and the same
3. little or no dividends are being paid
4. less than $10,000,000 in sales
5. fewer than 100 employees

HOW TO DEVELOP A SIMPLE, YET ALWAYS SUCCESSFUL,GAME PLAN

There is a tendency to approach the sale of a business with a good deal of fear and trepidation. As the sale or purchase of a business is not an everyday occurrence, there is a good deal of uncertainty as to the approach and the best way to facilitate the sale. One of the first weaknesses of the uninitiated and uninformed is that they have a tendency to look for simple answers. For example, if you are the owner of an insurance brokerage business and are trying to develop a reasonable purchase price, you listen to the old wives' tale that basically indicates that independent insurance agencies are sold at between one and one-half and two and one-half times the net premium dollar to the agency. The uninformed do not like to complicate the situation by asking such questions as the following:

1. Is the agency really worth that purchase price?
2. Can the purchaser pay for the purchase price out of future earnings?
3. What is the security if he defaults in payment?

Five Steps in Your Game Plan

Obviously, the best way to counteract the business clichés is to spend time familiarizing yourself with the necessary facts and information and to develop a logical, well-reasoned approach to the sale of the business. This approach would include the following:

1. Define the method for determining the fair market value under the traditional procedures. Beware, many of these "methods" are ill-defined and unless exact definitions are obtained, varying fair market values could easily be determined.

2. Determine the fair market value under the method set forth in Section 3 (see page 67).

3. Compare numbers 1 and 2, and if different, analyze the changes in the industry and determine if these changes have a positive or negative impact on the profitability.

4. Try to determine the future of the business. Is it a growth business? Is it stagnant? Is it in a decline?

5. Determine whether the future earnings will not only pay the purchase price but return sufficient profit to the buyer compared to the risk.

The owner of the business may become fixated on one point of the sale, such as attaining a certain purchase price. On the other hand, the buyer can become fixated on structuring the purchase so that only assets, not stock, are bought. In either case, this is a dangerous state of mind. It makes the sales process extremely difficult. Therefore, it is particularly important to discard the "old wives' tales" or "rules of thumb" especially where they no longer apply to the business being sold.

PUTTING YOUR GAME-WINNING TEAM TOGETHER

While the owner of the business is the captain of the ship, he must have a good crew in order to get the desired results. It cannot be overemphasized that the components of the team can make or break any possible sale. These members cannot sell the business; this is within the owner's control. What the team members can do is maximize the chance for success. Creative team members can make the impossible deal possible. The sales process is one of the most fertile grounds for inventiveness and ingenuity. There are many tools that are available and it is up to the team members to explain to the owner and purchaser which are most appropriate in the particular instance.

The members of this team should definitely include an attorney and an accountant. The accountant is going to be responsible for accumulating the information necessary to put together the sales package. He may also advise on the tax consequences and generally provides the financial information for the offering circular, supporting schedules, and background information.

In addition to drafting the sales document, the attorney will negotiate for and on the owner's behalf and will normally structure the transaction, unless this function is shared with the accountant. In today's age of specialization, it is important to choose your attorney and accountant wisely.

Many people rely on those individuals who have represented them in the past. This may or may not be wise or appropriate. Obviously an individual who has performed services for you in the past has a good deal of familiarity with your business. This can be invaluable. On the other hand, if both are not properly schooled in the fine art of buying and selling small corporations, they will not be able to perform as well as might be anticipated. In addition, personalities and expertise that were invaluable in counseling the business during its everyday existence are not always the traits or background that are required during the sales process.

There are often additional advisors to the team members required in specific situations. A perfect example would be a pension consultant. He would be particularly useful where the corporation has established a sophisticated pension plan and the early termination of the plan could create a substantial financial liability as well as tax problems. In this case, it may be possible, with the help of the pension consultant, to negotiate an obligation on the purchaser to continue the pension plan. A pension consultant in this case could be either an actuary or some other professional whose business is to help design pension plans.

There are also additional team members that may be needed, either at the inception or during the period of sale. The first and foremost, of course, is a business broker. Obviously if you are going to list the business for sale, the business broker will have to work closely with your accountant and attorney. Initially, the proper procedure is to contact the business broker once other decisions have been made. A full discussion of the utilization of a business broker will occur later. How each of the team members will interrelate and the individual functions of each member will be dependent on the fact situations present at the time. In many cases, the only team members needed are the owner, the accountant, and the attorney. In this case, the owner will determine the roles of each. In other cases, in more sophisticated sales, the roles and responsibilities of each team member will be segmented. To give hard and fast rules as to how each will act only would stifle the sales process. The sales process has to be a particularly flexible process at all junctures if it is to succeed.

Key Idea: It is absolutely necessary at the inception to put together a successful sales team. Although the owner or owners of the business are the captains of the ship, a competent crew is imperative. The two most important types of individuals in this crew are the accountant and the attorney. Choose them wisely. Remember, it is your business if you are the seller and your money if you are the purchaser. The ultimate responsibility for the success or failure should rest with you.

To sum up, the possible team members and their consultants who can assist the owner are as follows:

1. attorney
2. accountant

3. business broker
4. pension consultant
5. labor consultant
6. appraiser of business and real estate
7. insurance consultant
8. other

HOW THE OWNER SHOULD USE HIS TEAM AS A RAZOR-EDGED FENCING FOIL

The next question that is raised is, "What is the role that the owners of the business should play?" It is unwise to put all the trust in the other team members. It is the owner's business and the purchaser's money, and they should call the ultimate shots. The most effective role that the owner or purchaser can play is that of a fencer using his team members as a foil. It is inherent in the attorney's role that he be able to go back and apologize for misunderstanding or misconstruing his principals' intentions. The following example will illustrate how the purchaser can use his attorney as the "bad guy."

Example: A owns all the stock of XYZ Corporation and has had the company for sale. ABC Corporation, which is owned by B, wishes to purchase. ABC Corporation has high earnings and will be able to afford the purchase price if the appropriate terms can be negotiated. The problem is that ABC Corporation has all its capital tied up in its own business, and therefore has limited additional cash available for the down payment. Accordingly, terms (especially the down payment), rather than price, are the major concerns of ABC Corporation. A meeting is established to discuss price, terms, and security. B has instructed his attorney to act as the "bad guy." He is to hold the line on price, terms, and security, and to negotiate hard. He has also been told to be not only fair but abrasive. As has been planned by B and his attorney, the meeting "blows up." After the meeting, B contacts A and they go out and discuss the entire sales process. At this time, B opens his heart and soul to A and they discuss the mutuality and comity of interest, and how the merger would be a natural one for both parties. While B would like to be able to purchase the business, he cannot meet the terms or security requirements requested by A. At this time, B will probably agree that the business is worth what A is asking and will agree to pay the requested price. In this case, the prior bad feelings probably have been turned to B's advantage and a deal may be consummated. It might not have been possible to get the concessions needed without that crisis created at the meeting.

As can be seen in the above example, many deals have been consummated after impossibly divergent positions have been presented at a negotiation session. The two principals then have gone out for a drink together. During this time, they have struck the bargain. In essence, what has happened and what most informed principals fully understand is that they have wielded their foils in such a way as to crystallize the negotiating stance of the other party; then they have negotiated the final sale. This type of game playing is not always needed or wanted, but in the proper situation it can be effective.

This role-playing is most effective where the position of one party is ultimately reasonable but he cannot obtain his goals without a crisis. In our example above, A wanted price, terms, and security his way. Once the crisis occurred, he realized that the deal could only be consummated if he was flexible on terms and security.

Key Idea: Honesty and openness pay in virtually all segments of the sales process. However, from time to time, role-playing (good guy/bad guy) can bring the desired results.

Many owners of businesses, because it is their money, have taken the position that they should actively negotiate. This can be effective if they have received the proper schooling before coming to the negotiation table. For example, as explained in Section 4, security, terms, and taxes will play at least as big a role in the sale of a business as price. If the owners appreciate this fact and know what is and what is not negotiable in the other areas, they often can combine their superior negotiating skills and a good working relationship with the buyer to arrive at the basic terms of the contract.

How a Checklist Will Help You

It is worthwhile to prepare a chart such as the following prior to a negotiation session. This chart will highlight the areas of controversy between the parties as well as show those to which they have agreed. It is unbelievable that at times individuals lose sight of all that they have agreed on and focus only on the fact that they cannot agree on a purchase price or the amount of the down payment. In these cases, a checklist such as the one that follows will serve both the purpose of showing how far the negotiations have come as well as that which is still not resolved. It will also ensure that there is no misunderstanding between the parties as to what has occurred to date. Probably one of the most disastrous occurrences during a negotiation process is that the parties believe that they are in agreement as to a certain item when in fact there is a misunderstanding and this item is still at issue. This not only adds an additional factor yet to be resolved, but shakes the confidence of the individuals in the credibility of the others. As all contracts have only three major subdivisions—price, terms, and security—the checklist is relatively simple.

	Buyer's Position	Seller's Position	Agreed	Disagreed	Future Negotiating Position
Price					
Terms					
Security					

If the owner has done the negotiating, to the outside world he has used his accountant as an inactive advisor and his attorney as nothing more than a scrivener. Needless to say, the use of the owner as the chief negotiator is only truly effective if he receives the necessary background information before commencing his negotiations. The effectiveness of this particular method will usually depend on both a preexisting useful relationship between the buyer and the seller and the negotiating skill of the owner.

Key Idea: It is important for the principal in the sales process, be he the purchaser or seller, to determine what role he is going to take during negotiations. The choices are active participant or passive controller.

Warning: Even if the owner of the business is going to take an active role and utilize his advisors and other team members only in an advisory capacity, it is absolutely imperative that he be schooled as to what is and is not negotiable. For example, if the corporation owns a good deal of appreciated equipment that would give rise to investment credit and depreciation recapture, with the incumbent corporate tax, obviously it is necessary for him to strive for a sale of stock instead of assets. He should stress to the potential buyer the advantages of purchasing stock. These advantages include the benefits that can be obtained by not disturbing the continuity of existence; for example, the sale of stock normally will not affect any existing contracts with suppliers, existing creditor relationships, and the like. To use the old cliché, "Forewarned is forearmed."

WHAT TO DO TO MAKE YOUR COMPANY MORE ATTRACTIVE TO THE BUYER—CLEANING UP YOUR ACT

Once your team members are assembled, they will analyze the business with you. Many times the conclusion will be for you to clean up your act. It is important to realize that survival is the first concern of a closely held business. The second is that it return the maximum amount in after-tax dollars to its shareholder employees. There are no outside individuals that need to be satisfied. In a publicly held company, it is important to satisfy the investing public, the Securities and Exchange Commission, and your independent certified public accountants. In a closely held business, the shareholders, directors, and officers are usually one and the same. Their goal is to pay the least amount of tax and return the maximum amount tax-free or at minimum tax cost to themselves.

In the sale of a business, it becomes important to restructure the business and make it palatable to an outsider purchaser. This requires an analysis of certain assets, as well as adding a sales "sex appeal." The type of cleanup that is suggested or becomes imperative depends on a number of factors:

1. How much time there is between the commencement of planning and the time when the business will be offered for sale. Many times business owners will begin to talk about a sale many years before the contemplated sale. For example, they may discuss with their team members a sale timed with their retirement, which may be as much as five to ten years away. This lead time can be used effectively. You may have a long period in which to accomplish the necessary cleanup. On the other hand, the time may be short. Some problems may have come up that require an almost instantaneous sale.

2. The second question that has to be asked is, "What needs to be cleaned up?" There are two separate categories involved in answering this question—personal and business related.

As mentioned previously, a closely held business usually attempts to pay the least amount of tax and return the maximum amount of after-tax dollars to the individual owner/employees rather than report maximum income. Such things as fringe benefits, salaries, and so on may be manipulated to benefit these individuals without due regard to the effect that it has on the income of the corporation. Many owners view a part of their salary as a return on investment as well as compensation for the services rendered. This could be a tax disaster if the IRS can prove that the compensation paid was unreasonable. The expenditures, especially those related to salary, may not be reflective of the actual worth of the individual to the corporation and will have a tendency to distort the true corporate income. For example, an individual may be receiving a $150,000 salary. This salary was determined by the individual in conjunction with his tax advisors so that it would

1. minimize the corporate and individual tax,
2. maximize his deferred compensation plan, and
3. maintain his life style.

In developing a sales strategy, it is important to determine the worth of the individual in relation to what he has been paid. If it is found that the cost of a nonrelated replacement employee to serve in the same capacity will be $100,000, in essence, the income of the corporation has been understated by $50,000 less taxes. These are the personal type of expenses that will at least need to be examined, analyzed, and possibly explained to the potential purchaser. Several of the other personal type of expenses, which include fringe benefits, property owned by the business being used personally, and the like will be explained shortly.

Warning: With the enactment of the Tax Reform Act of 1986 and the lowering of individual tax rates, there will be increased pressure to maximize salaries in the future with the commensurate understatement of corporate earnings. Ascertaining the true earnings of the corporation will become even more difficult than it was in the past.

It should be noted that if there are business and personal expenses that are intertwined, it is necessary to develop a proper allocation between these mixed-use expenses and properties. The method used to differentiate personal versus business use will be discussed shortly.

WHEN TO SELL A PORTION OF THE BUSINESS FIRST

No matter how well-run and smoothly operating a closely held corporation is, there are always business steps that should be taken to put a corporation into a sales position. Some of the more common situations that you will have to deal with are as follows:

1. A division or some other portion of the business may not be directly related to the maximum production of income. An example of this problem can be illustrated as follows:

Example: Sales and Distribution Corporation is in the business of selling many items through a mail order catalog. For many years, a pet project of one of the founders of the corporation has been to maintain a printing press so that a major portion of the catalog can be printed in-house. A recent cost analysis of the printing department has shown that printing equipment is capital intensive and in this case yields little income. Prior to the sale of the business, it may be beneficial to sell the printing equipment. This would have the following benefits: (1) The corporation should show a better return on its investment. As the printing equipment is very capital intensive and yields no income, the actual return on invested assets should increase. (2) The remainder of the business may operate more smoothly. Some personnel can be eliminated. (3) It may be less taxing on the officers to bid out the mail order catalog rather than oversee its printing in-house.

As an alternative, if the corporation still does not deem it appropriate to sell its printing operation, it may be beneficial to spin off the printing operation into a separate and distinct entity and have this entity stand on its own. It could be part of the purchase or excluded from the purchase depending on the desires of the purchaser. The potential purchaser could buy the printing business or exclude it from his offer. The company could, in essence, offer two distinct purchase prices, one for the major portion of its business and the other incorporating the printing business.

2. The corporation may own extraneous assets. Some of these assets may be solely business related, such as vacant land where the business was going to expand. Some of the other assets may be mixed-use property such as an entertainment facility, a company plane, a company automobile, and the like. Again, many times it is beneficial, prior to offering the company for sale, to remove these assets.

HOW TO TREAT PERSONAL-USE EXPENSES AND ASSETS

There are usually no problems encountered in explaining the personal fringe benefits enjoyed by the individual owners of a closely held corporation. How to deal with these will be discussed shortly. If assets used for personal benefits are involved, it may be just as easy to sell these assets to unrelated third parties or to the owners of the corporation. Personal-use property and assets are simple to categorize and to analyze their total costs.

How to Determine the Cost of
Personal-Use Assets and Expenses

Personal-Use Asset or Expense	Annual Amount	Buyer's Replacement Amount	Savings
I. Personal-Use Expense			
A. Salary			
B. Fringe Benefits:			
1. Medical reimbursement			
2. Retired lives reserve			
3. Deferred compensation			
a. Qualified plans			
b. Nonqualified plans			
4. Insurance			
a. Key man			
b. Others			
II. Personal-Use Business Asset			
A. Car			
B. Country Club			
C. Boat			
D. Plane			
E. Travel and entertainment			
F. Other			

Mixed-Use Expenses and Assets

Mixed-use property poses an additional set of problems. It is necessary to ask not only how much it costs but also what portion is business and what portion is personal. The above chart can be used in the same manner for mixed-use expenses and assets. An example would be the cost of a car. If it is solely for personal use, completely unrelated to business purposes, it would show up on the first checklist. If there was a mixed use, the actual expense of the car would be reduced by the personal portion of the car use. The easiest way out of this complicated procedure may be to sell these unwanted assets to unrelated third parties or to sell them to the owner of the corporation.

Warning: When selling capital assets from the corporation to the individual shareholders, it is important that all transfers should be at fair market value. In all cases, the tax cost of this transfer should be considered prior to the sale.

Excess Fringe Benefits

Should excess fringe benefits be explained or eliminated? There probably is not a profitable closely held corporation in existence that does not have fringe benefits designed solely for the individual shareholder-employees. These fringe benefits range from those that are widely accepted and completely legitimate for tax purposes, such as health insurance, group term insurance, contributions to pension and profit sharing plans, disability insurance, and so on, to those that are not directly business related and are, for tax purposes, more suspect. These are divided into the purely personal esoteric type such as retired lives reserve, and those expenses where the direct business relationship is more tenuous (the company airplane, country club dues, some travel and entertainment, convention expenses, and so on). Accordingly, it is important to divide the more suspect fringe benefits into two separate categories:

1. Those fringe benefits not usual and normal in a closely held corporation; retired lives reserve, split dollar insurance, and the like.
2. Those fringe benefits whose substantiation as directly related business expenses are more tenuous; the company airplane, the company car, country club, travel and entertainment, convention expenses, and the like. We have already referred to these as mixed-use property or mixed-use expenses.

The first type of expenses are easy to value as a cost to the corporation and will be added to the normal fringe benefits and salary to determine the executives' compensation costs. With mixed-use property and expenses such as the company airplane, automobile, country club, it is difficult to determine the exact value to the corporation versus the personal benefit derived. Even with something as common as the company car, it is necessary to determine both the total cost and the portion of this cost that should be applied to the corporation and the portion that should be personal usage. These types of expenses should be eliminated or at least reduced to what will be considered as a reasonable amount, so that the valuation of the business and the subsequent sale will be easier. As noted earlier, if time permits, it may be advantageous to sell the mixed-use property.

Virtually all successful corporations will own automobiles for their executives, so this type of expense (even though it may not be completely deductible especially after The Tax Reform Act of 1984 as subsequently modified) is still well within the realm of justificability. The more exotic the expense or type of property, the more appropriate it is to reduce or eliminate it. Exactly what is done with the asset or expense will depend on the period of time between the discussion of possible sale and the actual offering the business for sale.

Key Idea: It is absolutely imperative that "you clean up your act" before the company is put up for sale. Cleaning up your act may involve spinning off unprofitable portions of the business, selling the assets of the business, eliminating costs, and categorizing certain fringe benefits. The exact steps you should take range from the sale of these assets to categorizing what these expenses are and valuing the worth to the corporation versus personal usage by the shareholder/employee.

Summarizing Three Steps in the Sale of the Business

The steps in the sale of the business are as simple as 1, 2, and 3 and can be summarized as follows.

1. Value the business.
2. Zero in on the potential purchasers.
3. Structure the sale.

However, before you can proceed with any of these steps, it is important that you have proceeded conceptually and put yourself into the proper mind-set for the sale.

Four Steps to Develop the Proper Mind-Set

1. Analyze whether or not it really is the time to sell. This analysis requires both an analysis of the intrinsic and extrinsic factors as well as the personal reasons for the sale. In all cases, it is imperative to acknowledge that timing is the key although this is probably the single element that is beyond everyone's control.

2. Analyze your business; classify and anticipate its potential. It is important to determine where your business has been, where it is,

and where it could be. In this analysis, it is important to determine not only your company's profitability but how the investing public values its segment of the economy. In addition, the economy itself will have an impact on your company's potential.

3. Put your sales team together. Determine who are the team members and also determine whether or not you will take an active or passive role in the sales process.

4. Clean up your act. It is always best if you can eliminate the extraneous assets or expenses. However, if you cannot eliminate you must classify, value, and allocate that which is personal from that which is business related.

Once these preliminary steps have been taken, the actual sales process will have begun. Step 1, which is the valuation of the business, will be discussed in Section 3. Step 2, which is zeroing in on the potential purchasers will be discussed in Section 4. The final step, structuring the sale, will be discussed in Section 5. The sales process is only bewildering to the unprepared and uninitiated. With the proper groundwork, the sales process will be neither intimidating nor complicated.

SECTION 3

HOW TO DETERMINE THE TRUE VALUE OF A BUSINESS

Determining the value of the business can be useful for both objective and subjective reasons. Objectively, it can help to determine whether or not there are sufficient funds for retirement, payment of debts, providing funds for other endeavors, and so on. It can also help determine whether or not there is an estate tax problem. Subjectively, it may satisfy the needs of the owner. There are always additional reasons for needing to ascertain a value which do not fit conveniently in either category.

Value will often play a rather unusual role. Some people will say "I will only sell when the business is worth $1,000,000." Thus, one of the reasons that a business is sold is that the individual has attained his or her subjective goal.

The layman's approach, which is utilized in this book, will provide a value within parameters. It will crystallize the otherwise unclear position of the owners of the corporation. Once the value has been obtained, the owners can determine whether a full-blown business appraisal is appropriate, or necessary, and can determine whether or not to proceed with the sales process.

Inevitably, the first question an owner of a business will ask is "How much is it worth?" The owner's desire may not solely be to obtain the objective information. In some cases, the "worth" subjectively reflects his or her degree of success during his or her business life. Discussing value with the owner should be done with discretion, as he or she will not be objective, and should be as dispassionate and removed as possible.

Obviously, there is a need to know. The question of whether the business is for sale may depend on its worth. In the example on page 22, the publishing business was only for sale once the worth was sufficient to provide the vehicle for retirement. Only if the value of the business was equal to or greater than the amount needed would the business be sold. In that example, our publishers looked to the sales proceeds to provide for their retirement.

Rather than providing funds to satisfy a need (such as retirement, payment of other debts, security) the sale of a business may be prompted by the evidence that its high value has produced an estate tax problem. The sales process is often a vehicle to obtain a goal or solve a problem. How value will affect the decisions that are to be made can be illustrated by the following.

EXAMPLE OF WHEN SELLING IS NOT PROFITABLE

A and B have, for five years, been operating Publishing, Inc. Publishing, Inc. is a capital intensive business. While A and B have been well paid (between $75,000 and $100,000 per year depending on the availability of funds), Publishing, Inc. has not had sufficient excess funds nor has it been economically feasible to establish either a profit sharing or pension plan. A and B have attained the age of fifty-eight and sixty respectively and wish to sell the corporation to provide for their retirement. If the value of Publishing, Inc. is determined to be $500,000, A and B may only realize $180,000 each in after tax income. This probably will not come close to providing them with the retirement income that they require. Accordingly, following an appraisal, they may decide that now is not the right time to sell. The answer may be different if Publishing, Inc., were valued at $1,000,000, $2,000,000, or more.

WHEN AN ESTATE TAX PROBLEM CAN BE CREATED BY CORPORATE VALUE

The value of the corporation may pose an estate tax problem. The phasing in of the provisions of the Economic Recovery Act of 1981 provides that a married couple, after January 1, 1987, with proper planning will be able to transfer $1,200,000 in assets to the next generation estate tax free. This can be accomplished with a marital deduction will and the appropriate ownership of property. If you couple this unified credit with the unlimited marital deduction (which, except in rare instances, eliminates taxation on the death of the first spouse) and the $10,000 per donee gift tax exclusion, it is easy to grasp that estate taxes really pose little if any problem to a married couple with an estate of less than $1,500,000. On the other hand, if a vast portion of the married couple's estate is represented by stock in a closely held corporation, there is still the potential for a high tax to be incurred on the death of the second spouse. In this case, there may not be sufficient liquid assets available to pay the tax. An example will illustrate this problem:

Example: Joe and Mary Close (age seventy-five and seventy-two respectively) own the following property:

1. House in joint tenancy	$400,000
2. Marketable securities	$400,000
3. 100% of the issued stock of Widget, Inc., a closely held corporation	$4,000,000
Total assets of Joe and Mary Close	$4,800,000

Widget, Inc., is currently managed by their son, Jim. They have provided income for their retirement through a pension plan established years ago. Under current law, there would be no estate tax on the death of the first spouse. However, when the second spouse dies, there would be a tax of $1,683,000, which is greater than the liquid assets of Joe and Mary combined. Accordingly, they have an estate tax problem.

Contrast this with the same fact situation except that the total value of Widget, Inc., is only $2,000,000. Again, there would be no tax when the first spouse dies and when the second dies, the tax, while still substantial, would only be $637,000. The value of this estate is within manageable limits. This tax can be reduced or eliminated by an estate plan using an appropriate gifting program, recapitalization, or through some other estate planning device that could be used to reduce the value of the corporate stock retained by the estate.

How Congress Has Helped Solve the Estate Tax Problem

It should be noted that Congress has been particularly aware of this problem and has attempted to provide tools, other than selling the business, to obtain the funds necessary to pay the estate tax, by enacting two sections into the Internal Revenue Code: Sections 303 and 6166.

The Benefits of Code Section 303 in Estate and Post-mortem Planning

Section 303 has had a checkered history and has been revised directly and indirectly several times since its enactment. Section 303 allows the redemption of stock from an individual's estate if it meets certain requirements. These requirements can be summarized as follows:

1. The stock must constitute more than thirty-five percent of the decedent's adjusted gross estate.

2. The stock redeemed must amount to at least twenty percent of the issued stock.

3. The redemption is limited to:

a. death taxes (attributable to the business interest)
b. funeral expenses
c. administration expenses

These funds are removed with little, if any, income tax as the redemption is treated as a capital transaction instead of as dividend income. In essence, Section 303 permits the estate, which owns stock in a qualifying closely held corporation with excess liquid assets, to redeem a portion of its stock without the estate incurring any income tax. In the above example, if Widget, Inc., had excess liquid funds, up to $1,683,600 of its stock could have been redeemed from the estate of the survivor of Joe or Mary Close and the estate would have incurred no income tax. The benefits of this Section can be illustrated by the following example:

Example: Widget, Inc., has $1,000,000 of excess liquid funds from the sale of a portion of its business. There is a desire to distribute these funds to the stockholders, Joe and Mary, in 1988. The three alternative tax ramifications can be summarized as follows:

1. The $1,000,000 is distributed and taxed as dividend income. The total tax liability should approximate $280,000.

2. The $1,000,000 is distributed so that it is taxed as capital gain. The total tax liability should again approximate $280,000.

3. A qualifying stock redemption under Section 303 could be accomplished after their deaths yielding little if any tax.

The advantages of using Section 303 then become obvious. It should be noted that the amount of stock that can be redeemed is limited to the sum of the death taxes and the funeral and administrative expenses allowed as a deduction to the estate.

The Benefits of Code Section 6166 in Estate and Post-mortem Planning

The second section that can be used to mitigate the liquidity crisis illustrated by the above example is Section 6166. The Economic Recovery Act of 1981 now provides that Section 6166 will allow for a fifteen-year installment payment of the estate tax attributable to the decedent's estate if the closely held business exceeds thirty-five percent of the adjusted gross estate. If the estate chooses this installment payout, only the interest need be paid annually for the first five years. Thereafter, the tax owed, plus interest, must be paid in annual installments over the next ten years. The interest charged will be at the rate of four percent of the tax due, if the tax liability is less than $345,800. If the tax liability exceeds $345,800 (less the appropriate unified credit) the interest on any excess will be at the normal IRS interest rates. The deferral of the payment of tax under this provision is limited to the tax attributable to the closely held business. While it is not the intent to make the reader an expert in estate planning, it is important to realize tools are available to help solve the liquidity crisis.

Key Idea: In the event that a business has not been sold prior to the death of the second spouse, either Section 303 or 6166 may allow for post-mortem estate planning to ease the liquidity crisis that results from the high value attached to the stock of a closely held corporation and the resulting estate tax. The sale of the business may not always be necessary.

HOW DIFFERENT METHODS CAN BE USED BY THE LAYMAN TO VALUE THE BUSINESS

The first and foremost approach utilizes a combination of the corporate earnings and book value (see page 65). In addition, the corporation's dividend payouts may also play a part in this valuation process. This is the method that will be explained later in this chapter.

The second approach that may have "some" applicability is the "rule of thumb" used in valuing businesses within an industry. Probably one of the prime examples of this is the insurance industry, discussed earlier. Insurance brokerage businesses are valued, according to the industry's rule of thumb, at between one and one-half and two and one-half times the net premium dollar to the agency. This provides a simplistic method that does not require many judgments or much analysis. However, these rules of thumb within the industry should be critically examined before being relied upon.

Remember: The problem with these historical methods is that they may no longer be indicative of the true value of the business.

Example: Changes in the insurance industry have had a two-fold negative impact on the profitability of the agency. First, the cost of various forms of insurance may have declined on a dollar basis. In other words, it may cost less to insure a $50,000 house today than it did five years ago. The second reason is that insurance companies have reduced the percentage of the commission dollar payable to the agency. This has completely upset the profitability of the agencies and has had an impact on the prior historical method of valuation.

In some cases, the independent insurance agencies continue to be sold on a historical basis because of special circumstances. For example, banks and other financial institutions have been expanding beyond their traditional functions. A logical expansion is into the insurance industry. These institutions have a special need to acquire preexisting agencies. Without their helping to maintain an inflated market value, the old rule of thumb would have completely disappeared from existence rather than being an anachronism.

Example: XYZ Insurance Brokerage Company ran an extremely successful business in a medium-sized community. Internal conflict had occurred between the older shareholders who were nearing retirement and the younger shareholders whose primary goals were instant gratification (high salary and fringe benefits) rather than providing retirement dollars for the older shareholders.

The buy/sell agreement entered into many years ago provided that the agency, for buyout purposes, would be valued at 1.25 times its net premium dollar. The accountant made an analysis and determined that it was impossible for the younger shareholders to purchase the retiring shareholder's stock using this method and still pay themselves a reasonable salary. After lengthy discussions, the agency was offered for sale. Even though it had been extremely successful, it was impossible to sell at 1.25 times its net premium dollar until a bank in the area purchased it. This special use situation maintained an artificial value and lent credence to a rule of thumb that is no longer financially applicable.

Historically, many of these inappropriate valuation techniques have been spawned by the service industries. The reasons for this are varied. One hypothesis is that these businesses are unique and the historical valuation methods would not have yielded the value that the businesses were intrinsically worth.

Note: It is extremely important to analyze valuation not only from the techniques utilized within the particular industry, but also to determine the reasons behind these rules and ascertain whether or not the assumptions that went into developing them are still applicable.

The Limitations on the Layman's Appraisal

The appraisal methods set forth in this chapter are not a substitute for a business appraisal. They should be used only as a planning tool to set the parameters of value. The value of a closely held corporation is an elusive quarry. Its determination is, at best, an art and not a science, and, at worst, pure conjecture. Because a closely held corporation is not a fungible commodity, determination of value is dependent on many imprecise factors, such as:

1. the number of possible buyers
2. the basic nature of a "single purpose asset"
3. the role of management
4. the dependency on a major supplier or customer
5. geographic location
6. niche in marketplace and dependency on factors beyond control, such as a strike at major customer.

These and other related factors make it impossible to consider the appraisal method set forth in this chapter as anything more than a guide. To do otherwise would be to misconstrue its intent and could lead to disastrous results.

Note: Many of the tools set forth in this book are not limited to closely held corporations, but can also be expanded to small publicly held corporations. A prerequisite to using this approach is the lack of an actively traded market. Many supposedly public corporations are so thinly traded that the value determined in the marketplace is not reflective of the true worth of the business. Therefore, while a publicly held corporation is theoretically valued by the marketplace, if the trading is small, this value can be at least partially disregarded and the approach set forth in this section can be utilized.

HOW INTRINSIC AND EXTRINSIC FACTORS AFFECT VALUE

We have already discussed how intrinsic and extrinsic factors affect the appropriate time to sell. The process of valuing the closely held corporation is also dependent on these two factors. The intrinsic factors that affect the value of the closely held corporation are those that relate to its financial condition, and include: (1) earnings capacity, (2) book value, (3) dividend paying capacity, and (4) good will.

These factors are contrasted with the extrinisic factors that involve conditions and situations outside the corporation that help determine its value. These extrinsic factors can be divided into two separate and distinct categories:

1. those that are within the control of the principals, including restrictions on the sale of stock set forth in the articles of incorporation, bylaws, or shareholders' agreement.
2. those that are outside the control of the shareholders, which include the general economic conditions and the specific economic conditions within the particular industry.

The major thrust of this book is to determine value unfettered by restrictions on transferability imposed by the shareholders themselves. Nonetheless, these restrictions can determine value and, therefore, it is important to understand how they can be used effectively.

Important Note: One of the most likely groups of potential purchasers of the business are the other shareholders. These individuals already have a substantial interest in the corporation. At times, they may wish to increase their commitment through additional purchase of stock. This is not only evident during the period of sale, but obviously is important throughout the corporate existence. Therefore, the shareholders, either at the inception of the corporation or at any time during its existence, may deem it worthwhile to restrict their sale of stock.

How Stock Restrictions Affect the Value of a Stockholder's Interest

Restrictions can be inserted in the bylaws or articles of incorporation; however, they are most commonly incorporated into a shareholder's agreement. There are basically two types of these agreements: stock redemption and cross purchase. In the stock redemption agreement, the corporation has the option or obligation to purchase the stock of a deceased or selling shareholder. In the cross purchase agreement, the remaining shareholders have the option or obligation to purchase the stock.

The effect that these agreements have on the value of the stock, either for tax or sales purposes, is dependent on such factors as whether the agreement is between family members, whether it is solely an option or a mandatory obligation, and whether it restricts the shareholder during his or her life as well as at death.

Warning: The major thrust of this book is to discuss the sale of businesses unfettered by any restrictions. If there is a preexisting agreement, this will have a definite impact on the sales process and should be considered before proceeding with any of the methods or suggestions contained in this book.

The remaining extrinsic factors are those outside the control of the shareholders that impact on the valuation process. The impact of extrinsic factors on valuation was discussed in Section 2 (see page 15).

HOW TO USE INTRINSIC FACTORS TO DETERMINE VALUE

Let us assume that the intrinsic factors of the business are known. To convert these intrinsic characteristics into a value, it is necessary to find a comparable company or companies. Without knowing the nature of the business, we could have the same intrinsic characteristics that would yield completely different results.

Example: If the corporation being valued turned out to be a corporation that supplied the high-tech industry with its high price earnings ratio, the value of the corporation would be significantly greater than if the corporation supplied the depressed agricultural market with its low price earnings ratio.

Example: A is attempting to arrive at a value of XYZ Corporation, a closely held corporation that manufactures products used in construction. A determines that the publicly held ABC Corporation is comparable. While ABC is better than twenty times bigger than XYZ, its earnings history is similar, it serves the same markets, and it sells comparable products. In addition, its financial ratios, such as debt to equity and current ratio, are similar. A ascertains that earnings are the determining factor in valuing a company within this industry. ABC is currently selling at twelve times its earnings. As XYZ Corporation's earnings are $250,000, if ABC is used as the comparable corporation, its value is $3,000,000. In the alternative, A could find DFE Corporation, which is also comparable in all intrinsic financial respects, except DFE sells to the agricultural market (which is currently extremely depressed) and therefore commands only a price earnings ratio of 6. If DFE is used as the comparable company, the value of XYZ would only be $1,500,000. As can be seen by this example, extrinsic factors can materially affect the value of the corporation that is being sold even though the intrinsic factors of earnings history and financial ratios are all similar.

HOW THE TYPE OF BUSINESS DICTATES VALUE ANALYSIS

For valuation purposes, there are not only the three types of businesses that were discussed earlier, but also corporations that are designated holding companies. Holding companies are corporations that do not actively engage in business, whose sole function is to hold assets, such as land, buildings, stocks, bonds, and so forth. The purchase and sale of these businesses are directly related to the underlying value of their assets. If the assets owned by the holding company are publicly traded stocks, bonds, or real estate that can be quickly and economically sold, the alternative is not to sell the business in its entirety but to sell the individual assets and then liquidate the corporation.

The need to determine a value is normally for gift or estate tax purposes. The IRS has developed various criteria in valuing these holding companies. Such companies are rarely sold in their entirety unless their assets consist of stock in closely held corporations. In arriving at the value of these corporations, earnings do not play the same role that they do in active corporations and adjusted book value becomes more significant.

Except for holding companies, the same general approach will be utilized for valuing the other three classifications of businesses. However, it should be noted that the capital intensive nature and relatively low return on investment of the manufacturing and merchandising businesses compared to the service businesses has had an impact on the alternatives available to the owners of these corporations.

HOW THE TYPE OF BUSINESS AFFECTS YOUR APPROACH TO DETERMINING FAIR MARKET VALUE

In manufacturing and merchandising companies, book value will play a more significant role than in service corporations. Even if the combination of the various factors that will help determine the fair market value of the business yields a value less than book value, it may be that the true value of the business will be more related to book value.

A viable alternative to a sale may be the liquidation of the business. Rather than selling the business as a going concern, the owners may elect a liquidation sale to maximize their return.

Example: ABC Corporation, a service-oriented business, has been generating after-tax profits of approximately $70,000 per year and has the following balance sheet:

	Book Value	Fair Market Value
Cash	$10,000	$10,000
Inventory	$10,000	$10,000
Receivables	$100,000	$100,000
Equipment	$20,000	$30,000
Total Assets	$140,000	$150,000
Accounts Payable	$100,000	$100,000
Capital Stock and Retained Earnings	$40,000	$40,000
Unrealized Appreciation	———	$10,000
Total Liabilities and Equity	$140,000	$150,000

If comparable companies indicate that the appropriate price earnings ratio for businesses such as ABC are between one and two times earnings, the value of this corporation as a going concern is between $70,000 and $140,000. On a liquidation basis, it probably would realize no more than $50,000. If ABC, instead of being a service-oriented business, was a manufacturing corporation with the same after-tax income but with the following balance sheet:

	Book Value	Fair Market Value
Cash	$10,000	$10,000
Inventory	$100,000	$100,000
Receivables	$100,000	$100,000
Plant and Equipment	$125,000	$70,000
Total Assets	$335,000	$480,000
Accounts Payable	$200,000	$200,000
Capital Stock and Retained Earnings	$135,000	$135,000
Unrealized Appreciation	———	$145,000
Total Liabilities and Equity	$335,000	$480,000

If comparable companies to ABC were only selling at between one and two times earnings, liquidation might be a viable alternative. On liquidation, the return to its shareholders could be as much as $280,000.

Note: The capital base (inventory, receivables, plant, and equipment) of a service business is usually significantly less than that needed by a manufacturing concern of similar sales.

Beware: Fair market value determined on a going concern basis is rarely equivalent to liquidation value, for manufacturing and merchandising businesses, the liquidation value may actually be determinative of true fair market value.

Example: A classification of business that illustrates this concept is Wisconsin's small town furniture stores. The small town furniture store has historically been capital intensive. In the last decade, these businesses have been particularly susceptible to competition from discounters and, therefore, have yielded a small return on investment. Often, it has been impossible to yield a return higher than financing rates.

In attempting to sell a store such as this, the owner will not only look at all the prospective purchasers but also will analyze the yield that a going out of business sale would bring. The demise of the small town furniture store in Wisconsin indicates that this, in many cases, has been an extremely viable alternative and has been particularly appropriate when the owner of the business does not own the real estate.

Remember: Service businesses or merchandising businesses that do not have a substantial amount of physical assets and are not capital intensive normally will not have this as an available option. Liquidation for these corporations is not a viable alternative as their true value is maximized solely as a going concern.

Be Aware: The capital- and noncapital-intensive nature of the business will have an impact not only on the valuation process *per se* but on the other available options.

Example: A capital-intensive corporation does not always equate to a high liquidation value. Many capital intensive businesses, especially in manufacturing, would find it very difficult to liquidate at anywhere near their fair market value. Specialty equipment is difficult to sell, and inventory, even if it is properly valued (going concern valuation method), can rarely be disposed of at its cost to the corporation. However, merchandising businesses with high inventory and relatively low investment in furniture, fixtures, and equipment lend themselves to a liquidation sale.

USING IRS REVENUE RULING 59-60 IN DETERMINING VALUE

An appropriate starting point for the determination of the valuation of the corporation has been established by the Internal Revenue Service in Revenue Ruling 59-60, which outlines in considerable detail the factors that should be considered. The IRS has in the past, and continues to be interested in, developing a proper procedure in valuing small closely held corporations for estate and gift tax purposes. Accordingly, they have devised a list of criteria (intrinsic and extrinsic) that is used in valuing these corporations. Among the most important are the following:

1. the nature of the business and the history of the enterprise from its inception
2. the economic outlook in general and the condition and outlook of the specific industry in particular
3. the book value of the stock and the financial condition of the business
4. the earnings capacity
5. the dividend paying capacity
6. the intangible value (goodwill, for example)
7. the market price of stocks or corporations engaged in a similar line of business having their stocks actively traded in a free and open market, either on an exchange or over the counter

While the above is a list of those criteria that are most important in determining value, it is not a definitive list of all that is necessary. In addition, in the event that the sale of the corporate stock is restricted (through a restriction inserted in the bylaws, articles of incorporation, or through a stock purchase agreement) this extrinsic factor could have a definite negative impact on the value of the stock.

Example: A and B each own one-half of the outstanding common stock of Widget, Inc. They, many years ago, entered into a shareholders agreement that provided for a mandatory purchase at one and one-half times the book value of the stock of the corporation on the death of either of the shareholders. A dies. The analysis of the value of Widget, Inc. (taking into consideration all factors other than the shareholders agreement) would indicate a value for A's stock of $250,000. If the book value of the stock is $100,000, the purchase price for the stock would be fixed at $150,000. In this case, if A and B were not related, this would in all likelihood be the true fair market value of A's stock in his estate.

HOW APPRAISERS DETERMINE FAIR MARKET VALUE

There are an infinite number of sophisticated methods for valuing a corporation. These involve numerous economic and mathematical assumptions and approaches that require a background far beyond that which is available to anyone but a professional appraiser. In the final analysis, these methods involve one or more of the classical approaches that provide the basis for appraising real estate: income, market, and cost.

1. The income approach (known in the real estate trade as the capitalization method) capitalizes the net after-tax earnings at a reasonable rate of return considering the investment and risk. A simple example will illustrate this concept:

Joe Smith owns a twelve-unit apartment building. Its income and expenses can be summarized as follows:

Rent		$58,000
Real estate taxes	$10,000	
Utilities	$ 5,000	
Maintenance and repairs	$10,000	
		$25,000
Net income before debt service and depreciation		$33,000

If apartment buildings, considering the type of investment and risk, generally yield a return of twelve and one-half percent, the fair market value will be $264,000. To determine the capitalization value, divide the net income before debt service and depreciation by the capitalization rate. In this particular instance, the net income before debt service and depreciation was $33,000. This is divided by twelve and one-half percent.

The capitalization rate, even for the same investment, may differ depending on certain factors, such as geographic area. The sunbelt may have a lower capitalization rate than a region that is experiencing little growth. The capitalization rate should be understood for exactly what it is and that is a "general" rate of return for like and similar investments. It does not attempt to equate or produce a rate of return for a specific investment.

2. The second method, known as the market approach, determines the value of the company under analysis by multiplying its adjusted earnings by the price earnings ratio of a comparable company in the same industry, which is traded in the marketplace. This can be compared to the real estate appraiser who, in determining the fair market value of the twelve-flat in the above example, ascertains sales of like buildings in the same general geographic area.

For example, a sixteen-unit apartment building in the same geographic area and in the same condition was sold for $384,000, or $24,000 a unit. The market approach would indicate a value for the twelve-flat at $288,000 (twelve units times $24,000 per unit). If the company under analysis has adjusted earnings of $250,000 and if a comparable publicly traded company is selling at ten times its adjusted earnings, the value of the company would be $2,500,000.

3. The third method is the cost approach, which involves a determination of the depreciated cost of the underlying assets. In the above example, the cost of new construction for the twelve-flat would be determined and this cost could be depreciated to reflect the age of the twelve-flat. If a new twelve-unit apartment building could be built for $35,000 a unit and if the appraiser determined that approximately one-third of the economic life had already elapsed, the per unit depreciated cost would be two-thirds of $35,000 or $23,333. The total value would be $279,996.00 (per unit depreciated cost times number of units).

Differences Between Income and Market Approach

It should be noted that the income approach and the market approach are similar. The income approach, which is a capitalization of net earnings, may not take into consideration the specific type of industry. The proper capitalization rate for general manufacturing companies may be ten percent, while widget manufacturers may be yielding fifteen percent.

The market approach does not consider only the income from the company but other intrinsic factors (such as book value). The prime tool in developing a value for the closely held corporation is the market approach, or if not, the use of a combination of the income and the market approach.

Before developing a valuation using a comparable company (market approach), it is important to determine the adjusted income of the company to be analyzed. The question that may be raised is "Does the income or capitalization approach alone have any use in valuing a closely held corporation?" The answer normally is, only as a last resort. In other words, it is important to find a comparable company. Only when this becomes impossible should an analysis be based only on the capitalization approach. The approach used in developing the fair market value of the closely held corporation is a combination of an adjusted market (the income is adjusted and the valuation is determined with comparable companies) and adjusted cost.

HOW TO USE VALUATION TOOLS TO DETERMINE FAIR MARKET VALUE

How to Determine Value Based on the Earnings Approach

Why is it impossible to compare the earnings of a publicly held corporation with those of a closely held corporation without adjustments? The earnings of a publicly traded corporation are more indicative of the true income of the corporation than the income reported on the statements of a closely held corporation. The officers and directors of a publicly held corporation are subject to two separate and conflicting pressures that affect the decisions they make.

The first set of pressures involves survival and paying the lowest possible income tax. The other set of pressures involves the obligation to the shareholders. The obligation to the shareholders necessitates the maximization of income and the payment of dividends to maintain the market value of the shares. Both of these are, tax wise, disastrous. The closely held corporation is not under the constraints placed by the investing public.

A perfect example of this concept is the compensation package provided for the chief executive officer who is also the majority shareholder. This compensation package seldom will be solely reflective of his worth to the business. Rarely will this compensation package be structured to consider what minimum amount the corporation will have to pay so that the executive officer will not go looking for another job. His or her compensation reflects a combination of the parties' needs and the tax advisor's desire to produce the maximum tax results while at the same time maintaining the shareholder's life style.

Before you can compare the earnings of the closely held corporation to the earnings of a publicly held company, it is important to make certain adjustments to income. Some of the most common are:

1. compensation paid in excess of replacement salaries
2. fringe benefits above and beyond those that are usual in the industry and those that are geared for the maximum benefit of the shareholder/employee
3. adjustments to inventory, LIFO, and others
4. adjustments related to the personal use of corporate assets
5. costs that were expensed rather than capitalized

While the appropriate starting point is the after-tax income as reported on the financial statements, the above after-tax effect of the adjustments should be added to or subtracted from the book income to determine the true earnings capacity of the corporation.

Example: It is determined that XYZ corporation is paying $50,000 of excess compensation to its chief executive officer, who is also its majority shareholder. The corporation is in the forty percent combined federal and state tax bracket. Accordingly, a net after-tax adjustment of $30,000 should be added to book income.

HOW EARNINGS TRENDS AFFECT FAIR MARKET VALUE

The basic supposition in the earnings approach of valuation is that the future earnings of the business can be predicted from its prior earnings history. In other words, prior earnings are the most reliable guide to what the company will earn in the future. Once the expected earnings of the company has been determined, this figure is multiplied by the price earnings ratio of comparable publicly traded companies. The price earnings ratio is defined as the market price of a share of publicly traded stock divided by its per share earnings. For example, if a company is trading at $45 and if its earnings are $5, the price earnings ratio is nine.

A determination of the future earning power of the company requires an analysis of the prior years' adjusted earnings and earnings trends. There is no doubt that earnings trends are extremely significant in determining the value of the corporate stock. An example of the impact of these trends can be seen by studying the following example.

Example:

Corporations A, B, and C have the following per share earnings

	1981	1982	1983	1984	1985
A	\$1.00	\$1.20	\$1.44	\$1.73	\$2.08
B	\$1.50	\$1.48	\$1.51	\$1.47	\$1.49
C	\$2.10	\$1.75	\$1.42	\$1.20	\$ .98

Each of these companies has an average per share earnings for the five-year period of \$1.49. Corporation A's earnings are growing at twenty percent, compounded per year; Corporation B's earnings are static; and Corporation C's earnings are declining. Obviously, the future earnings of each corporation would have to take these trends into consideration. The Internal Revenue Service has acknowledged this fact and will accord more weight to the most recent years. A simplistic way of approaching the weighting of earnings trends was set forth in *Central Trust Company v. U.S.* (305F.2d.393,424 (Ct. Cls. 1962)), which weighed the earnings on a scale from five for the most recent year to one for the last of the five years.

If this particular approach was used in the above example, the following table would result.

	1981	1982	1983	1984	1985	Total
Corp. A	1x(\$1.00) +	2x(\$1.20) +	3x(\$1.44) +	4x(\$1.73) +	5x(\$2.08)	= \$25.04
Corp. B	1x(\$1.50) +	2x(\$1.48) +	3x(\$1.51) +	4x(\$1.47) +	5x(\$1.49)	= \$22.32
Corp. C	1x(\$2.10) +	2x(\$1.75) +	3x(\$1.42) +	4x(\$1.20) +	5x(\$ .98)	= \$19.56

Average Earnings of Corp. A $\frac{25.04}{15} = \$1.67$

Average Earnings of Corp. B $\frac{22.32}{15} = \$1.49$

Average Earnings of Corp. C $\frac{19.56}{15} = \$1.30$

The weighted earnings of Corporation A are approximately twenty-eight percent higher than that of Corporation C, although the average earnings of A, B, and C are all the same. For those who are enamored with procedures using exact formulas, this has particular merit. There probably is little relationship between the value of Corporation A and Corporation C. Realistically, an analysis such as this has little meaning without understanding the reasons behind the trends. Before arriving at a value for either A or C, a complete analysis should be made of the reasons for the increase or decrease in the earnings. Remember, the object is to determine the future earnings. This only can be predicted by the past if the constants remain the same.

The above earnings trends should reflect the adjusted net earnings of the company and not the net earnings as reported on the financial statements of the company. An indication of how these earnings have been manipulated to reflect tax motivated considerations has already been set forth. In addition, adjustments should also be made for nonrecurring factors that have a material impact on earnings. These include such things as capital gains, strikes, abnormal retirement payments, fire, or other disruptive events.

How to Determine the Accurate Price Earnings Ratio

Once the appropriate earnings have been determined, the task remains to find an appropriate multiplier. The best guide is the price earnings ratio of a comparable company whose shares are publicly traded.

The obvious problem is that a truly comparable company rarely exists. Even if a company is found in the same industry manufacturing the same products, it is doubtful that it would be the same size. Normally, traded companies are larger and have a different market position than the company under valuation. Even if a comparable company is found, its past history and earning's record may not be the same. If the publicly traded company had the earnings trend of Corporation C in the above example, while the corporation that was being valued had the earnings trends of A Corporation, truly comparable companies have not been found.

As truly comparable companies are difficult to locate, the valuation of the company may be based on other businesses with common characteristics. Sometimes it is impossible to find a company that will be acceptable. In those cases, it will be necessary to find a price earnings ratio that would be indicative of a similar investment. In other words, apply an appropriate capitalization rate.

The classical thesis is that a risky business should be acquired at a lower price earnings ratio than a nonrisky, stable business. The factors that could be taken into consideration are the nature of the business and the stability or irregularity of the earnings. Because the capitalization rate is based on subjective factors that are hard to justify, finding a comparable company is extremely important.

HOW TO USE BOOK VALUE IN THE VALUATION OF THE BUSINESS

Book value is defined as the net assets of a company as presented on its financial statements; in other words, the gross assets less the liabilities. The stated assets as reflected on the company's books will almost invariably be reflected at cost or sometimes, as in the case of inventories, at the lower of cost or market. The depreciated cost rarely bears any relationship to the fair market value of the underlying assets in an operating company. An example will illustrate this concept.

Example: XYZ Corporation owns the following assets subject to the liabilities set forth below. The information from its financial statements is reported at cost (depreciated cost where applicable) or as in the case of inventories LIFO (Last In First Out). The second column represents the actual fair market value of the underlying assets.

	Per Financial Statements	Fair Market Value
Cash	1,000.00	1,000.00
Receivables Net of Bad Debts	10,000.00	10,000.00
Inventory Based on the LIFO Method of Accounting	20,000.00	40,000.00
Equipment	10,000.00	30,000.00
Land and Buildings	50,000.00	75,000.00
Patent	10,000.00	100,000.00
TOTAL ASSETS:	$101,000.00	$256,000.00
Liabilities	50,000.00	50,000.00
Capital Stock and Earnings	51,000.00	51,000.00
Unrealized Appreciation	0.00	155,000.00
TOTAL LIABILITIES AND EQUITY:	$101,000.00	$256,000.00

If XYZ Corporation has 1,000 shares of issued common stock, the book value, as represented on its financial statements, would be $51 per share. If the book value was adjusted for the market value of the underlying assets, it would increase to $206 per share. In determining book value for sales purposes, it is necessary to make adjustments similar to those that were made in determining adjusted net income. Among those items that would normally have to be adjusted are the following.

1. Inventory. If inventory for financial statement purposes is reflected at lower of cost or market, then the book value of the inventory should be fairly reflective of its true value. If inventory is valued pursuant to LIFO, it has a tendency, in periods of inflation, to be undervalued. In this case, an adjustment should be made.

2. Equipment. For those purchases after the Economic Recovery Tax Act of 1981 and before January 1, 1987, the depreciated cost of equipment rarely equals its fair market value. The ability to amortize in five years the entire cost of the machinery and equipment rarely approximates the actual useful or economic life of the equipment. Accordingly, equipment may also be undervalued when it is reflected on the financial statements at depreciated cost.

3. Land and Buildings. This is another area where the fair market value may vary significantly from depreciated cost. For tax accounting purposes (prior to January 1, 1987), the entire building could be amortized in 19 years. After the Tax Reform Act of 1986, the normal amortization period for residential real property will be 27½ years and commercial and manufacturing real property 31½ years. It should be noted that financial institutions will normally allow for the purchase of the building to be paid in 25 years. Land and buildings have historically appreciated while on the books of the corporation they are subject to depreciation. Therefore, they may be significantly undervalued on the financial statements. With the changes in the depreciation schedules enacted by the Tax Reform Act of 1986, the disparity between the value of the land and buildings for book purposes and the true fair market value may lessen unless inflation again rears its ugly head.

4. Intangible Assets. Intangible assets such as patents, covenants not-to-compete, and the like may be worth a good deal more than the amount reflected on the financial statements.

DETERMINING THE DIFFERENCE BETWEEN BOOK VALUE AND LIQUIDATION BASIS

The next question that must be asked is, "Should book value be determined on a going concern basis or on a liquidation basis?" For example, on a going concern basis, the inventory listed on the financial statements is determined at lower of cost or market. Under this method, the corporation has determined its cost basis for the inventory. On an item by item basis, it has been ascertained whether the inventory should be reduced because of a decrease in the cost of the item, damage, obsolescence, and the like.

This method should normally be reflective of the true fair market value of the inventory on a going concern basis. Upon liquidation, it is common for a company not to receive the full cost for its inventory because there will not be a commercially saleable method available. A bulk sale or other device to "dispose," not sell, the inventory must be found.

Another example of the difference between going concern and liquidating value is equipment. It is relatively easy to determine the cost of new equipment and determine how much less than cost this used equipment should be reflected on the books (economic depreciation versus tax depreciation). In the event that the company had to be liquidated, the ability of the corporation to realize this fair market value is doubtful. Normally, adjusted book value is based on the assumption that the corporation will continue to operate. In the following instances, this assumption may be inappropriate.

1. the future operation of the corporation is in doubt
2. liquidation is being considered as a viable alternative to continuation of the business

For example, a furniture store is attempting to determine its fair market value for the purposes of sale. As liquidation of the business is a realistic alternative to sale as a going concern, there may actually be two sets of valuations. One set will be based on a continuing operating basis using weighted earnings and adjusted book value, with the other set using liquidation value. The furniture, fixtures and equipment used in the operation of the business will probably have different values on each of these two statements. For example, as a going concern, the depreciated value based on an economic basis is appropriate while on a liquidation sale the furniture, fixtures and equipment will probably be listed at salvage value.

In a sales and merchandising corporation where the major portion of the assets are invested in inventory and receivables, the ability to liquidate at near the adjusted book value may be practical. However, if the corporation is a manufacturing corporation, the ability to liquidate this corporation and realize the full fair market value is doubtful. This fact, along with the consideration that earnings in an operating company is the primary factor in valuing a corporation, makes book value of questionable use. While earnings appear to be a cornerstone in the valuation process of a majority of businesses, it requires a number of subjective determinations, such as, weighting for earnings trends, comparable PE, capitalization rate, and so forth. On the other hand, the determination of book value, while it may be subject to differing opinions as to the underlying value of the assets or approaches (liquidation value or operating company value), is relatively easy to grasp and to set margins for error. Therefore, as both the buyer and seller can relate to and understand book value, it probably has an inordinate weight in the valuation process.

Key Idea: While a business may be bought and sold based on projected earnings, buyers and sellers feel more comfortable when the actual price relates to book value.

How Other Factors Can Affect Valuation

There is no doubt that the payment of dividends has a definite impact on the valuation of publicly traded corporations. The investing public weighs any investment for both its current income and its anticipated appreciation in value over a period of time. Many corporations will decide to maintain a dividend history in order to support the price of its stock.

At the other end of the spectrum are the owners of closely held corporations. Except at the time of sale, their desire is to maintain a low value (for gift and estate tax purposes) rather than to attain the highest attainable value. Other than in special situations, a closely held corporation, because of the adverse tax ramifications, will rarely pay dividends. If a publicly held corporation paying dividends appears comparable on all other counts, the value of the closely held corporation will tend to be discounted. An example will illustrate this point.

Example: XYZ, a publicly traded corporation, has been selling at a price earnings ratio of ten, and currently has been traded in a range between thirty-nine and forty-one. It has established a dividend history over the last ten years and is currently paying a dividend of $2 a year. Even if the closely held corporation is comparable to the publicly traded corporation except that it has not been paying a $2 a year dividend, it would be inappropriate to utilize the price earnings ratio of ten in determining the value of the closely held corporation. The value must be discounted.

HOW TO ARRIVE AT THE COMPOSITE VALUE USING BOTH EARNINGS AND BOOK VALUE

Valuation of the corporation usually combines both the earnings potential and book value. As with all general rules, there are exceptions. One of the most obvious is where liquidation is a realistic alternative. The net proceeds from a liquidation sale may exceed the amount that could be obtained from the sale of the business as a going concern. In these cases, the earnings approach would yield a value less than the adjusted book value as reflected on a liquidation basis.

Key Idea: Normally, the valuation of a business involves weighing both the adjusted book value of the corporation and the potential earnings. An exception is where the adjusted book value determined on a liquidation basis would yield a greater return than the value determined using a multiple of earnings.

Unfortunately, there is no mathematical determination as to exactly how much weight should be accorded each factor. The imprecise nature of these determinations is best addressed by the Internal Revenue Service's position as set forth in Rev. Rul. 59-60:

> That because valuation cannot be made on the basis of the prescribed formula, there is no means whereby the various applicable factors in a particular case can be assigned mathematical weights in deriving the fair market value.

It would appear that the IRS does not want to promulgate a predetermined formula as they obviously believe it can only be used against them. The courts that have to deal in these matters often do not detail the reasoning giving rise to their decisions. One exception was the court in *Central Trust Company* (305F2d.393,424 (Ct. Cls. 1962)) which weighted the valuation as follows: fifty percent to earnings, twenty percent to book value, and thirty percent to an approach that based its value on capitalizing dividends.

In the case of *Bader* (172F Supp.833 (D.C. Ill. 1959)), the earnings were again given a fifty percent weight; dividend and book value valuations were each given twenty-five percent. While these cases involved determining value for tax purposes, they illustrate the prevalent reasoning, which is to give a greater weight to earnings than to book value or capitalizing dividend payments.

Key Idea: While there is no precise formula for weighing the various factors, normally earnings will be given the greatest weight. This can be two, three, or four times greater than book value. If, in addition, the closely held corporation is paying dividends, it would also be necessary to capitalize the dividends to determine a valuation for the corporation.

WHEN THE COMPOSITE VALUE SHOULD BE DISCOUNTED

Once a per share value has been arrived at by weighting earnings and book value, it is necessary to analyze whether or not it is appropriate to discount this value. The two major factors giving rise to a discount are:

1. minority interest
2. lack of marketability

How to Arrive at a Minority Discount

In a small, closely held corporation there is a disparity of worth between the majority and minority interests. In the absence of corporate agreements, minority shares are worth substantially less than a majority interest in the corporation. Any party who has represented the holders of a minority interest in an intracorporate dispute knows how little leverage the minority shares have in absence of any protection through corporate agreements. For this reason, a minority interest should be discounted. The question is, "how much?"

This, like many other decisions that are made in the valuation process, must be made on a case by case basis. Obviously, if more than fifty percent (50%) of the stock is being transferred, there is no minority discount. On the other hand, if fifty percent (50%) or less is transferred, the parties will disagree as to how great this discount should be. The seller will normally downplay the importance of this discount. The purchaser, on the other hand, will dwell on the problems inherent in purchasing less than a controlling interest. Accordingly, a discount from as little as zero to as much as fifty percent may be applied in each case.

How to Arrive at a Discount for Lack of Marketability

Sometimes it is appropriate to discount the stock for lack of marketability. It is necessary to distinguish the concepts of marketability and minority discounts. These concepts are often confused because the rationale in allowing the minority discount is essentially the same as that for the lack of marketability. In both cases, it is difficult to sell the shares for the price at which publicly held shares with comparable earnings would be sold. The distinction between lack of marketability and minority interest is that the former could apply to a controlling as well as a minority interest. In the sales process, it is not a good idea for the seller to discount the value for lack of marketability. The courts, however, have allowed a marketability discount of between ten and twenty percent.

How to Arrive at a Discount for Nonvoting Stock

The final discount that may be applied is for nonvoting stock. In a closely held corporation, the majority with voting control will, in all likelihood, dictate the distribution of a good percentage of the earnings through salaries, bonuses, and fringe benefits rather than dividends. The stockholder owning nonvoting stock is in the same position as the minority stockholder. The discount for nonvoting stock should be comparable with the minority discount.

GETTING THE MOST OUT OF THE VALUATION LETTER

General concepts are best illustrated by specific examples. We have described how to determine earnings potential and adjusted book value. Now it is important to apply these general concepts to a particular fact situation. The application in this particular case will be through the use of a valuation letter. For purposes of illustration, two different fact situations will be explored. The valuation letters detailing the reasoning behind the process are set forth in Appendices A and B.

The best way to approach this subject is to ask "Now that you know the value, what is the best way to use it?" Or, to put it another way, "What good is the analysis if nobody else knows it?" Rarely will it be worthwhile to obtain a valuation and not have the facts, reasons, and conclusions summarized in the valuation letter. There are exceptions to this general rule, especially where the owner may suspect the potential purchaser is only on a fishing expedition and may not be truly interested or financially capable of purchasing. An example will illustrate this particular exception.

Example: Jake runs Jake's Pizza Parlor, a very profitable business. He is approaching retirement age and has been approached to sell numerous times. His old buddy Joe has approached him at the country club after golf and casually discussed the possibility of purchasing Jake's Pizza Parlor. Jake does not believe that Joe has the financial wherewithal to secure this purchase. He does not want to expend too much of his professionals' time and therefore his money in valuing the corporation and determining terms on which he would be willing to sell.

Accordingly, a letter setting forth the general parameters of the purchase excluding the reasoning behind the valuation may be all that is needed. A full valuation such as that set forth in Appendices A and B would be superfluous as the primary problem is not the value of the corporation but the financial instability of the purchaser.

The valuation letter can be utilized in the same manner as the written real estate appraisal. If the prospective purchaser is not known at the period of time the appraisal is obtained, there probably is little reason to have it written. If the prospective purchaser is already known, it may be an extremely effective sales' tool. As in the sale of real estate, where there is a tentative agreement between the parties to sell at the "fair market value," it is incumbent on the seller to obtain an "appraisal" to add validity to the asking price or, in the case of the buyer, to add validity to the offering price. If the other party feels that the appraisal is inappropriate (not the true fair market value) he or she must obtain a second appraisal to counteract that which has already been presented. In this case, the other party is responding to somebody else's initiative and a responder in the negotiating process is normally at a disadvantage.

The valuation letter is used primarily in two instances:

1. where there is a preexisting relationship, or
2. where the prospective purchaser is known and has already evinced an interest in purchasing the business.

A preexisting relationship will include those situations in which the prospective purchaser is a fellow shareholder or employee, or has some form of business relationship with the seller, such as a purchaser or supplier of goods to the corporation.

The valuation letter can also be used effectively where the prospective purchaser is known and prior discussions between the parties have shown he has an interest "if the price is right." An example of how to use a valuation letter in these instances is as follows.

Example: Joe Jones has been an employee of Worldwide Widgets for many years. This was a "family business." However, his was not the side of the family that controlled the business. While Worldwide Widgets was a fiscally substantial business, it was not publicly traded. In the past, its employees had been encouraged to purchase stock. Joe has indicated that a vast portion of his retirement assets are invested in the illiquid stock of Worldwide Widgets. The financial information is set forth in Appendix A, Schedule I. He was unsure as how to proceed. Certain factors were apparent:

1. Worldwide Widgets, Inc., had been extremely successful during the period 1981 through 1984. Like other manufacturing companies, they are currently suffering from foreign competition, and the future, while not insecure, is not projected to be as profitable as the past.
2. Joe has indicated that he does not want to "rock the boat." This is a family matter and he does not want to upset his good relationship with the remainder of the family.
3. There was both voting and nonvoting stock outstanding.

The approach that was deemed most likely to produce the desired result was a valuation letter directed to Joe from his attorney, a copy of which is set forth in Appendix A. This valuation letter attempted to establish a purchase price at a "high reasonable value." Joe then distributed the letter to the family. The goal was to use the objective third party appraisal, through the valuation letter, to morally force the family into making the correct decision.

How to Use the Valuation Letter When There Is a Prospective Purchaser

Many times you will be dealing with a situation in which the parties have already begun to discuss the possible purchase of the business. For example, the owner of the business, who is a superb negotiator, has decided that he wishes to actively participate in the sales process. Personal motivations have determined that it is the right time to sell the business.

As will be indicated in Appendix B, this was not the appropriate time to sell according to an analysis of the intrinsic factors, but the extrinsic factors were positive. In the case of Widget Inc., the widget industry had made a turnaround and the investing public was favorably valuing the future of the widget companies. The price earnings ratio was higher than that which could be reasonably expected. In preparing a valuation letter for this company, interesting problems presented themselves.

1. Even though Widget, Inc., had been profitable for many years, it had fallen on hard times. Schedule I attached to Exhibit B illustrates the adverse current financial information. The owner had indicated to me that the company had turned the corner and that the future was again profitable. As shown in Section 2, this is one of the most difficult situations in which to justify the "true fair market value."

2. Not only did the owner want to know the true price, he wanted the highest price that could be realistically obtained. He knew that the prospective purchaser was a hard negotiator and all matters would be subject to fierce negotiation.

3. The owners had been very tax conscious and, accordingly, the corporation in the past had been used to maximize tax planning. There were excess as well as esoteric fringe benefits.

4. Because the corporation was a manufacturer and lessor of its widgets, as well as a distributor for the various peripheral items that are used in the widget industry, it had, in the past, attempted to expense rather than capitalize as much of its production costs as possible. The problem was further complicated by the fact that the inventory of Widgets, Inc., had increased substantially. It was necessary in determining the real income for each and every year to counterbalance the excess depreciation (if all widgets had been capitalized) against the costs that had been expensed rather than capitalized.

5. In determining book value, the nature of the company's products indicates Widget, Inc., produced a specialty widget. There was no real market for the inventory of Widget. Accordingly, the only true use of book value would be on a continuing not a liquidation basis. The prospective purchaser knew that the sellers had no real alternative other than to "sell the business;" liquidation was not a viable alternative.

In this, as in most cases, the valuation letter has a twofold function:

1. to indicate, within parameters, the true value of the business, and
2. to use as a sales tool.

Many times the valuation letter is prepared to educate the client as to the value of the business. In these cases, the client may not be convinced by just one opinion. Separate valuations by an attorney, accountant, and business broker may be needed. Valuation is an art and not a science. These letters are used only to avoid disaster where either the purchase price is so unreasonably high that potential purchasers are "scared off" or so low that the sale would be at a price less than its true fair market value. How to use these valuation letters not only for information but also as a sales tool will be discussed later on in Section 4.

In the example of Widget, Inc., the valuation letter was solely used as a sales tool. The owner of the business had in his own mind decided what the value of the business was and no amount of reasoning could convince him otherwise. He finally acknowledged that the price that he asked was high, but he believed that it would be used as a tool in his negotiations. This proved to be correct and a subsequent sale was negotiated, although at a price significantly less than the value set forth in this letter.

Key Idea: In preparing a valuation letter, it is important to keep in mind for what purposes it is to be used. The two most common purposes are to determine the true value of the business or to use as a sales tool. In each instance, the structure and presentation will be slightly different. In all cases it is important to discuss in the letter both the positive and negative factors that have gone into the valuation process. Otherwise, the conclusions would be suspect as the other party will be under the impression that not all factors have been considered.

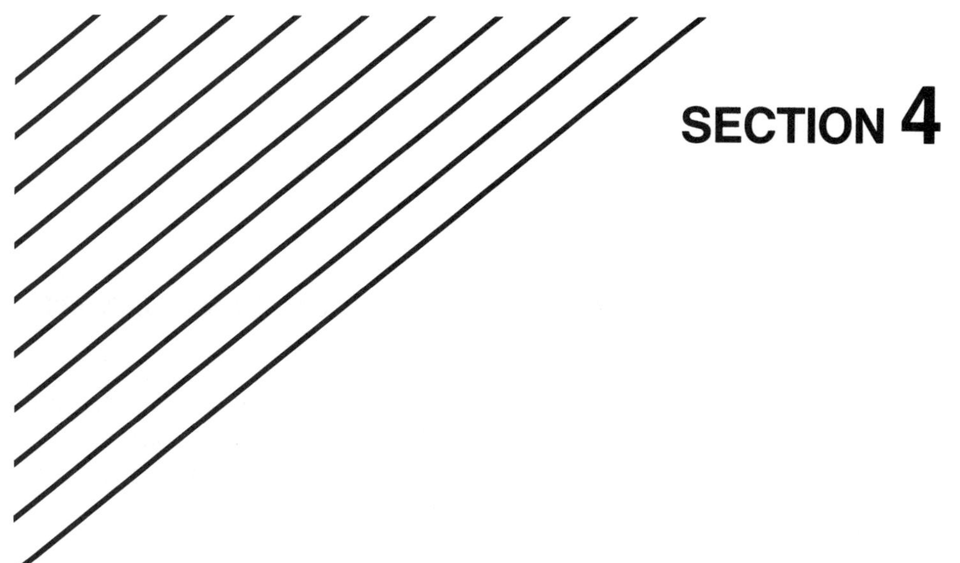

SECTION 4

HOW TO INITIATE THE SALES PROCESS: "PUT YOUR HOUSE IN ORDER AND ZERO IN ON POTENTIAL PURCHASERS"

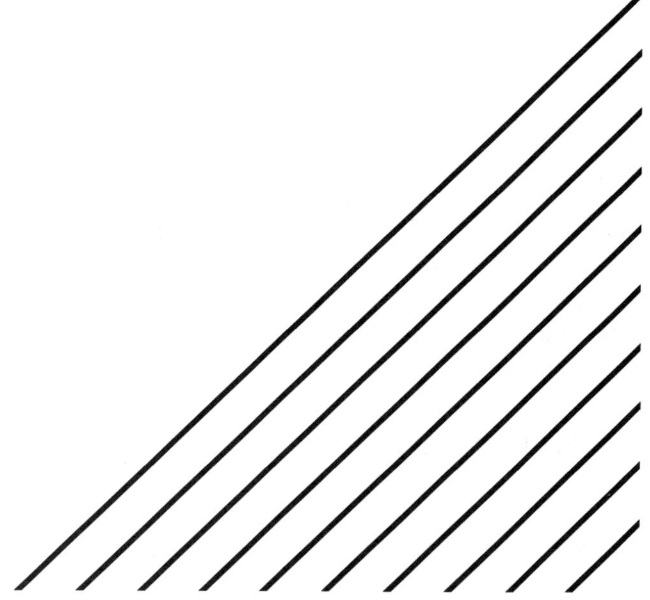

ANALYZING AND COORDINATING YOUR OWN NEEDS WITH THE SALE

The first affirmative step in the sales process is to analyze your net worth. You must decide whether the income from your current assets is sufficient to maintain your life style, both with and without the proceeds that could be realized from the sale of your business.

Example (1):

Joe owns the following:

Assets:	
House	$300,000.00
100% of Widget, Inc.	$1,000,000.00
Marketable Securities	$100,000.00
	$1,400,000.00
His current income is:	
Salary	$150,000.00
Interest on Investments	$10,000.00
Miscellaneous	$5,000.00
	$165,000.00

Obviously, if the income necessary to maintain his life style is $100,000, a sale of the business, either for cash or pursuant to a promissory note, will in all likelihood be necessary.

Example (2): Use Example (1) with the following changes: In addition to the above assets, Joe is age seventy and has $600,000 in a profit sharing plan. Assuming a ten percent return on his money, his $600,000 could guarantee a $95,149 per year payment for the next ten years. Joe need not sell the business in order to retire.

FIVE TAX-PLANNING TOOLS THAT MINIMIZE TAXES

It is important to coordinate your income requirements with the desire to minimize taxation upon the sale. The key is not cash flow or gross income, but after-tax income. Accordingly, your current as well as prior tax planning must be analyzed. The tax-planning devices that are available to the corporate client for the minimization of taxes are limited in number. These planning tools take different forms at different stages in the corporate existence, but they all involve:

1. dividing the income,
2. shifting the income,
3. converting income from ordinary income to capital gain, (This technique, which is no longer applicable, was extremely useful prior to January 1, 1988.)
4. recategorizing income or properly paying expenses,
5. timing of income.

Many of the tax-planning tools involve the shifting of income between entities and persons, or from one period of time to another. The first question that is asked is, "What are your after-tax income needs?" The answer to this question is pivotal. As with all tax planning, the most difficult client will be the one who needs all his income to maintain his desired life style. An example will illustrate the disastrous tax results that this type of client can present.

Example: Joe Doctor discusses tax planning on an annual basis with his advisors. Every year he establishes a game plan to minimize his taxes. His plan has involved reducing his taxable income through the implementation of qualified deferred compensation plans, and retaining surplus income in his service corporation. If Joe Doctor follows his advisors' suggestions, his $150,000 of earnings (gross income less expenses of maintaining his practice) would be reported, taxwise, as follows:

1. Joe would receive a salary of $100,000 from his service corporation.

2. Of the remainder, $25,000 would be contributed to the qualified deferred compensation plans established by Joe Doctor's service corporation.

3. The final $25,000 could be retained in his service corporation.

With the above planning, Joe Doctor's total federal tax liability would be determined as follows:

Corporate Tax	3,750.00
Individual Tax (assuming other income equals itemized deductions in excess of the zero bracket amount and exemptions)	25,537.50
Total Family Tax Liability:	29,287.50

As it turns out, Joe Doctor does not pay this tax. He pays a tax on $150,000 of taxable income, or $42,000. This is just under $13,000 more than would be required if the above game plan had been established. The reason for the doctor's disastrous tax situation is that his financial needs are such that he requires all the income to be paid to him individually in order to maintain his life style. All tax planning has the quid pro quo—the loss of control.

Note: The prior illustration shows that the financial needs of the seller may dictate the method of proceeding. For example, if the owner has substantial personal indebtedness, the required down payment must be an amount sufficient to satisfy his personal obligations. This may not be desirable taxwise, but any amount less than this might not be feasible.

Example: George has the following assets and liabilities:

Assets:	
House	$700,000.00
100% of Widget, Inc.	$2,000,000.00
	$2,700,000.00
Liabilities:	
Mortgage on Home	$600,000.00
Secured Indebtedness (Stock of Widget, Inc. pledged)	$400,000.00
	$1,000,000.00
Equity	$1,700,000.00

In this case, George may require at least $1,000,000 downpayment on the sale. Anything less would leave him at the mercy of the payments from the purchaser to meet his debt obligations.

As with Joe Doctor and his yearly income requirements, the most difficult seller to plan for is the one who will need the total proceeds paid in cash at closing. The example of Joe is not meant to illustrate maximum tax planning as it utilizes only elementary planning devices. It illustrates the point that the final decisions as to the requested asking price and terms of sale can only be ascertained after a determination of the individual owner's net worth and the income needed to maintain his life style.

PINPOINTING YOUR CURRENT NET WORTH AND INCOME FLOW

The first step for any seller is to prepare a balance sheet of the total assets and liabilities.

Any of the financial statements supplied to your bank when obtaining a loan or a form similar to that could be utilized for this purpose. From this information, it is necessary to determine your income (see Appendix C). It is also advisable to review the last three years' personal tax returns so that the sources of your income can be analyzed. In determining your future income, certain items from the tax return should be modified. The appropriate modifications are set forth as follows.

1. Tax exempt securities. If you own tax exempt securities, the income generated by these are to be included in your income.

2. Social security payments. If you will receive social security in the near future, the amount for both you and your spouse must be determined and included in income.

3. Cash flow and non-taxable income from rental properties should be considered. Anticipated income should also be reflected, for example, if the mortgage has been substantially reduced and could be paid off, the anticipated cash flow is included in income.

4. Projected profit sharing payments are income. The amount included should be determined as a single life annuity if single. If you are married, a joint and survivor annuity should be the frame of reference (see Appendix D). An example will indicate how the amount of income can be determined.

Example: Joe Owner has $200,000 accumulated in a profit sharing plan for his sole benefit, in which he is 100 percent vested. He is sixty-five and his wife is sixty-three. They are interested in purchasing a joint and survivor annuity. According to the tables, male sixty-five, female sixty-three, they should receive $7.74 per month for each $1,000 invested (see Appendix D). The monthly annuity that can be purchased with the $200,000 is $1,548. This annuity would be paid until both Joe and his wife are deceased.

5. IRA, Individual retirement account. The analysis will be the same as that set forth in paragraph 4.

6. Pension plan. The payments to be received will be specifically set forth in the plan. The amount of retirement income will usually be dependent on salary, years of service, and age at retirement.

7. Other income will include such items as, commissions, royalties, director's fees, and the like.

8. Tax sheltered investments. During the last two decades, the investment by high-income individuals in tax sheltered investments has been common. It is important during this analysis to determine whether or not these investments will provide a cash flow in the future and, if so, how they will be taxed. Also, if the seller had anticipated his future tax needs to be mitigated by these tax shelters, he should closely review the impact on the utilization of these passive losses against his other income after the Tax Reform Act of 1986.

Once the total income is ascertained, state and federal income tax should be calculated so that the net after tax income can be determined. The tax returns, in conjunction with the net worth statement, will provide both a determination of the pre- and post-sale after-tax income.

HOW TO ADJUST PROJECTED INCOME TO MEET PERSONAL FINANCIAL GOALS

Once you have prepared an analysis of your projected after-sale income, it is important to determine your needs and ascertain if there is any shortfall. Unfortunately, the analysis is not always as simple as it appears. This analysis presupposes using only the income from investments and exhausting the qualified deferred compensation and IRA funds. Some owners of a business will be solely concerned about providing sufficient income for themselves and their spouses during their lifetimes. They are not interested in leaving estates to their heirs. Other individuals feel an obligation to the next generation. Between these two extremes, there is an infinite number of variations depending on the individual's desires.

Key Idea: It is imperative at the first possible opportunity to analyze your individual income requirements as well as your sources of income both prior to and after sale.

Key Idea: As an advisor, when you are discussing both sources of income and income needs with the individual owner, it is usually a good idea to broach the subject of whether or not he feels any obligation to leave an estate to the next generation. Normally, during the first inquiry, his answer may be undefined as he may not have previously considered this. It is a good idea to reask and rephrase this question at various times throughout the sales process. This will give the seller an opportunity to crystallize his own thoughts and desires.

Restructure Investments

Another factor to be considered is that the post-sale investments can be restructured to produce additional income. For example, the presale income may have been exceedingly high because of the high salary. Therefore, a substantial portion of the liquid assets may have been invested in tax-free municipals or tax deferred annuities. After sale, it may be appropriate to change the tax deferred annuities into taxable annuities and to convert some of the municipal bonds into higher yielding corporate or treasury bonds.

Example: Joe Owner has just sold all of the stock in Widget, Inc., in 1986 and has realized $500,000 in after-tax proceeds. His before- and after-sale assets and taxable income before adjustments are as hereinafter set forth. It is assumed that he is married and his other income equals his exemptions and itemized deductions in excess of the zero bracket amount.

I. Calculation of Taxable Income	1986 Before Sale Income	After Sale Income Assuming 1988 Rates
Salary	$120,000	–
Net Taxable Income from Investments (1)	($ 40,000)	0
Covenant not-to-compete	(0)	$ 25,000
Taxable Income	$ 80,000	$ 25,000
Tax	$ 23,159	$ 3,750
After-tax Taxable Income	$ 51,841	$ 21,250
II. Calculation of Cashflow		
After-tax Taxable Income	$ 56,841	$ 21,250
Plus Cash Flow Non-taxable and elimination of non-cash flow loss	(2) $ 50,000	(3) $ 50,000
Cash Flow	$ 106,841	$ 71,250

(1) $400,000 of assets were invested in tax shelters. These tax shelters produced a minimum cash flow of $10,000 and a yearly taxable loss of $40,000. All the loss was allowed prior to the Tax Reform Act of 1986. As this was a passive activity in which the taxpayer invested prior to the date of enactment, the disallowance of the loss would have been phased in. For the sake of simplicity, I have assumed in this example all loss was available in 1988.

Tax Shelter Loss	($ 40,000)	
Income for Sale Proceeds ($500,000 × 8%)	$ 40,000	
Net Taxable Income from Investments	0	
(2) Net Taxable Income Investment		
Must add Non-taxable cash flow	$ 10,000	
Plus eliminate Non-cash Flow Loss	$ 40,000	
	$ 50,000	
(3) 1988 Net Taxable Income from Investments (must add same as 2 above):		
Assets:		
Stock	$ 500,000	0
Cash Equivalents	0	$ 500,000
Tax Deferred Annuity	$ 350,000	$ 350,000
Tax Shelter Investments (1)	$ 400,000	$ 400,000
House and Personal Assets	$ 300,000	$ 300,000
Total Assets	$1,550,000	$1,550,000

It is assumed in the above example that the only initial change that was made by Joe was that his non-income-producing asset of the closely held common stock was converted into income producing assets at eight percent. After discussion with Joe, it is determined that he needs about $90,000 in after-tax cash flow to maintain his life style and currently there is a substantial shortfall. Positive steps that he could take in this case are:

1. Convert the tax shelter into tax exempts yielding six percent. It should be noted that tax shelters are usually illiquid and difficult to convert to cash. However, Joe, with the help of his advisors, did purchase the tax shelters at a period of time that they will "mature" and be converted into cash at the time of the sale of his closely held corporation.

2. Convert the tax deferred annuity into payment of interest only at eight percent. If these steps were taken, he would have the following income in 1987:

Salary	0
Income from Investments:	
Tax Deferred Annuity	$28,000.00
Municipals	$24,000.00
Cash Equivalents	$40,000.00
Covenant not-to-compete	$25,000.00
Total Cash Flow	$117,000.00
Tax	$ 23,227.50
After-tax Cash Flow	$ 93,772.50

Obviously his income could be supplemented from principal distributions in the tax sheltered annuity.

Key Idea: Tax exempts are worth "more" to a higher-basis taxpayer than a lower-basis taxpayer. The following chart will indicate the advantages of each of the various investments, depending on the individual tax bracket. The chart will illustrate how you can determine whether the municipal or the taxable investment is taxwise the most beneficial:

Individual Tax Bracket	Municipal Bond Rate
15%	×/.85
28%	×/.72
33%	×/.67

If X is the municipal bond rate, then the municipal bond investment is the superior investment, assuming all other factors being equal, if the taxable investment yields less than the "Equivalent Taxable Rate." The taxable investment is the superior investment, again, all factors being considered equal if it yields greater than the equivalent taxable rate.

Example:

Municipal Bond Rate—6%

Individual Tax Rate	Municipal Bond Rate		Equivalent Taxable Rate
15%	.6/.85	=	7.06%
28%	.6/.72	=	8.33%
33%	.6/.67	=	8.96%

Note that in 1988 and thereafter, there are only two rates for individual taxpayers:

	Married	Single
15%	0—$29,750	0—$17,850
28%	$29,750 and up	$17,850 and up

However, the benefit of the fifteen percent rate is phased out for married individuals with taxable incomes between $71,900 and $149,250. This phase out occurs for single individuals between $35,950 and $113,300. Therefore, a third-rate bracket amounting to thirty-three has been added. Municipals will be most beneficial taxwise to those individuals whose income occurs within those brackets.

PLANNING FOR THE UNPLANNED: DEATH OR DISABILITY

When analyzing your financial needs, it is also a good idea to make the same analysis considering unplanned for events such as death or disability. This is particularly useful if the planning occurs significantly before the proposed sale or retirement. An analysis such as the one above may indicate that even with a realistic sales price for the company, the cash flow after the sale would not be sufficient to maintain your life style. In this case, it may be appropriate to institute other planning devices, such as establishing qualified deferred compensation plans, purchasing rental real estate, or utilizing other tools and investments to ensure that additional income will be available.

Caution: This analysis may also indicate the need to supplement both life and disability insurance. In the example on page 84, if Joe Owner died or became disabled prior to sale, it could have a catastrophic effect on his family and business. His (or his estate's) need for personal funds could necessitate a forced sale of his home and business at a distressed price. In this instance, the purchase of life insurance to provide liquidity to the estate upon death and to supplement his income upon disability through disability insurance are appropriate expenditures.

It may also be necessary to develop a strategy such as this so that as many alternatives remain available to the owner as possible.

Example: An individual may have been depending on his investment in the business for his retirement. If a family member becomes interested in continuing the business, this could have a disastrous effect on his family relationship if he does not have alternative sources of income. As with most planning, flexibility remains the key.

TWO IMPORTANT STEPS BEFORE YOU PRESENT A COMPANY FOR SALE

There are certain steps that are worthwhile to take prior to offering the business for sale. The positive steps were discussed in Section 2. These involve eliminating extraneous assets or taking steps that may make your business more saleable.

Example: If you have two businesses, one categorized as high-tech and the other woodworking, it may be beneficial to spin off the woodworking division of the business, even if it is profitable, before attempting to sell the business as a whole. If the woodworking division of the business is included in the sale, even if it does not constitute a material portion of the total sales, earnings, or assets, it will have a negative impact on the sales process in the following ways:

1. It may classify the entire business, not as a high-tech, but as a woodworking company. Woodworking companies have historically sold at lower price earnings ratios than high-tech industries.
2. It may discourage certain purchasers who feel that they are paying too great a price for the total assets purchased.
3. The combined purchase price may be such that it is beyond the reach of many of the potential purchasers.

If the businesses are complimentary, the spinoff may not be a good idea. In these instances, it may be the only way possible to use the physical plant and personnel to the maximum advantage. An example of one of these exceptions may be a ski and dive retail outlet. Scuba diving is a capital-intensive retail business that requires specialized equipment and personnel; however, it may be an appropriate complement to a ski shop. Who wants to buy snow ski equipment in July?

Presale Planning Can Add "Salable Sex Appeal" to Your Business

It is also important to review the business to see if there is some way to add or create "salable sex appeal." The development of a new product, the establishment of a branch office, or the purchase of a competitor are examples of the positive steps to be taken. Any one of these will have the impact of adding a little extra appeal to the business that is being sold. Obviously the steps that can be taken and how useful they are will depend on the time span between the initial decision that a sale is appropriate and the beginning of the sales process.

HOW TO DETERMINE WHAT INFORMATION TO SUPPLY TO THE PROSPECTIVE PURCHASER

The sales process is fraught with many problems. One of the first is "What information do we supply to potential purchasers?" Obviously, without the necessary information, the potential purchaser cannot make an intelligent decision as to the advisability of purchasing the business. However, if the potential purchaser is a competitor and if your business is in a competitive industry, disseminating information can work to your disadvantage.

The principle questions you should ask are, "How confidential is the information?" and "How can it be used against me?" The answers to these questions will normally give rise to the scope and nature of the information that can be supplied. As a general rule, the more competitive the industry, the greater the detriment. Therefore, in competitive industries, generalized information should be supplied. With a less competitive industry, more specific information can be supplied without jeopardizing the business. In those industries in which your business may be adversely affected by the dissemination of this information the utilization of a nondisclosure document can lessen the possibility of an adverse impact on disclosure.

The second area that causes problems is the multi-business corporation. Some corporations operate multiple businesses. For example, they may manufacture pallets and fences. Pallets are sold directly to big corporations. Fences are sold either to the retail market or to the wholesale market. The question presented is "Do you combine or do you separate the financial information?" If the financial information is consolidated, it will be less useful to the potential purchaser. In the above example, the gross profit margins within the company may vary as follows:

	Gross Profit Margin
Pallets	20%
Fences sold at retail	50%
Fences sold wholesale	30%

If the information is combined and the gross profit margin is thirty-five percent, the result may be a meaningless figure, absolutely useless to the potential purchaser. However, if the information is broken down and supplied in great detail, it will be definitely more useful to the potential purchaser, but the possibility that it may be used to your disadvantage increases. The basic approach is to supply as little information as possible to keep the potential purchasers interested until you are able to separate those who are real potential purchasers from those who are just looking.

Key Idea: One of the first questions that must be asked is, "In how much detail should the financial and other information be presented?" The rule of thumb is to give the minimum information necessary to keep the potential purchaser interested. Full disclosure should occur at the latest possible time in the sales process and only to those who the seller has determined are truly interested.

Using a Nondisclosure Document

The nondisclosure document, a sample of which is set forth in Appendix E, attempts to restrict the use of the information supplied. The seller wishes to obligate the potential purchaser to use the supplied information solely to determine whether or not to purchase the business and not to reproduce or distribute it for any other purposes.

The nondisclosure document can be a formal or letter agreement. Sometimes it can be a useful tool for the purchaser as well as providing protection for the seller. Unschooled sellers are often hesitant to supply any information. An offer to execute a nondisclosure agreement by the potential purchaser who needs the information will often help alleviate the seller's hesitancy.

There is no doubt that the nondisclosure document is a validly binding agreement. The question that is raised is, "What good is it?" Trial attorneys would probably enjoy litigating the question of whether the disclosure of information has been detrimental to the seller and what damages resulted. As a practical matter, the nondisclosure document is a good will gesture and should be used for that purpose. It will, in all likelihood, weed out those individuals who wish to utilize the information solely to your disadvantage.

How to Develop an Offering Circular

While you are analyzing what information can be supplied, it is also useful to consider developing an offering circular. The offering circular should at least contain the following information:

1. a description of the nature and history of the business
2. a description of the workforce and whether it is unionized
3. a description of the key personnel, their shareholdings, and whether they have executed employment contracts
4. financial information for the last five years
5. the requested terms and conditions of sale

The usage of the offering circular as well as its contents will depend on numerous factors. The first factor is whether or not the information is to be widely distributed or supplied to a select group of potential purchasers. If a business broker is involved, he normally will work with the owners of the business to develop exactly what he deems appropriate.

Note: If self-marketing is the method to be used, it is normally prudent to treat all inquiries as individualized. The difference is not so much in content as in presentation. In an individualized approach, the offering circular will be customized. However, if there is a mass marketing effort, the individual receiving the information is attuned to the fact that he has not been personally approached but has been approached as part of a general solicitation. In this case, unless the information is professionally produced, it may not be favorably received.

HOW TO ZERO IN ON POTENTIAL PURCHASERS

Locating potential purchasers of a business, while not scientific, does have its guidelines. It can be analogous to the search for the great musky by the Northern Wisconsin Fisherman. Regardless of the size of the lake on which the fisherman pursues his quarry, there are only a limited number of places where the musky will normally congregate: rock bars, weedbeds, dropoffs, sunken logs, and the like. The musky fisherman will not randomly cast his lure into the water, but will concentrate his efforts in the areas of the lake that have one or more of these characteristics.

In the same way, random mass mailings for the sale of a business will normally have little, if any, effect. A well-defined approach geared to reaching those individuals and corporations that exhibit one or more of the characteristics discussed below will give the greatest chance for success. You must also keep in mind that although the fisherman concentrates his efforts on favored locations, he will from time to time catch a musky where all his knowledge and experience indicate there are none. You too should concentrate on the individuals or corporations possessing the following characteristics, but do not limit your search to these parties. A potential purchaser may be found in some of the most unexpected places.

1. Expertise and experience. Try to locate the individuals or corporations that are in the same or similar business. The most likely purchaser is probably your competitor. Another likely individual or group of individuals are the key employees. This group also has the necessary know-how and experience to run the business; however, they may lack the financial wherewithal to purchase the business. The use of venture capital and leveraged buyouts can increase the ability of this group of individuals to purchase the business.

2. Financial wherewithal. Purchasers with "deep pockets" are prime candidates. The deep pocket gives the individual a great deal of flexibility. If you approach him when the time is right, you may locate a potential purchaser where normally you would not expect to find one. Some of the circumstances that will help make the "time right" are as follows:

Does a successful family corporation have too many family members actively participating in the business? If the answer is yes, they may be looking for an additional business to purchase. An example will illustrate this concept:

Example: Reed and Harpo for many years jointly owned a retail music store. It grew beyond their wildest imagination. Two children on each side of the family decided that they were interested in perpetuating the business. Originally Reed and Harpo were ecstatic that their children were "following in their fathers' footsteps."

It soon became evident that while the business was big and successful enough to accommodate and support all family members, personality conflicts were arising. Subconsciously, they were prime targets for expansion. At the same time, a music store in an adjacent community was offered for sale. Reed and Harpo, to alleviate family conflicts and to protect the business, purchased the music store.

The sellers of this music store were intelligent enough, when they were considering the sale of the business, to approach all of the other music stores within a fifty-mile radius to determine whether or not these individuals were interested in purchasing their business. Neither Reed nor Harpo nor their children would have considered the purchase of this business if they had not been approached.

But they were approached when they had sufficient capital (deep pocket) and when the purchase not only was a good business move but also alleviated the conflict that was developing internally. The sellers made the right move at the right time.

3. Excess retained earnings. The potential purchaser may have an accumulated earnings problem. The penalty tax imposed by Section 531 applies to any corporation that has permitted its earnings and profits to be accumulated instead of distributed. The statute imposes a tax on earnings of a corporation (after certain credits) that accumulates income in excess of its reasonable needs or reasonably anticipated needs.

Another Potential Purchaser

One of the accepted anticipated business needs is to provide assets to acquire another related business or to expand the existing business. It is not unusual for a corporation faced with an accumulated earnings problem to investigate expansion of its business through acquisition. The business acquired could be vertically or horizontally integrated into the main business. An example will illustrate how this threat of an accumulated earnings tax can be used to the advantage of both the purchaser and the seller.

Example: Darwin owns an office supply company with his wife. It started ten years ago as a "garage industry" and has now grown to sales of well over $1,000,000. Darwin and his wife are very frugal and have felt that the best way to ensure their well-being is to retain money in the corporation. The corporation currently has about $500,000 of accumulated earnings and no debt. Excess funds have begun to accumulate in the corporation in the form of savings accounts and treasury bills for which there is no current use. The company is vulnerable to the imposition of an accumulated earnings tax.

Now is the time for Darwin to look to purchase another office supply company or expand into a new area. If there was another office supply company for sale, either in town or in a neighboring community, there is no doubt that Darwin and his wife would at least be interested in investigating the possibility of purchase.

Their business would also be a prime candidate as far as the seller was concerned. Their financial stability would allow them either to purchase for cash or make a substantial downpayment. One of the major concerns of a seller when a portion of the purchase price needs to be financed, is security. In this case, the transaction would be extremely secure.

4. Need to diversify. A segment of an industry may be dying and the company wishes to expand in other areas. An example of this concept involved my grandfather whose company manufactured women's hats. During the 1920s, 30s, and 40s, millinery was a thriving industry. If he had foreseen the change in the industry and if he had wished to perpetuate the business, he should have expanded his business to include other products such as belts, scarfs, and the like. He could have used his expertise, equipment, and personnel to maximum advantage. The purchase of an existing business might have facilitated his entry into one of these other areas.

5. Need. There is little doubt that need is one of the most significant characteristics. Need comes in many forms. Some of the more common instances where the seller can locate a buyer through need will be set forth:

A. To guarantee the source of supply. If your company is supplying a particular material, or parts used in a bigger product, the customer may wish to vertically integrate to ensure his source of supply.

Example: Cut Rite is manufacturing lawnmowers. For many years, it has purchased all its gears from Gear Corporation. Gear Corporation has made castings of these gears and, while there could be alternate sources of supply for Cut Rite Corporation, it would take time to develop and could affect overall production. Accordingly, if Gear Corporation were for sale, it would be a natural acquisition for Cut Rite.

B. To guarantee a purchaser for its products. It may also be proper for the supplier to vertically integrate by purchasing the customer. In the above example, all the gears were produced by Gear Corporation. Gear Corporation may be manufacturing gears for other corporations. If Cut Rite were for sale, this might be a natural acquisition for Gear Corporation.

Key Idea: It is normally a good idea to look to both suppliers and customers as potential purchasers of the business.

C. To eliminate a competitor. Many times, a particular market cannot support competing businesses. In this instance, need is equated to survival. Only one business is going to survive and a merger of the two competitors may be a viable alternative.

D. To gain control of the business. The most obvious purchaser, when there is more than one shareholder, is the remaining shareholder or shareholders. Some of the reasons that interest the remaining shareholders in purchasing are:

1. they wish to consolidate their control,
2. they think it is a good investment,
3. they may be able to use the excess corporate funds to facilitate the purchase,
4. they have worked well with the existing shareholder but may not look forward to working with any of the prospective purchasers, or
5. they wish to provide jobs for their children.

These factors, combined with your moral obligation to deal with the other shareholders, gives them a great deal of leverage in a proposed sale.

Example: Widgets International had been a family corporation for many years. Each of the three children, Fred, Wilma, and Betty, owned approximately twenty-four percent. Five retired employees of the company owned twenty-four percent. The chief executive officer for the last twenty years was Wilma. At a board of directors meeting, she announced, at age sixty-one, that she had worked enough. She was going to retire from the business in one year whether or not a sale was consummated.

Widget International was a very successful business and she initiated the sale at a time when the intrinsic and extrinsic factors were positive. The first question that was raised to Wilma by her financial advisors was "Why not sell it to the children?" The other sister, who owned twenty-four percent, was not active in the business and Fred, who also owned twenty-four percent of the business, was a bachelor. Both indicated that any sale that was acceptable to Wilma was acceptable to them. Wilma had two sons and a son-in-law who were employees in the business and each owned approximately one percent of the outstanding stock.

It became evident that Wilma did not have enough confidence in her sons' and her son-in-law's abilities to profitably run the business. Accordingly, she was looking to an outside purchaser, not for the maximum purchase price, but to ensure that the purchase price agreed to would be paid and the business would prosper.

In this case security was the key. The children had no significant independent assets and therefore could not "guarantee the payment." Their outlook appeared bleak, even though they actively pursued the purchase. Because of the reasonable purchase price, the profitability of the business and the fact that the business itself was a natural extension of other businesses, two potential purchasers were quickly located. One of these purchasers had all of the positive characteristics that would make the sale feasible, including a substantial net worth.

As soon as the third parties made offers, problems occurred. Even though the potential purchaser assured her that her children would always have a job, Wilma began to question whether this would be true. In the final analysis, she did a complete flip flop and sold the business to her two sons and her son-in-law. The purchaser crystallized the issue and she did what she considered "morally right." There is a happy ending to this story; Widgets International has grown, Wilma has been paid off and the kids, who theoretically could not run the business, have turned Widgets International into a major force in their industry.

E. To keep one's job. Our current economy, with its contracting employment in basic industry and shifting employment needs, has awakened employees to the value of a good job. This particular value is relevant in those industries that are now facing outside competition. In the past, because of the lack of competition, employees in various segments of the economy have been receiving a greater salary than the value of the services performed would normally warrant. While the managers of the business may not admit it, it would appear that a part of the earnings of the business were actually being paid, not to the shareholders as dividends, but to unrelated parties (employees) as a distribution of earnings. This was an acceptable situation when the business was growing and profitable. However, in many of our basic manufacturing businesses now subject to foreign competition, the payment of these salaries is a luxury they can no longer afford. In cases such as this, it behooves one to consider the use of an Employee Stock Option Plan (ESOP). While a full discussion of the utilization of an ESOP is beyond the scope of this book, it is necessary to understand that the ESOP allows for the payment of the stock in before-tax dollars rather than after-tax dollars. This can permit a higher purchase price to be paid by the employees than by an outsider. While the purchase price seemingly costs the employees more than the outsider as the funds are being paid in before- rather than after-tax dollars, the actual after tax cost to the employees is significantly less.

Example: The employees of ABC Corporation wish to purchase the company's stock. The founder of ABC Corporation, Mr. X, is willing to sell. Assume ABC Corporation is in the effective thirty-four percent tax bracket. If X sells all of the stock in ABC for $1,000,000 to an ESOP, ABC Corporation will make contributions to the ESOP (really nothing more than a form of profit sharing plan) and the $1,000,000 of deductions would cost, in after-tax dollars, only $660,000. An outsider purchasing the business in after-tax dollars would have in essence paid a $340,000 premium.

If the company's employees fit into either of the following two categories, an ESOP should be investigated:

1. there are employees who are overcompensated for the jobs that they perform
2. there are highly paid employees who may be worth what they are paid and have a vested interest in the business itself

While ESOPs are currently in vogue and therefore sellers have recognized their potential, in a good many cases, an independent group of individuals who are sometimes overlooked are middle management personnel who could take advantage of an ESOP.

These employees normally are not thought of as potential purchasers unless they are also related to the seller. The reason for this is that they usually lack the financial wherewithal to accomplish the purchase and are also faced with the purchase in after-tax dollars. To accomplish this sale, the seller will have to take some risks.

There are several interesting methods that can be utilized to facilitate purchases in these instances, such as preferred stock recapitalizations, redemptions, use of holding companies, and the like. Accordingly, individual employees, if they have the proper prerequisites, should not be overlooked. It is a good exercise to analyze the workforce to determine whether or not there is an individual or individuals who could act in concert to buy the business.

Key Idea: In the last decade, management has had a new tool to accomplish the purchase. This is the leveraged buyout. The techniques have been available for a long period of time; however, the ability of management to purchase has been enhanced by the new pool of venture capital. If you are interested in purchasing and are part of the management team, you should discuss acquisition with corporations offering not "financing" but "venture capital."

DEALING WITH OUTSIDER AND INSIDER PURCHASERS

The first group of potential purchasers are the outsiders. These are the individuals and corporations with whom you have neither a working relationship nor a preexisting rapport. Most times when dealing with an outsider, it is best if you use an intermediary. If, during negotiations, there are personality conflicts or widely divergent positions that cause antagonism, the intermediary (usually the attorney) can save face by stating that he has misunderstood or misconstrued his client's position.

While the various classifications of outsiders will be set forth shortly, the definition of "outsider" encompasses all potential purchasers with whom you have not developed a rapport. A competitor is normally an outsider. However, many businesses have "friendly competitors" and the principals may have become friendly during their attendance at conventions or participation in trade groups or a chamber of commerce.

When the competitor fits into this class, the term outsider would most likely be inappropriate. Thus, the definition of outsider may, at times, be a misnomer.

The rapport that has been established may be disturbed if they get an "informal" letter from an attorney stating that your business is for sale. They may feel this an affront to them and a rejection of the "relationship" that had been established. The intermediary should normally be used with any of the following categories of outsiders only if the seller has no preexisting rapport.

1. Competitors. As stated previously, this category will usually contain at least one potential purchaser. In most cases, the competitors will be outsiders and the intermediary should be used to make the approach.

2. Suppliers or customers. Many businesses like to vertically integrate. The goal of these types of companies is to own a chain of businesses from manufacturing to retail. If this type of company is known or if there are either suppliers or customers for a substantial portion of your business products, these parties should be approached. This category can contain both insiders and outsiders, depending on the nature of the industry. The possibility of finding potential purchasers in this group was greater fifteen years ago when companies were frequently acquiring either purchasers or suppliers of their products. This trend has slowed down. In addition, many prior purchases have not produced the desired results and therefore this category is less likely to contain viable purchasers.

3. Financial institutions. Financial institutions, which historically were in business solely to lend money, have expanded in such diverse areas as leasing, insurance, data processing, and so forth. This is one segment of the economy that is still interested in acquiring peripheral, but related businesses. If your business is ancillary to that of a financial institution, then discreet inquiries should be made. Normally the initial inquiry will be from the seller to his contact person at the bank. Once interest has been established, the professionals will normally take over. Bankers are accustomed to dealing with attorneys.

4. Dissatisfied outsiders. Many companies split up. It is not at all unusual, that, after the split-up, you actually have two potential purchasers rather than one. The problem in this instance is that after the split-up, both of these potential purchasers have a reduced financial base. Accordingly, you may have potential purchasers who do not have the financial wherewithal to secure the purchase. Notwithstanding this fact, if you know of an employee of a competitor or someone else who is unhappy, discreet inquiries may be in order.

5. Others. There are always individuals who do not fit into any specific category. Included within this category are the rich man's son, a completely unrelated corporation wishing to expand its business, or a myriad of other possibilities. Whether they are insiders or

outsiders and how inquiries should be made will depend on the particular fact situation.

Key Idea: Normally, those potential purchasers who are designated as outsiders should be approached initially by the seller's attorney. On the other hand, any individual who is considered an insider should, if at all possible, be approached initially by the seller himself. Any other inquiry may disturb the preexisting relationship and the rapport that has been established.

The above contained the usual list of outsiders. As noted, several of the categories may also contain within their parameters individuals who can be categorized as insiders. As will be discussed shortly, the method of approach is significantly different for outsiders and insiders.

While the potential number of purchasers from the category designated as outsiders is almost infinite, the number of insiders is normally small. They usually belong to one of two categories: employees or shareholders.

As most shareholders in a closely held corporation are also employees, this further reduces the total number of potential purchasers from the insider group. The concept of outsider and insider is not only a process of categorization, it also requires a determination of whether there was a preexisting relationship between the party and the business that is being sold. While there are really only two categories of insiders, a person who normally would be considered an outsider may, because of a preexisting relationship, be defined and require treatment as an insider. The converse is rarely true. In a small corporation, rarely will an insider be treated as an outsider.

Relationships in small corporations are normally of the love/hate variety. A lukewarm relationship rarely exists. If the potential purchaser is a fellow shareholder and if the relationship is not positive, in all likelihood there will be an existing feud. This necessitates a whole different approach. In a case such as this, legal proceedings, if not in process, may be threatened. A solution to the deadlock may be the purchase of the interest of one of the shareholders. Accordingly, the attorneys themselves may be pressuring the clients to commence the negotiation process.

With insiders, the approach normally should come from the principal and not from the attorney. This should not be construed to mean that the seller should not do his homework and confer with the attorney and accountant, but solely that the approach should be personal in nature.

For example, if there are two fifty percent shareholders and if one of them is older and wishes to retire, even without a preexisting agreement restricting the sale of stock, it would be ludicrous for the older individual's attorney to approach the younger shareholder to buy his stock. While a full discussion as to the methods of purchasing a corporation, either by outsiders or insiders, will occur in Section 5, it should be noted that insiders will have an inherent edge for several reasons.

The Insider's Edge

1. They have a preexisting relationship with the seller.
2. They already know the business and a smooth transition can occur.
3. The purchase price will be less. If the fair market value of the corporation is $1,000,000, and if the insider owns twenty percent of the common stock, the cost of the business to him would be $800,000 while an outsider would have to pay the full $1,000,000.
4. Unconventional methods may be more easily used by an insider than an outsider. Such methods will include redemption of stock, use of an ESOP, and purchase through a leveraged buyout.

It should also be noted that insiders have to be handled more delicately than outsiders. If the sale is not consummated, you must still live with the insider. In the above example, of the two fifty percent shareholders, one being the older individual who wishes to retire, if he cannot sell to either his fellow shareholder or a third party, he must maintain a working relationship in order for the business to prosper.

If he is unable to sell, it may be beneficial for him to negotiate some form of semi-retirement, in which his employment obligations will be reduced and an income flow maintained. If he has alienated the younger shareholder, this option may not be available. If the older shareholder had alienated an outsider, it will have little adverse impact on either him or the business. Dealing with insiders is always more difficult than dealing with outsiders.

DETERMINING WHO SHOULD MARKET YOUR COMPANY

Should you attempt to self-market the corporation or should a professional broker be given the responsibility? The answer to this question lies in understanding the scope of the problem. The approach is similar to that used by a fisherman. If he is in familiar waters and knows the lake, he does not need a guide. On the other hand, if he is fishing new waters, then a guide is both useful and necessary if he wishes to catch fish. A guide, in addition to familiarizing the fisherman with the lake and the various types of structure, will also demonstrate how to fish these waters.

This analogy can be usefully applied to the problem of how best to sell the corporation.

1. The first factor is the makeup of the potential class of purchasers. If the most viable purchasers are insiders and if you have competent advisors, then you do not need a business broker. Even if the potential purchasers are outsiders but are a known set of individuals, it may not be necessary or cost efficient to retain a business broker. In other words, the more limited the number of potential purchasers, the more likely that self-marketing will be the best choice.

2. The second factor that will help make your decision is the quality and experience of your professional team. If you have confidence in its knowledge and ability, you may wish to commence self-marketing. In the normal case, a discreet inquiry to those individuals identified on page 103 is the first step. You can always go to a mass marketer, the professional broker, at a later date to try to reach those individuals who are unknown to you. If you list your business with a broker first, the business community will quickly become aware that it is for sale. Discreet inquiries at that time are usually too late to be beneficial.

3. The third factor to consider is the type of business you are attempting to sell. If yours is a business that requires little specialized expertise and there is already a well-established organizational structure, a mass marketer may be more beneficial. An example of this situation would be a string of franchise restaurants with capable managers in each location. It should be noted that few small businesses are likely to be in this category.

Note: The type of industry will also impact on how the business will be sold. Some industries appear to be subject to the control of business brokers. Some franchises have their own internal sales staff, or utilize outside brokers. If you are in one of those industries, then you should go with the crowd, at least after you have made your own initial inquiries.

Key Idea: A discreet approach to the group of potential purchasers who are considered insiders is usually the best initial approach. Mass marketing is normally a fall-back position if self marketing fails.

Another factor is "How hot is the market?" Certain segments of the business community have been sold during the recent past at substantial premiums. Two examples are small newspapers and banks. In these instances, sophisticated brokers may have the contacts necessary to maximize the return to the stockholders.

How to Locate a Competent Business Broker

If you have decided that the most expeditious way to proceed is through a business broker, the question becomes, "What types of brokers can help me market my corporation and locate a buyer?"

The first question is whether the real estate/business broker has a place in the sales process. Many real estate brokers claim that they sell businesses. There is some truth to this statement; however, their real usefulness is limited. They fill a real need in marketing the corner tavern (real estate plus liquor license), small grocery, hardware store, or supper club. Real estate brokers are most effective when the primary asset to be sold is real estate, with other hard and soft assets not being a material portion of the sales price. Two examples will contrast those cases in which the real estate broker fills a real need with one in which his retention probably would be inappropriate.

Where a Real Estate Broker Is Useful

Example: Sara owns a very successful downtown restaurant and bar. She has been operating this as a sole proprietorship for many years and there is no indebtedness against this property. The adjusted book value of the business is as follows:

Land and Buildings	$420,000.00
Equipment	40,000.00
Inventory (estimated)	10,000.00
TOTAL ADJUSTED BOOK VALUE	$470,000.00

It is determined that the true "fair market value" is $525,000.00. This situation lends itself to marketing by a real estate broker.

Where a Real Estate Broker Is Not Appropriate

Example: D.J. owns a Northeastern Wisconsin franchise for a well-established hamburger chain. He has been operating the business as a corporation under the name "Hamburger, Inc." His business has been growing and Hamburger, Inc. now operates six locations. At two locations, it owns the land and building. At the other four, it has favorable long-term leases. The adjusted book value of Hamburger, Inc. is as follows:

Land and Buildings	$300,000.00
Inventory	50,000.00
Equipment	$250,000.00
Franchise Rights	$100,000.00
TOTAL ASSETS	$700,000.00
Liabilities	$250,000.00
Equity	$450,000.00
TOTAL LIABILITIES AND EQUITY	$700,000.00

Hamburger, Inc., after paying a reasonable salary to D.J., has been earning $200,000 a year in before-tax income. D.J.'s advisors have informed him that the fair market value for his stock is approximately $1,200,000.00. In this case, a real estate broker probably would be inappropriate to handle the sale.

Key Idea: The real estate business broker is most useful where the assets to be sold consist primarily of real estate and other hard physical assets and little, if any, value is attributable to goodwill. What the broker lacks in business expertise in these cases is usually more than compensated by his knowledge of the marketplace.

The Business Broker

The other classification of brokers is the pure business broker. His sole source of income is from commissions earned on the sale of businesses. There is no doubt his fee is negotiable; however, he may charge as much as ten percent of the sales price and will enter into an agreement similar to the listing agreement for the sale of real estate. The problem is that the business broker for small businesses is a relatively new breed. Therefore, it is difficult to find one who is both knowledgeable and honorable. The goal is to locate an individual with whom you feel comfortable and who has had success selling comparable businesses.

If you are a member of a trade organization, it behooves you to discover from the state or national office which businesses have been sold in the last couple of years and determine who has been successful in marketing them.

Word of mouth and personal referrals are probably your most reliable guide. If you cannot learn of an appropriate business broker in this manner, read the trade magazines. They normally will have businesses in the classified section for sale by brokers. Contact those brokers and determine their expertise, experience, and prior success by asking questions such as:

1. What businesses similar to yours do they have currently for sale?
2. What businesses have they sold in the prior couple of years?
3. How would they market your corporation?
4. Would they provide you with a sample copy of a selling brochure for one of the businesses that are currently for sale?
5. Where do they have offices and how many different brokers do they employ?
6. Any other questions that would give you some idea as to their expertise within the industry as well as their ability to sell your business.

A final source that may be useful in locating the appropriate business broker is through your professionals. They may have dealt with an individual or firm in the past and will inform you as to their experience.

Key Idea: It is extremely difficult to locate a business broker who is both knowledgeable and reliable because the business broker for small businesses is a relatively new breed. Word of mouth referral is probably the most reliable guide in locating the appropriate firm. Contacting your trade organization or working through the industry trade magazines may provide an additional source of leads.

HOW TO SUCCESSFULLY SELF-MARKET YOUR BUSINESS

The ability to successfully self-market your business requires the implementation of the following procedure.

1. Develop an expert sales team and allocate responsibility.
   A. Determine your team members. These include at least your attorney and accountant.
   B. Allocate responsibility for preparation of financial information as well as planning and tax responsibility.
   C. Determine whether you are going to take an active or passive role in the negotiation process.
2. Clean up your act. Make your business as "saleable" as possible.
3. Determine the true value of your business. (Section 3)
4. Develop and classify the information that you wish to supply.
   A. Analyze how detrimental specific financial information would be in the hands of a competitor.
   B. Determine whether to supply detailed or general financial information.
   C. Develop a five-year presentation of financial information as well as future projections if you deem them necessary.
   D. Put together an appropriate tickler letter.
5. Interest those individuals who are potential purchasers and approach them correctly.
   A. Discuss the possible purchase with those insiders who are shareholders and key employees.
   B. Approach the outsiders with whom you have developed a rapport.
   C. Approach outsiders who you deem are potential purchasers.
6. Maximize the talents of your sales team.
   A. Once the potential purchaser has been located, determine who should lead the negotiation process—you or your attorney.
   B. If your accountant is a strong communicator, determine whether or not he can be useful in supplying the financial information or if this will all be funneled through the attorney.

The first step in this process, after the sales team has been assembled, is to reach the most likely purchasers and supply them with enough information to spark their interest. Often this can be accomplished through the utilization of a tickler letter that contains a general description of the business, a summarization of the financial information, and the requested purchase price and terms of purchase. Before describing exactly what information is to be supplied in the tickler letter, you should review your role as owner in the sales process. The use and tone of the tickler letter (for a complete discussion see page 94) may depend not only on your desires, but also on who the potential purchasers are.

For example, you may have to take an active role with those individuals who are insiders and with those outsiders with whom you have developed a preexisting rapport. In this case, the active role may be nothing more than a personal call from you stating that you are contemplating the sale of your business. If he expresses interest, you will have your accountant and attorney supply him with the necessary information. When this occurs, you, with your advisors and sales team, should decide exactly what information to supply.

HOW TO DECIDE WHICH POTENTIAL PURCHASER TO APPROACH FIRST

The first discussion with your sales team will involve determining the potential purchasers and deciding how to approach each of them. The hierarchy as to who is to be approached is usually as follows:

1. inactive shareholder
2. shareholder/employee
3. key employee
4. outsider with whom you have developed a rapport
5. outsider with whom no rapport has been established

Normally, the first individuals to be approached are insiders. There are both moral and practical reasons for approaching the inactive shareholders or shareholder/employees first. You are morally obligated to your fellow shareholders even if you are not bound by any restrictive shareholders agreement. Even without this moral obligation, if you propose the sale to outsiders before dealing with these insiders, you could create dissension that could manifest itself before, during, and after the sale.

The second group encompasses the key employees. Even though these employees may not be financially able to accomplish the purchase, it is usually a good idea to make them aware of what is happening. The last thing you need during the sales process is to have two or three of your key individuals quit to take different jobs. While your other employees probably fall within the definition of insider, they should not be approached at the same time as the key employees.

The only way the other employees can realistically purchase the business is through an ESOP. This is a tool of last resort when it applies to all employees. It may have a viable use as part of a buyout by highly placed key personnel to help finance the purchase in before-tax dollars.

If at all possible, the proposed sale should not be made public knowledge until the last possible moment. The sale of a business has, in the best of times, a disruptive effect on the business. You do not wish to disturb the efficiency or productivity of the company any more than necessary during the sales process.

The next group that should be approached includes those outsiders with whom you have established a rapport. Many times they have already approached you with the comment "When you are ready to sell, give me a call." Give them the opportunity! If you do not approach them first and they learn of the sale from other sources, they may suffer such an affront that you will have inadvertently alienated the most viable of the potential outside purchasers.

Key Idea: The first group of persons to approach is the shareholders and key personnel. This should be on a personal basis and not through your legal advisor.

Key Idea: The second group is those outsiders with whom a rapport has been established. Again, the approach with the greatest chance of success will be personal contact from the owner of the business.

After you have exhausted these groups of individuals, then you can distribute a tickler letter to the last group of outsiders who are known or may logically have an interest in purchasing your business. There are several decisions to be made in structuring the tickler letter. These decisions involve the following.

1. Should it be a blind letter, or should it state the name of the business to be sold?
2. What facts should be included?

In addition, there is the question of on whose stationery this tickler letter should be written. Normally, in presenting the corporation for sale to outsiders, the use of your attorney is worthwhile. If the tickler letter is on the lawyer's stationery, it can be either a blind letter or state the name of the business to be sold. The use of the blind letter has several advantages.

1. It does not list the business to be sold for all to know. Usually it does not do you any good to let the business community know that your business is for sale until it is actually listed with a business broker or has been sold through your own efforts. Once a company is known to be for sale, both its business relationships and its workforce's efficiency can be disrupted.

2. It adds an aura of mystery. Even though the name of the selling business may be self-evident because of the descriptive information contained in the tickler letter, it provides a psychological lift by letting the potential purchaser in on your "secret" when the seller's name is revealed. The disclosure of the name of the selling company has been kept from the general community but now you "trust" the potential purchaser enough to divulge this piece of information.

Each tickler letter is custom designed. How much information can be supplied without damaging the business has been discussed on page 94. Nonetheless, all tickler letters should contain the following:

1. A description of the business. The minimum is a general description; for example, a manufacturer of pallets, a business supply house, retail men's store, manufacturer of agricultural equipment, and the like.

2. Gross sales. The current as well as the past sales should be indicated. For example, the current sales of the company are $1,200,000 and they have been increasing at the rate of ten percent during each of the last five years.

3. Profitability. This should be the adjusted income of the corporation. The decision whether or not to include before- or after-tax income must be made on a case-by-case basis.

4. Summary of requested purchase price and terms of sale.

While it is neither necessary nor appropriate in the tickler letter to describe in detail the asking price and terms, it is usually a good idea to summarize the most favorable conditions of purchase.

For example, the letter may state that the purchase price for 100 percent of the stock of XYZ Corporation will be $1,000,000, to be paid in cash at date of closing. This sets the parameters, although it does not preclude a potential purchaser from offering $950,000, $250,000 down with the remainder payable pursuant to a promissory note in equal monthly payments over fifteen years.

The insertion of price and terms into the tickler letter has a twofold positive effect; it sets the parameters and commences the negotiation process. An example of a tickler letter is set forth in Appendix F. While this tickler letter was utilized as a response to inquiries of management as to whether or not the corporation was for sale, this could just as well have been utilized to sell the corporation to outsiders.

How a Purchaser May Respond to a Tickler Letter

From time to time, a potential purchaser may hear of a business being sold and may wish to pursue the purchase. He may also be the recipient of a tickler letter. The question in these instances is, "How will he proceed or respond?" Obviously, if he has the necessary rapport, the simplest way is to pick up the phone.

In a vast majority of cases, if this alternative had been appropriate, he would have already received a personal approach. To follow through, he would prepare a letter requesting detailed information about the business. This letter, a sample of which is set forth in Appendix G, should be prepared by your attorney (with your input) and written in a correct, formal, comprehensive, and professional style.

The letter serves a number of purposes. It shows the seller that you are interested enough to spend some money to obtain professional advice. Secondly, it indicates that if the negotiation process is to proceed, it will be the responsibility of the professionals. The potential purchaser may have begun his own orchestration of the negotiation process. He may have indicated that while he is in control of the negotiations, the process itself will be the responsibility of the professionals. The logic and professionalism of this approach should be appreciated by the seller.

As the potential purchaser, he will wish to obtain the maximum information so that he can spend the minimum amount of time analyzing the viability of the purchase. On the other hand, if the request is too detailed, it may make the seller suspicious of the purchaser's true motives and create an atmosphere of distrust.

Many professionals do not view the sales process as adversary in nature. They treat the process as one of mutual self-interest. While in some cases this is correct, it is not wise to rely on this fact as self-interest is the primary concern of both purchaser and seller. This first becomes apparent with the request for information. The seller wishes to distribute the minimum information to keep the purchaser interested while the buyer wants to obtain the maximum information without disturbing the sales process. The problems and possible solutions have already been discussed. The response to the tickler letter, consciously or unconsciously, commences the negotiation process.

How to React to the Purchaser's Response to the Tickler Letter

There will be two separate and distinct types of positive responses to the tickler letter. The first will be either a letter or personal communication from the potential purchaser. The second will be communication from his attorney. While this is a select community that you have solicited, you may not know much about the potential purchaser.

Once you receive a positive response, you should proceed with care. If there is an axiom at this juncture of the sales process, it is, "The more you know about the potential purchaser, the greater the chance for success." Accordingly, before responding to any positive inquiry, you should attempt to obtain as much information as possible about the potential purchaser. There are two sources of this information: primary and secondary.

It behooves the seller to exhaust all secondary sources before trying to obtain the information from the purchaser. One of the cheapest and easiest sources of secondary information is contained in Dun and Bradstreet reports. It is inappropriate to rely on all the information that is presented on a D & B report. The reason for this is that a vast majority of the information has been supplied by the company with little outside verification. However, it is a proper first step and can supply information as to the name of the principal officers, the gross sales, the type of assets, liabilities, and timeliness in making debt payments. These reports will eliminate those parties who are obviously not capable of purchasing the business. If you have a business that is for sale for $2,000,000 and if the potential purchaser has yearly sales of $400,000, obviously he alone is not a suitable candidate. If your business does not subscribe to the D & B reports, you can obtain them through your local banker for a minimal fee.

Key Idea: It greatly enhances the seller's chance for success to know as much as possible about the potential purchaser. All information should be obtained from secondary sources at the first possible opportunity.

Key Idea: One of the cheapest and easiest sources of secondary information is the Dun and Bradstreet reports. Beware of those companies that are not listed with Dun and Bradstreet or refuse to supply them with necessary information.

If the company that has responded to the tickler letter is publicly traded, there are several other sources of useful secondary information.

There are two distinct types of publicly held corporations, those with widely traded stock and those that, while public, are not actively traded. The availability of information will vary depending on how widely traded the stock of the potential purchaser is. With the widely traded companies, information can be obtained readily from your securities broker. He can supply you with copies of the Standard and Poor's or other financial services' reports. Those corporations that are not actively traded have little available public information prepared for use by the investing public. In these cases, the stockbroker will inform you that the company is traded over the counter, but has minimal, if any, financial information.

Nonetheless, all publicly held corporations must file annual and quarterly reports with the Securities and Exchange Commission. These reports are Forms 10-K and 10-Q. They are open to public inspection. There is a service that will obtain this information for you for a fee. This company is Disclosure, 5161 River Road, Bethesda, MD 20816; telephone number (301) 951-1300.

The information required on the Form 10-K is extensive and will include such items as:

1. legal proceedings
2. full financial statements including the appropriate footnotes
3. a description of the principal security holders and the stock that is owned by management

4. a description of the directors and executive officers
5. a description of the renumeration of the directors and officers
6. increases and decreases in outstanding securities
7. various other necessary and useful information

While the report will not answer all your questions, it will supply information not only about the financial wherewithal of the purchasing corporation but also about who the controlling parties are. This information obtained through secondary sources, will give you answers to the following questions.

1. Will security be a problem? (Contrast the potential purchaser, Fly By Night, Inc., with General Motors.)
2. Why do they want to purchase?
3. Have they been expanding or contracting?
4. Where are they located?
5. How widely traded is the corporation?
6. How much of the ownership is controlled by management?

Key Idea: All secondary sources of information should be exhausted before direct inquiries are made from the potential purchaser.

The question then becomes, "Is it appropriate to ask for information from the potential purchaser before negotiation actually commences?" There is no doubt that once serious negotiations have commenced it is appropriate to get current financial statements from the potential purchaser. It has been my experience that unless the information is obtained early, the request gets "lost" in the negotiation process. Serious negotiations can commence in this instance without the seller knowing the financial stability of the purchaser.

The need for security may not be realized until late in the negotiation process. The question then is, "When is the earliest date this information can be requested?" The answer to this question is not simple. It is obvious that the need is greatest when you cannot get the information from secondary sources and you are suspicious of the party's motives. If, for example, you get a detailed letter such as the one set forth in Appendix G, the company is not publicly traded, and Dun and Bradstreet does not have any information regarding the party, it would be prudent to know something about the inquiring party before supplying information.

Key Idea: The less information available from secondary sources, the greater the need to obtain this financial information directly from the potential purchaser.

Supplying detailed information to a blind buyer, such as an attorney, as set forth in Appendix G, can only be detrimental. The best answer to the prior question is "You request financial information when it is not available from other sources and you do not feel comfortable supplying requested information." If you are reasonably certain as to the financial stability of the purchaser, this step is not necessary. The more uncomfortable and the less knowledge you have, the greater the need.

HOW TO STAY FLEXIBLE IN NEGOTIATING TO NAIL DOWN THE SALE

The sales process requires flexibility at almost every turn. The key to selling is not conflict, but cooperation. From time to time, you will receive a detailed letter such as that set forth in Appendix G, and yet you will not feel it appropriate to request financial information from the potential purchaser. Rather than denying all the information and wishing to show "good faith," you may want to supply information that will not be detrimental to you. The sales process requires some risk taking and, accordingly, it is necessary to weigh the risk against the potential reward. It is normally possible to supply selected information that may already be available from secondary sources. A full discussion of what and how information should be supplied has already been set forth on page 94. Exactly what response you should make, of course, depends on the existing fact situation.

Once you have screened the response and determined that it is legitimate, the next step will be dictated by the potential purchaser. Sometimes, with the information you have supplied, he will commence the negotiation process; however, in a vast majority of cases, he may also request additional information. Part or all of the information that is requested in Appendix G is normally appropriate. Sometimes it may be more useful to summarize the information rather than to supply copies of the primary information. At other times, it may be more appropriate to eliminate this step and supply the primary information. The factors that determine how extensive the information should be are two fold:

1. whether the information can be detrimental if it gets into the wrong hands (see page 94)
2. whether or not you are confident that the party is truly interested in purchasing the business for the proper reasons and is financially able to make the purchase

During the sale process, it will be important to determine whether a logical step-by-step approach should be followed or if certain steps should be eliminated for the sake of expediency. The quicker the sales process proceeds, the greater the chance for success. The corollary is the longer the sales process, the more problems will occur and the less likely the chance for success. If you follow the step-by-step approach and supply the offering circular, it would be premature to have him execute a nondisclosure agreement. As previously discussed, the nondisclosure agreement is a statement signed by the potential purchaser that indicates the information supplied will be used solely for the purpose of evaluating the feasibility of purchase.

Notwithstanding the difficulty in enforcing these documents, there is no doubt that a nondisclosure agreement should be signed before any specific documentation is supplied to a potential purchaser who is either a competitor or could use that information against you. A sample of a nondisclosure statement is set forth in Appendix F.

The question then becomes "Is it necessary during the disclosure process to lay it on the line and set forth the parameters of negotiation that include price, terms, and security?" If the tickler letter has been properly drafted, it should set forth these parameters and normally it will not be necessary to expand on your position during the disclosure stage of the sales process. If, on the other hand, the tickler letter was meaningfully vague, it is important to set forth your requested terms at the earliest possible time. If you fail to do this, you will have lost the advantage of initially setting forth your position. This advantage can shift to the purchaser and he may use this opportunity to set forth the terms and price in either a formal or informal offer to purchase.

HOW TO HANDLE SERIOUS NEGOTIATIONS

If the proper groundwork has been laid, the negotiation process is not difficult. It is only when the foundation is weak or nonexistent that the negotiation process is time-consuming and many times fruitless, even when success would seem assured. An interested purchaser, if he has been properly schooled, should realize that in the long run there probably is little difference if he pays $1,250,000 or $1,350,000. It is either a good or bad deal and marginal differences in the purchase price may make little difference if he can negotiate the proper terms. Successful negotiation is an art in itself.

A full discussion of the various negotiation techniques is beyond the scope of this book. The negotiation process may involve correspondence, head-to-head negotiation sessions, or a combination of both interspersed with telephone conversations.

While normally the professionals will carry the ball in the negotiation process, the principals may have to become active participants. The proper procedure is for the parties and their professionals to evaluate, prior to the onset of the negotiation process, their strengths and the other party's weaknesses. If the principal is a successful negotiator, the goal of the negotiation process should be to allow the principals to do most of the negotiating. If, on the other hand, the individual is reserved and not particularly successful in the art of negotiation, he should leave the entire process to his attorneys.

If negotiation proceeds to a "meeting of minds," the question is "what is the next step?" There are two ways to proceed. The first is through a letter of intent, which can either be a binding or nonbinding agreement. The alternative is a full fledged sales agreement. A comprehensive sales agreement is a complicated document for which there is "no real form." Each business is distinct. Each has its own set of problems and, accordingly, each sales agreement will need to be custom designed. The more confidence there is that a "true meeting of the minds" exists, the less need there is for a letter of intent.

In virtually all cases, because of the time lag between the initial "meeting of the minds" and a "formal sales agreement," a letter of intent setting forth the basic terms and conditions (whether binding or nonbinding) should be executed. This is to morally bind the parties to complete the sales transaction as proposed and make sure that there is a "true meeting of the minds." It is extremely important that one or more parties have not misconstrued the terms and conditions of sale. It is amazing how parties participating in the same conferences have differing opinions as to the agreement reached.

The way to alleviate misunderstandings is by the letter of intent. The letter of intent is designed to set forth in nonlegal terms the general provisions of the sales agreement. A copy of a nonbinding letter of intent is set forth in Appendix H. The question then becomes, "If we have this letter of intent, why do we need a sales agreement?"

The sales agreement sets forth the basic provisions such as the assets to be sold, the price to be paid, the terms of payment, the security for payment, and the additional ancillary documents that may need to be signed (for example, leases, employment contracts, consulting agreements, covenants not-to-compete). It also provides the potential purchaser with the terms and provisions that are considered the "necessary boilerplate" to guarantee that he receives good title to all assets purchased free and clear of any current or contingent liabilities.

These provisions contain the representations and the warranties of the seller, covenants of both parties, contingencies that must be satisfied before closing, and provisions as to indemnification if there is a breach of representations and warranties. These terms will provide answers for such questions as:

1. If the stock of the corporation is to be purchased and if at a later date there is an Internal Revenue Service audit that determines taxes have been underpaid, who is liable for the payment of these taxes?
2. What happens if there is a material distortion in the financial statements that have been supplied?
3. What happens if the chief customer of the business ceases to purchase after sale?

These questions illustrate the problems not usually covered in the informal nonbinding letter of intent. They are not all inclusive as the necessary "boiler point" must be custom designed to the type of transaction as well as the type of business being sold.

Finally, the English language is inexact and the letter of intent, whose purpose is to present in nonlegal terms the general intent of the party, may be ambiguous. The final sales agreement, if properly drafted, will have only one interpretation. Therefore, either a very comprehensive letter of intent (see Exhibit I) or a sales agreement is usually called for in these instances. A sample of a sales agreement for the purchase of assets of a corporation is set forth in Appendix J. This book is not intended to analyze all the terms of the sales agreement, but solely to make you aware of their implication and impact. The effect and impact of the terms and conditions must be explained by the professionals to the client.

The final step in the sales process, and a step which will only be alluded to, is closing. At closing, the parties will execute the documentation necessary to implement the transaction. Normally, even in the simplest of closings, there will be a great deal of documentation that must be signed. These documents will include promissory notes, security agreements, employment contracts, leases, minutes of director and shareholder action, bulk sales agreements, and the like. The key in all these cases is to focus on those documents that set forth the basic terms and provisions of the transaction; in other words, what is to be sold, the price to be paid, how it is to be paid, and what is the security for payment. While it may be proper to rely on your professionals to ensure that the proper boilerplate is in the documents and in, event of default, that you are properly secured, there is no substitute for a detailed review of these documents with your attorney.

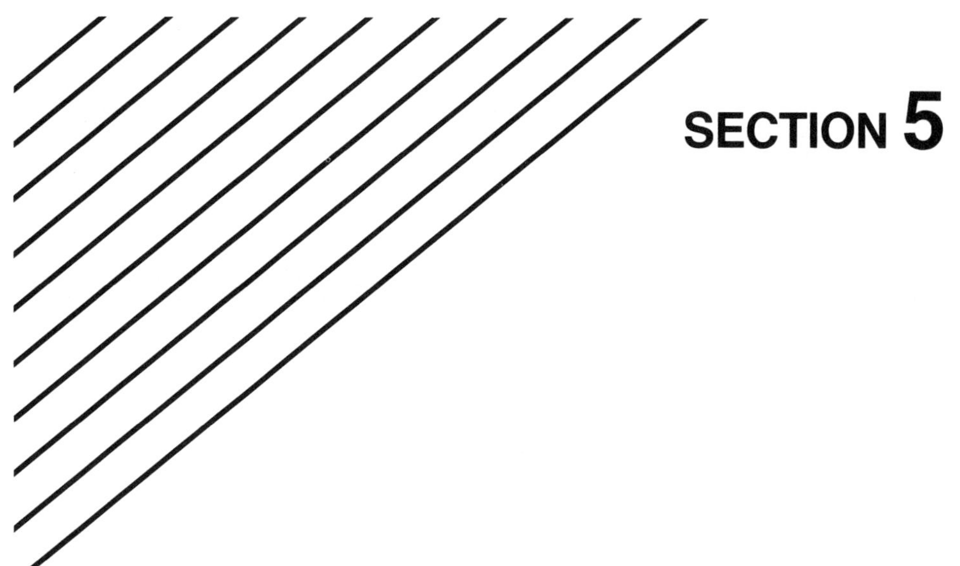

SECTION **5**

HOW TO STRUCTURE THE SALE TO ENSURE PAYMENT AND MAXIMIZE AFTER-TAX PROCEEDS

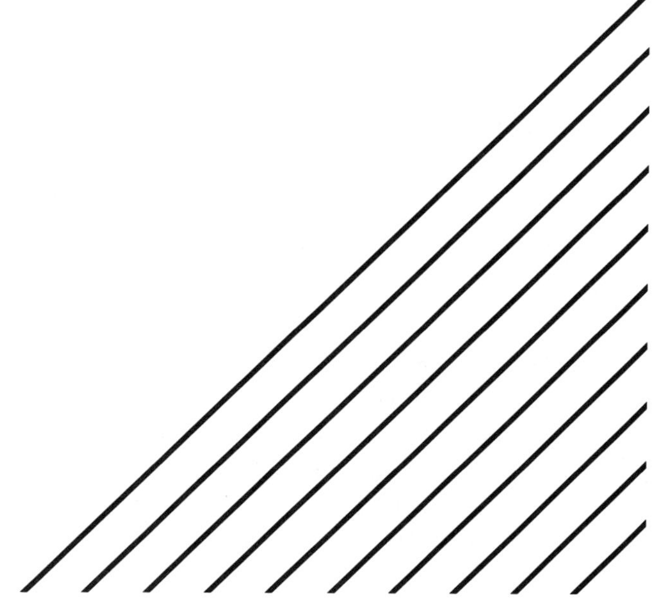

PART 1

THE KEYS TO ANY SALES CONTRACT

THE PSTT CONCEPT: HOW TO USE IT TO YOUR ADVANTAGE

All sales contracts, whether they are a comprehensive agreement (see Appendix J) or an informal letter of intent (see Appendix H), have four elements in common. These elements are "Price, Security, Terms, and Taxes." This section will provide you with the tools to ensure that you receive the maximum benefits from the sales contract.

It may also be appropriate to include an additional "P", "Property to be sold" as the fifth element of the sales contract; however, I include this "P" within the definition of "Terms." The property to be sold is either the stock of the corporation or a portion or all the assets that are owned by the corporation. In either case, the purchaser normally wishes to acquire all the operating assets (versus all assets) of the corporation either directly through their purchase or indirectly through the purchase of stock. The operating assets will include the inventory, equipment, and good will. The nonoperating assets will include cash, securities, receivables, and may also include the land and buildings if owned by the corporation.

While the purchase of a business is not an adversary proceeding, usually what is good for one party will either have a neutral or detrimental impact on the other. A perfect example applicable to the law prior to the changes made in the Tax Reform Act of 1986 is as follows:

Example: We assume the assets of the corporation are being purchased and if a part of the purchase price is allocated to a covenant not-to-compete, these payments are tax deductible by the purchaser. This is obviously beneficial to the purchaser as the most viable alternative is to designate these payments as good will, which normally cannot be amortized and will be paid in after-tax dollars.

From the seller's perspective, if a portion of the purchase price is designated as a covenant not-to-compete, he will have to report all payments as ordinary income rather than capital gain. This is just one factor in the negotiation process, which has varying impacts on the parties. While this example has current limited applicability, it does illustrate the general rule which is "What is good for the seller is bad for the buyer and vice versa."

Note: Because of the elimination of the tax benefits of capital gains in 1988, a greater allocation will probably be made to covenants not-to-compete, especially if the stock of the corporation is being sold. These covenants are taxwise beneficial to the purchaser because they are deductible and there will not be the corresponding detriment to the seller. There are two caveats in this matter:

1. Taxwise, it may not be possible to disguise all the good will as covenant not-to-compete.
2. Covenants not-to-compete are difficult to secure.

On the other hand, it is inappropriate to look at the sales process exclusively as an adversary proceeding. This is especially true if a portion of the total purchase price is not to be paid in cash at closing but by the execution of a long-term installment note. Then the seller has a vested interest in the future success of the purchaser. It is extremely detrimental for him to structure the transaction in such a way that the purchaser is incapable of meeting his financial obligations from the available cashflow.

Example: A owns all of the stock of Widget, Inc. He has negotiated the sale of Widget, Inc. to B for $1 million. The available after-tax cashflow is projected at $100,000 a year. If A, because of personal needs, demands that the entire payments be spread over no more than five years at twelve percent interest, the yearly cash requirements would be $266,934. These payments could not be made from the cashflow of the business and probably would necessitate a default by B unless he had other assets with which he could satisfy the financial obligations. The default that would ensue probably would not be beneficial to A.

HOW TO USE THE SIX COMPONENTS THAT COMPRISE PURCHASE PRICE

The purchase price consists of six component parts. It is not reflected solely as the price paid for the stock and assets. In the sale of small closely held businesses, a portion may be allocated to other items. A discussion of the five most common components of the purchase price other than the assets purchased follows.

An Employment Contract

Many purchases are made with the understanding that the sellers remain as employees during a transition period. During this transition period, the sellers will remain as employees and will be compensated solely for the services that they perform; no part of the purchase price will be allocated to the employment contract.

Some of the selling shareholders may view the sale of the business as premature. In this case, in order to consummate the sale, these shareholder/employees may require employment contracts after closing. This category of selling shareholder may need a salary to supplement his other income until he receives social security. He may also need additional years of service to qualify him for pension payments, or for numerous other personally motivated reasons such as:

1. high educational costs—children still in college
2. workaholic
3. no outside interests

When the compensation paid is in excess of the value of the anticipated services to be rendered, a part of the purchase price has been consciously or unconsciously reallocated from the assets purchased to the employment contract. Even if the compensation is commensurate with the services to be rendered, some of the purchase price has been allocated to this employment contract.

There are two reasons for this. The employment contract restricts the flexibility of the purchaser in operating the business. It is also inappropriate to expect that the prior owner of the business who "ran the show without the need to report to anyone" will be a truly valuable long-term employee. The change in status after many years will be extremely difficult. If the selling parties remain as employees through the transition period, it is normally in the best interest of all to terminate their employment as soon as possible, following the takeover and transition.

As a selling shareholder, it is dangerous to designate a part of the purchase price to an employment contract for the following reasons:

1. They are difficult to secure.

2. The expectation of the parties as to the services to be rendered is rarely synonymous.

The difference in expectations of the parties could cause problems after the sale and raise numerous legal questions as to whether or not a default has occurred. Notwithstanding this fact, many times a part of the purchase price is consciously or unconsciously allocated to an employment contract.

An example will illustrate when an employment contract can be used effectively.

Example: Widget, Inc. is owned as follows:

	Stock	Age	Function
Young	20%	57	CEO
Older	40%	68	Semi-retired
Ancient	40%	75	Retired

Young was hired as the Chief Executive Officer five years ago and was allowed to purchase twenty percent of the outstanding stock (he still owes a substantial amount of the purchase price pursuant to a promissory note). At that time, a new pension plan was established. To receive maximum benefits, he must be employed for ten years. In order to acquiesce to the sale, Young required a five-year employment contract.

Key Idea: Normally, it is not good practice to allocate a portion of the purchase price to a long-term employment contract. They are difficult to secure. In addition, because of the varying expectations of the parties as to the services to be rendered, they may cause friction after the sale.

Key Idea: Sometimes it is necessary to negotiate an employment contract as part of the sales price. This occurs most frequently when one or more of the selling shareholders is younger and there will be a significant period of time between sale and when his income is supplemented by social security and/or payments from qualified deferred compensation plans.

Covenants Not-to-Compete

Selling shareholders should expect that for a period of time after the sale of the business they will not directly or indirectly enter into competition with the business sold. To compete would be both immoral and usually against their best interests.

Buyers usually look to the future income to pay the purchase price. If a part of the purchase price is paid pursuant to a promissory note and the seller works for a competitor or goes into competition, this could jeopardize the purchaser's ability to make payments.

The question becomes "Should a portion of the sales price be allocated to a covenant not-to-compete?" Obviously, the facts in each case will differ. The age of the seller as well as the nature of the business appear to be the two prime factors. At the one end of the spectrum is an individual, age seventy, in a highly capital intensive business who sells. In this case, a covenant not-to-compete is probably not necessary to protect the purchaser from competition by the seller. On the other end of the spectrum, is an individual, age forty-five, in a service-oriented business (sales agent, consultant, attorney, accountant) whose business is being purchased. In this case, obviously some protection to the purchaser may not only be taxwise appropriate but it is definitely needed and warranted by the circumstances.

Warning: In all cases, whether or not a portion of the purchase price is allocated to a covenant not-to-compete, a covenant not-to-compete should be inserted in the sales agreement. Temptation and future problems should be anticipated and eliminated whenever possible. Only in the most unusual cases will the person who is selling the business anticipate at the "time of sale" that he will utilize the proceeds from the sale to go into competition. Normally, there are good "personal" reasons for his attempting to sell and the last thing he contemplates at that time is to go into competition after the sale. However, he may be disillusioned with retirement or may find the new business venture he has undertaken not as financially or personally rewarding as his prior business. Unless he is prohibited from going back into competition one of his most obvious alternatives is to reestablish the business that he knows will be successful—that which he has already sold.

Prior to the Tax Reform Act of 1986, two negative factors undermined the purchaser's attempts to allocate a substantial portion of the purchase price to the covenant: taxation and discounting. See pages 136 and 139. With this acts enactment, unless the receipt of the covenant can be taxed to the corporation (instead of to the shareholders), only discounting will be a negative factor.

Key Idea: Where stock is being sold the allocation of a part of the sales price to a covenant not-to-compete may be taxwise beneficial to the purchaser.

Payment of Fringe Benefits

An integral part of the sales contract often is the continued payment by the purchaser of various fringe benefits. The most common of these fringe benefits are medical insurance (at least until the time that the selling shareholder qualifies for Medicare) and qualified deferred compensation plans. The high cost of medical insurance coupled with the fact that many selling shareholders may not even qualify for insurance unless they are a part of a group will often necessitate the continued employment by one or more of the selling shareholders.

Key Idea: Even though it is usually not a good idea to apportion a substantial part of the purchase price to employment contracts, if an employment contract is desired, it is in the best interest of both that a substantial portion of the costs should be allocated to fringe benefits. This will have the positive effect of converting income into tax-free payments and ensure future communication between the parties.

Beware: Where employment contracts are entered into without the expectation of the rendering of substantial services, the Internal Revenue Service can redesignate the payments and disallow the salary deduction to the purchaser.

Rental of Real Estate from the Selling Shareholder

Proper tax planning normally dictates that the real property is owned by the individual shareholders and leased to the corporation. While there are many reasons why this is advantageous, at no time during the corporate existence (with the possible exception of retirement) do the benefits of this planning become clearer than at the time of sale. The positive impact of this planning can be illustrated by comparing the following examples:

Example 1: Proper Planning

Joe has sufficient assets to purchase the operating assets of XYZ corporation ($550,000), but not the land and buildings ($150,000). If the land and building are owned individually and if all the operating assets are owned by the corporation, then Joe can purchase all the stock owned by the selling shareholders. The seller can lease the land and buildings to Joe and also grant him an option to purchase. If the selling shareholders had a basis of $100,000 in the corporate stock, they would have to report a $450,000 gain with a maximum $126,000 in federal tax.

Example 2: Improper Planning

If XYZ corporation not only owned the operating assets but also owned the land and buildings, taxwise it might be a great deal more difficult for Joe to purchase the business. As the corporation owns the operating assets and the land and buildings, it will not be possible for Joe to purchase the stock of XYZ corporation. XYZ corporation would have to sell the operating assets and then distribute the after-tax proceeds to the shareholders. Assume XYZ corporation has the following balance sheet:

ASSETS

	Book Value	Fair Market
Cash, Receivables, and	$ 20,000	$ 20,000
Inventory	$ 50,000	$ 50,000
Equipment (net of depreciation)	$350,000	$550,000
Land and Buildings	$150,000	$150,000
Total Assets	$570,000	$770,000

LIABILITIES AND SHAREHOLDER'S EQUITY

Accounts Payable	$140,000	$140,000
Capital Stock	$100,000	$100,000
Retained Earnings	$330,000	$330,000
Unrealized Appreciation	———	$200,000
Total Liabilities and Equity	$570,000	$770,000

A sale and subsequent Section 331 liquidation would give rise to the following tax results:

XYZ corporation realizes a $200,000 gain upon the sale of the assets ($550,000 sales price less $350,000 cost basis). The Federal tax at the corporate level would be $61,250. The individual shareholders then would have to realize a gain of $468,750 upon the liquidation of the corporation. This gain would be determined as follows:

Cash, Receivables and Inventory		$70,000
Proceeds from Sale		$550,000
Land and Building		$150,000
Total Assets Distributed		$770,000
Less		
Corporate Tax Paid	$61,250	
Accounts Payable	$140,000	
		$201,250
Net Value of Distribution		$568,750
Basis of Stock		$100,000
Gain on Distribution		$468,750

This could yield a federal tax of approximately $131,250. The total tax liability would then be $192,500. The above example assumes a sale for cash.

Neither example precludes the seller from receiving a portion of the purchase price through the execution of an installment note. However, the type of planning will usually dictate the minimum amount that must be paid in cash at date of closing. If "proper planning" had previously been implemented, the necessity of a substantial downpayment would be greatly reduced. If improper planning had occurred, the downpayment must at least be equal to the total tax liability of the selling shareholders.

Warning: In the event that the corporation owns not only the operating assets but also the land and building and the purchaser wishes to purchase only the operating assets, it is imperative to receive a significant downpayment if the seller is to finance a portion of the transaction. This cash will be necessary to satisfy the tax liability at both the corporate and individual levels.

When the real property is not sold by the seller, a problem could occur if the purchasers are not committed to continue the lease or eventually purchase the premises. The reason for this is that often the real estate is a single purpose use property and is not readily marketable to third parties. Proper planning would be to negotiate a reasonably long-term sales contract (little money down) rather than a lease with an option. Another alternative in these situations may be a long-term lease. When analyzing the purchase price, it should be determined whether or not the lease that has been negotiated is representative of the fair market rental.

Key Idea: In all cases in which the purchase does not include the land and building, the seller should analyze the marketability of the land and buildings in the event that the purchaser decides to build or lease other property at the end of the lease term. In the event that the seller owns real estate that is a one-purpose white elephant, he should either negotiate:

1. a long-term land contract; or
2. a long-term lease with substantial penalties upon cancellation in order to protect his interests.

In these instances, even though the purchaser may not be financially "capable" of purchasing, the use of a long-term sales contract with little money down should be considered. The benefits of knowing that the problem is "solved" (building sold) may outweigh the lack of proper security. The seller should realize that by granting the favorable contractual provisions, the purchaser may actually have reduced the net purchase price received.

Example: XYZ Corporation operates a very successful business in a small town in Wisconsin. Land Baron, the owner of all the stock of XYZ, also owns the land and buildings. Big Corporation, whose headquarters is in Chicago, wants to buy all the stock of XYZ Corporation and consolidate the operating assets in Chicago. If, as a concession to Land Baron, they enter into a long-term lease for the premises, they may discount their offer because of the inconvenience they suffer by having to maintain the business at its current location. On the other hand, Land Baron may not be able to afford to have the premises vacated even if he receives his purchase price for the stock in XYZ Corporation. The value of the land and buildings may be a significant portion of the total purchase price, and unless the property is sold or a significantly long-term lease is entered into, an otherwise satisfactory purchase price for the business may be unacceptable.

Key Idea: Any time that a sizeable portion of the total value of the business is comprised of land and buildings (especially land and buildings that are specially designed for the business), it is imperative that the seller negotiate either (1) a long-term lease; or (2) a sales agreement for the land and buildings. Remember, it is better to convert these assets to cash or cash equivalents rather than be stuck with a "white elephant." Seller's greed (desire to maximize his return) in these cases can be disastrous. If he does not negotiate correctly, he can receive the maximum value for the active assets and yet be left with a sizeable portion of the total value being in nonproductive land and buildings. Instead of a cash inflow, it can result in a cash outflow.

Consulting contracts and other gimmicks. There are many times when the seller will negotiate independent contractor agreements as part of the sales agreement. This may be a consulting agreement, sales agency agreement, directorship or some other form of contract. At any time that the services rendered do not justify the payments, we must consider that a portion of the purchase price is contained in this agreement, and add this amount to the purchase price.

Example: A was selling XYZ Corporation. Prior to the sale, he had determined from the social security office that in order to receive maximum social security benefits, it was necessary that he receive maximum coverage under FICA during the next five years (he is currently fifty-seven). As part of the negotiations with B, who was purchasing XYZ Corporation, he attempted to obtain an employment contract. However, B felt that his presence at headquarters would be counterproductive. Instead of a salary, he offered him a sales territory with a guaranteed commission at least sufficient to maximize the social security payments. If the actual services to be rendered are not significant, a portion of these payments could be considered as payments of the purchase price.

Key Idea: At times it is necessary to allocate a part of the purchase price to other than the assets sold. Specialized consulting agreements or other gimmicks can be useful especially where it is necessary to pay an individual as an independent contractor. In these cases, it is extremely important to be able to justify the payments if they are questioned by the Internal Revenue Service.

Key Idea: With the enactment of the Tax Reform Act of 1986, the benefits of receiving capital gains have been removed. This, in conjunction with the fact that the social security payments have become significant, will probably call for more employment contracts and greater amounts being allocated to them. This will maximize the social security benefits to those individuals who may not have been entitled to them. The sole cost would be the additional FICA tax, which must be paid during the term of those employment contracts.

Warning: While increased usage of employment contracts will probably occur after the Tax Reform Act of 1986, individuals who are over the age of sixty-five and less than seventy should be particularly careful that the receipt of income pursuant to an employment contract will not reduce the amount of social security benefits that they are entitled to.

PART 2

HOW TO DETERMINE THE TRUE PURCHASE PRICE

The goal in tax planning is to maximize the after-tax income, not necessarily the gross proceeds. The payment of the total purchase price should be analyzed as to both its financial and tax impact. The "frame of reference" in all purchases is the payment of the entire purchase price for stock at date of closing. This definition is derived from the manner that stock is bought and sold on the various securities markets. Any sales terms that differ from this will discount the purchase price.

The definition of after-tax income is the total purchase price less the sum of the costs of sale plus applicable income tax. The tax structure commencing in 1988 has three tax rates. In addition, there are four different schedules depending on whether you are single, married filing separately, head of household or married. For married individuals the applicable marginal tax rates are as follows:

Taxable Income (TI)	Tax Payable
0—$29,750	15%
$29,750—$71,900	$4,462.50 + 28% of (TI—$29,750)
$71,900—$149,250	$16,264.50 + 33% of (TI—$71,900)
$149,250 and up	28% of TI*

*a phaseout of the personal and dependency exemptions can increase the tax rate on a portion or all of the income above $149,250 by as much as 5 percent.

As a starting point in determining the tax impact on the seller, it is necessary to determine his marginal tax rate. The marginal tax rate is defined as the amount of tax to be paid on the next dollar of income earned.

For example, if a married taxpayer has a projected after-sale taxable income of $90,000, his marginal tax rate would be thirty-three percent. If he was to receive a covenant not-to-compete for five years at $10,000 per year, he should expect to pay a $3,300 tax on each payment received.

Long-term capital gains beginning in 1987 are taxed at the lesser of ordinary income rates or twenty-eight percent.

Prior to the Tax Reform Act of 1986, the question from the seller's viewpoint was, "How do you obtain more capital gains and less ordinary income?" The answer, of course, was to have the greatest part of the purchase price possible allocated to capital assets or assets used in the trade or business (commonly referred to as Section 1231 assets) not subject to depreciation recapture under either Section 1245 or 1250. Capital assets, according to Code Section 1221, have been defined in the negative and exclude such items as inventory, accounts receivable, and the like. Section 1231 assets include equipment, land, buildings, goodwill, and the rest. The need for this planning, except in specialized situations, is no longer necessary. Accordingly the need to consider whether or not the sale will result in ordinary income or capital gain except in those situations is normally not significant.

Taxation can occur at both the corporate and individual level. The key for the seller after the Tax Reform Act of 1986 will be to avoid double taxation. It is therefore important to determine who will report the gain (seller, sellers' corporation, or both). The question of whether it is ordinary or capital gains is now less important than it was prior to the Tax Reform Act of 1986. As was stated previously, what is good for the seller is bad for the buyer. The initial conflict will occur when the parties are discussing what assets are to be sold. For the seller, the taxwise optimal result will be to allocate the entire sales price to stock. On the other hand, the optimal tax result as far as the purchaser is concerned will be to allocate the purchase price to depreciable assets, employment contracts, and covenants not-to-compete.

Example: A owns all of the stock in XYZ Corporation. XYZ Corporation has the following balance sheet:

	Book Value	Fair Market Value
Assets:		
Depreciable Equipment	0	$100,000
Total Assets	0	$100,000

Liabilities and Equity:		
Unrealized Appreciation		$100,000
Retained Earnings	($10,000)	($10,000)
Capital Stock	$10,000	$10,000
Total Liabilities and Equity	0	$100,000

Assume that A is in the twenty-eight percent marginal tax bracket and the corporation is in the combined Federal and State marginal tax bracket of forty percent. If B purchases all of the assets of XYZ Corporation for $100,000, the after-tax proceeds to A will be calculated as follows:

Gain on sale of assets by XYZ Corporation	$100,000
Tax on gain	$40,000
Proceeds to A in Liquidation	$60,000
Gain on receipt of proceeds by A assuming A has no basis in the stock	$60,000
Tax on receipt of proceeds by A	$16,800
After-tax proceeds to A	$43,200

If, in the alternative, A sold the stock to B for $100,000, then:

Gain on sale of stock by A	$100,000
Tax on gain	$28,000
After-tax proceeds to A	$72,000

Accordingly, in the above scenario, by selling the assets instead of the stock, A has realized sixty percent of the after-tax proceeds that he would have received if he could have sold the stock.

In trying to determine the tax effects on the seller, even after the Tax Reform Act of 1986, it may in certain instances still be important to understand the concept of recapture. "Depreciation recapture" is a term of art that refers to recategorizing capital gain as ordinary income. Investment credit recapture requires the repayment of a part or all of the investment credit previously claimed by the taxpayer.

For example, an item of personal property subject to depreciation and investment credit has an initial cost of $5,000 and was depreciated on a straight-line basis over five years. After three years, it was sold for $4,000. The $2,000 gain [$4,000 sales price less $2,000 ($5,000 original cost less $3,000 depreciation taken)] would have to be reported as ordinary income. In addition, there would be investment credit recapture because the original credit was taken on a five-year basis at ten percent. As it was held only three years, six percent was allowable. Therefore, four percent of the original cost of $5,000 or $200 of the original $500 credit would have to be repaid to the government (recaptured).

The prior example has been simplified because, under the tax law, the basis of the property would have to be reduced by one-half of the investment credit taken and this factor did not enter into the above computation. The effect would have been to reduce the depreciation deduction. Depreciation recapture is the exception to the general rule that capital assets or 1231 assets give rise to capital gain. If the above item of personal property had been sold for $6,000 instead of $4,000, there would have been a gain of $3,000:

Selling price	$6,000
Basis	$3,000
Gain on sale	$3,000

$2,000 of the gain would be taxed as ordinary income and $1,000 as capital gain. Note that the amount of ordinary income is limited to the lesser of the total gain or depreciation recapture.

Note: While the negative impact of depreciation recapture has been reduced by the Tax Reform Act of 1986, it can still have adverse tax ramifications in certain sales and liquidations.

Prior to the Tax Reform Act of 1986, to determine the "True Purchase Price" it was necessary to discount any sale proceeds received as ordinary income instead of long-term capital gain. This exercise, while it may still have some viability depending on how the law is interpreted, has minimum impact and can be discarded in most computations after January 1, 1988.

HOW DISCOUNTING AFFECTS AMOUNT RECEIVED

Discounting involves the time value of money. In other words, a dollar received today is worth more than a dollar received at a later date, unless an appropriate interest rate is paid. The need to discount the price received will usually appear in three different situations:

1. There is no interest to be added to payments to be received in the future. An example of this is a covenant not-to-compete payable at the rate of $10,000 per year over ten years without interest.

2. The interest rate paid is lower than that which the market would dictate. (such as the purchase money promissory note calls for interest at nine percent while the appropriate interest should be eleven percent.)

3. There is no interest inherent in the transaction. The contract negotiated on its "face" matches future payments with services rendered or other value received. However, when parties do not realistically value the future services, these contracts are part of the purchase price and must be discounted.

An example would be an employment contract of $25,000 per year when the selling party is not expected to perform any substantial services. The purchaser is obligated for this contract and its cost must be added to the purchase price. The method of determining the cost of this contract will be illustrated shortly.

It is obvious that the $100,000 covenant not-to-compete payable in five equal installments of $20,000 without interest is not worth $100,000. To determine its actual worth, it is important to ascertain an appropriate discount rate. While this may seem to be a matter of pure conjecture, the general method of determination is not that difficult.

In essence, the five-year covenant not-to-compete can be equated to an installment note to be paid off annually without interest. Your banker or securities broker can help determine an appropriate rate by ascertaining what bonds or loans of a like term and security are paying. If this discount rate is determined at ten percent, then the value in today's dollars of the $100,000 payable in five years, $20,000 annual payments, can be determined as follows:

DATE OF PAYMENT	APPROPRIATE DISCOUNT APPLICABLE TO THE PAYMENT	GROSS AMOUNT OF PAYMENT	DISCOUNTED VALUE OF PAYMENT
1st year from date of closing	90%	$20,000	$18,000
2nd year from date of closing	81%	$20,000	$16,200
3rd year from date of closing	73%	$20,000	$14,600

4th year from date of closing	66%	$20,000	$13,200
5th year from date of closing	59%	$20,000	$11,800
Total		$100,000	$73,800

Accordingly, while the face value of the payments to be made is $100,000, the discounted value applying a ten percent discount rate is only $73,800. For tax purposes, the seller will report ordinary income at the rate of $20,000 per year.

Key Idea: An easy way to approximate the current value of payments to be received without interest is to review an "Equal Monthly Mortgage Amortization Schedule." For example, if the above payments were made monthly, ($20,000/12 = $1,667 per month) instead of annually, the ten percent tables, five years, should be analyzed until the monthly payment is matched.

MONTHLY PAYMENT NECESSARY TO AMORTIZE LOAN
INTEREST AT 10%

TERM/AMOUNT	5 YEARS
$75,000	$1,593.53
$80,000	$1,699.77

Accordingly, the true value of the monthly payment is $78,458.

Note: Mutual Advantage The second area where it is appropriate to discount the value received is when the interest paid to the seller is less than what the market dictates. This is an area where planning within parameters can be extremely beneficial to the purchaser. Because of the changes in the Tax Reform Act the seller does not care if the payment is interest income or a principal payment on the assets sold as both will result in virtually the same taxation to him. Accordingly, higher (rather than lower) interest rates may be in vogue in 1987 and thereafter.

Prior to the Tax Reform Act of 1986, if the interest determined by the parties was not market value interest, the purchase price received had to be discounted. After the Tax Reform Act of 1986, there may in certain cases be interest determined at higher than market value and accordingly this may result in a premium in the note. In these cases, to protect the sellers the promissory note must either prohibit prepayment or provide for a prepayment penalty.

Example: If the current market interest rate for fixed ten-year obligations is twelve percent and if the interest rate applicable to the purchase money obligation is only nine percent, the favorable terms have in effect reduced the actual price paid by the borrower.

In determining the fair or appropriate interest rate to be charged for the portion of the sales price that is financed, there are three perspectives:

1. The first is that of the buyer. His frame of reference could be the alternative interest rates available to him from a lending institution. If the seller offers him more favorable terms, he has in effect received a discount on the purchase price paid.

2. The second is that of the seller. He will look to the rate that he can earn through alternative investments. The difference between what the seller can earn on his funds and what the buyer must pay is the profit of the lending institution. The spread will usually be at least two points.

3. The third is one of mutual self-interest. This perspective probably can best be illustrated by the question "Does the seller not only wish to sell his business but is he also willing to act as a lending institution?" In a majority of instances the answer is a simple no. In these cases, there is no mutual self-interest and again the buyer and seller are in adversary roles.

Four Reasons the Seller May Act As a Lending Institution

There are several factors that may sway the seller into acting as a lending institution. These can be summarized as follows.

A. If he acts as the lending institution and can offer more favorable terms than the lending institution, the number of potential buyers will probably increase.

B. The number of impediments in the transaction is reduced since there will be no need for a financing contingency.

C. Because most of the sales price will not be paid in cash but represented by a promissory note, the seller's investment strategy will be simplified. He will not have cash assets to invest but will convert his investment in the company into an installment note. As long as the security is good, he may actually receive a better return than he would using alternative investments.

D. An installment sales contract will be a tax advantage and although it will not reduce the total tax paid, it will spread the tax over a number of years and will increase his after-tax return as interest is being paid on untaxed profits.

Example: A has the alternative of selling the business for $100,000 in cash, or receiving an installment note payable annually at $20,000 per year plus interest at ten percent. Assume that A is in the twenty-eight percent marginal tax bracket and that he can earn ten percent on the after-tax proceeds. How much better off will he be if he receives the funds on an installment basis rather than in cash at closing?

1. A determination of the total net after-tax funds available after five years assuming the $100,000 is paid in cash at date of closing.

Year	Principal Payments	Net After Tax Value of Principal Payments	Interest on Promissory Note	Net After Tax Proceeds on Interest from Promissory Note	Earnings on Invested Assets	Net After Tax Income on Invested Assets	Total After Tax Investment Funds
1	$100,000	$72,000	0	0	$7,200	$5,184	$ 77,184
2	—	—	—	—	$7,718	$5,557	$ 82,741
3	—	—	—	—	$8,274	$5,957	$ 88,698
4	—	—	—	—	$8,698	$6,386	$ 95,084
5	—	—	—	—	$9,508	$6,846	$101,930

2. Determination of after-tax funds assuming installment payment.

Year	Principal Payments	Net After Tax Value of Principal Payments	Interest on Promissory Note	Net After Tax Proceeds on Interest from Promissory Note	Earnings on Invested Assets	Net After Tax Income on Invested Assets	Total After Tax Investment Funds
1	$20,000	$14,400	$10,000	$7,200			$ 21,600
2	$20,000	$14,400	$8,000	$5,760	$2,160	$1,555	$ 43,315
3	$20,000	$14,400	$6,000	$4,320	$4,332	$3,119	$ 65,154
4	$20,000	$14,400	$4,000	$2,880	$6,515	$4,691	$ 87,125
5	$20,000	$14,400	$2,000	$1,440	$8,713	$6,273	$109,238

As can be seen in this example, the receipt of the same purchase price in installments has increased the after-tax funds by about seven percent. The tradeoff is twofold: the lack of security and illiquidity of the investment.

The above has summarized the general concepts. The question now is "How do we determine the amount of discount that can be applied?" This is a complex actuarial determination; however, a simple method of approximating the amount of the discount can be illustrated as follows:

A is selling the stock in his corporation for $100,000 payable in 120 equal monthly installments of $1,266.76 with interest at nine percent. He discusses the appropriate interest rate with his banker and is informed that if the buyer had come to the bank, he could have obtained a loan with the same terms at an interest rate of twelve percent. All that needs to be done is to review the equal monthly amortization schedules and determine what the value of 120 monthly payments at $1266.76 a month would be at twelve percent interest.

MONTHLY PAYMENT NECESSARY TO AMORTIZE LOAN
INTEREST AT 12%

TERM/AMOUNT	5 YEARS
$85,000	$1,219.51
$90,000	$1,291.24

Accordingly, the true value is approximately $88,294.00.

The third area where discounts need to be applied is in those contracts that do not always reflect the proper charges for services rendered or for the rental of property. The concept of redistributing a portion of the sales price to a tax deductible form such as employment contracts, consulting contracts, or lease agreements has already been discussed.

The first step in determining the amount of the discount is to determine what is the true value for either the services performed or lease payments. The difference between the true value and the amount charged will be subject to discounting in the same manner as has been discussed when determining the true value of covenants not-to-compete.

Key Idea: Any time the purchase or sale anticipates installment payments, a lease, or an employment contract, it is important to determine whether the interest is appropriate for the term and security of the note, the lease payments match the fair market rental and the employment contract is for services actually to be rendered. At any time that this is not the case, it is imperative to determine the true interest rate, the true rent, and the true value for services rendered. The difference between the actual amount being charged and the true value reflects an additional increment to the purchase price. The actual amount to be added to the purchase price must be determined under the concept of discounting.

Key Idea: While the concept of discounting involves fairly complex actuarial determinations, simple methods can provide you with a "ballpark amount" as to the correct increment to the purchase price.

WHAT IS THE MEASURING STICK USED TO DETERMINE TRUE FAIR MARKET VALUE?

Every system that measures and compares has a basic frame of reference. In our monetary system, it is the dollar; in the metric system, it is the meter; in the English measuring system, it is the foot. For the owner of stock in a closely held corporation, the measuring stick is determined by the securities market. This measuring stick becomes a cash sale for stock at closing which results in capital gain. Any owner of publicly traded stock at any time can sell his stock for cash and will be taxed at capital gains rates for tax purposes. Any result other than a cash sale of stock at closing yielding capital gains will have to be discounted so that it can be properly compared to the measuring stick.

An example will show how to analyze and determine the true value of an offer.

Example: Joe owns 100 percent of XYZ, Inc. His advisors have informed him that his corporation's true value is between $225,000 and $275,000. He is incredulous and believes that anything under $400,000 is a steal. To support his position he has obtained an offer to purchase on the following terms:

A. $150,000 for the stock—no money down, with principal and interest (six percent) in 180 equal monthly installments of $1,265.80.

B. $150,000 for a covenant not-to-compete—$30,000 per year, for each of five years.

C. $200,000 for an employment contract—$40,000 a year for each of the next five years.

How do you analyze this offer? To determine the true fair market value you must discount each of the three components of the purchase price. For the purpose of this analysis, it will be assumed that the appropriate interest rate (seller's perspective) is eleven percent. It will be assumed that Joe is in the twenty-eight percent marginal tax bracket and he has no basis in the stock. Using the measuring stick (a cash sale at closing for the stock yielding capital gain), this offer will be compared to that common denominator. Assuming the true fair market value of the stock as determined by the advisors is $250,000, Joe would receive the following in after tax proceeds if he received a cash offer to buy his stock at that purchase price:

Sales price	$250,000
Basis	-0-
Gain on sale	$250,000
Less	
Tax on gain	$ 70,000
After-tax proceeds	$180,000

The true purchase price of the offer that Joe obtained will be determined as follows:

A. The purchase price is discounted for the difference between the interest charged and the market interest rate. Using the technique set forth on page 144, the discounted value of the purchase price for the stock is $111,500.

B. The covenant not-to-compete is discounted because no interest is charged on the covenant. Discounted at eleven percent, the true value of the covenant is $107,100.

C. The employment contract is discounted in three ways:

1. The amount to be paid for the services that will be rendered (not part of the purchase price) must be determined. In our example, it will be assumed that he is to work sixty percent of the time and that his services have been valued at $20,000 a year.
2. The receipt of salary is ordinary earned income not capital gain. While the prior advantages of long term capital gain receipts over ordinary income have been minimized by the Tax Reform Act of 1986, ordinary income is still subject to:

a. A FICA tax of approximately 7.15 percent on the social security base by both the employer and employee. The employee's portion of this payment is not deductible.

b. The reduction of social security benefits if he is receiving these while under the age of seventy.

The minimum discount to be determined would be as follows:

Purchase Price of Employment Contract	Discount Rate Applied to each Payment	Present Value of Payments
$10,000	.89	$ 8,900
$10,000	.79	$ 7,900
$10,000	.70	$ 7,000
$10,000	.63	$ 6,300
$10,000	.56	$ 5,600
		$35,700

Therefore, the true before-tax proceeds to Joe can be determined as follows:

Discounted value of the $150,000 Promissory note	$111,500
Discounted value (time value of money) of the covenant not-to-compete	$107,100
Discounted value (time value of money and reduction for worth of services rendered) of employment contract	$35,700
Total Proceeds	$254,300
Applicable Tax	$71,204
Total After-Tax Proceeds	$183,096

Warning: While it would have appeared that a portion of the purchase price had been converted from ordinary income (interest payments) to principal payments by charging a commercially unreasonably low interest rate as set forth above, the IRS had developed under Section 483 the imputed interest rules applicable to installment sales. This of course had sizable tax benefits prior to the enactment of the Tax Reform Act of 1986. After the Tax Reform Act of 1986, this Section may instead of providing minimum interest rates be utilized to provide maximum interest rates.

These rules state that you cannot arbitrarily set the interest rates on installment sales. If you do, a portion of the "principal payments" will be redesignated as "interest." Accordingly, in the above example, while the parties may have established a six percent interest rate, the IRS is not bound by this rate and a portion of the principal payments will be considered as interest income. See page 216 for a more comprehensive discussion of the imputed interest rules and how the parties can determine within parameters the interest for their mutual self-benefit.

Warning: Before establishing an appropriate interest rate, it is imperative that the parties review the rules under Section 483 to ensure that the interest charged is within the parameters set by that Section.

Part Two has discussed the components of the purchase price and how to determine what you are truly receiving if you are the seller or actually paying if you are the buyer. It became apparent that the "true value" was not always determinable from the legal documentation. For example, an employment contract with a stated salary might not equate to the actual worth of the services to be rendered. Any time the contracted value is not commensurate with either the services performed, the interest, or the rental, it is necessary to add an incremental value to the purchase price. This part also indicated the difference between the securities market, which establishes the measuring stick on which all sales are determined, a cash sale of the stock at closing resulting in capital gains, from the complexities that involve the sale of a closely held business. The sale of a closely held corporation's stock was compared to the measuring stick to determine what was the true value of the sale of the business. Once this value has been determined, the question becomes how do we ensure that the purchase price agreed on is paid? This raises the question of how do you adequately secure the transaction and is discussed in Part Three, which follows.

PART 3

HOW SECURITY ENSURES PAYMENT OF PURCHASE PRICE

The purpose of security can be summarized as follows:

"The purchase price has no worth unless it is paid."

While this statement is axiomatic, many people are seemingly unconcerned about the security for future payments. There appear to be two reasons for this. The first is the general naiveté of the seller. They have always paid their bills and assume that the purchaser will pay his. The second is a self-confident clairvoyance and innate trust in the purchaser.

From the attorney's frame of reference, which has developed over the years of only hearing from the clients when they have problems, security becomes paramount. The last thing an attorney wishes to do is structure a transaction that cannot work and therefore will not be paid. In the event of default, his client, the seller, may not be able to convert the remaining unpaid portion of the purchase price into cash. Therefore, security should not be the stepchild in the negotiation process.

FORMS OF SECURITY

Security comes in many forms. Some of the most common are:

1. Cash

2. The unsecured promise of either the purchaser or the corporation incorporated by the purchaser to buy the business. The unsecured promise is a promissory note without the pledge of any specific assets. The sole security is the general credit of the purchaser. If a corporation has been formed to accomplish this purchase, security can also take the form of the general credit of the corporation and the guarantee of the shareholders.

3. The secured promise is a promissory note that in addition to the general unsecured promise of the purchaser contains provisions, that in the event of default, payment will be made from specific assets to the exclusion of any other creditors.

4. Alternate third party security. This can take many forms, such as, a first or second mortgage on real estate, a guarantee of a third party or the bank's letter of credit. The use of a letter of credit has become extremely popular in recent years. The banks, in effect, guarantee the payment of the promissory note in the event that the purchaser defaults. They charge a fee (zero to two percent) on the principal balance each year for issuing this guarantee.

All forms of security involve a commitment by the purchaser. Normally, the purchaser's intent is to pay the purchase price out of the future profits of the business. Security comes into play only in the event that the planned income does not materialize.

In order to evaluate the security offered, some of the questions that must be asked are;

1. "What other income is pledged?"
2. "What assets have been pledged and how much are they worth?"
3. "Has the seller individually guaranteed the payments?"
4. "What creditors have superior claims to your security?"
5. "What does the seller lose if all goes wrong?"

Key Idea: Be wary of the purchaser who is hesitant to pledge sufficient collateral. This could indicate one or more of the following:

1. He is not confident that the business will succeed.
2. He is not sufficiently committed to make all payments.
3. He does not have sufficient collateral to pledge.
4. His financial stability may not be what has been represented.

HOW TO ANALYZE THE SECURITY OFFERED

The prime security for the purchase of a business is cash. Nonetheless, few businesses are purchased for cash either because it is not possible or taxwise it may be too costly. Accordingly, the unpaid portion of the purchase price will be in the form of a future promise to pay, which is usually represented by an installment note. This note may be secured or unsecured. Whatever security is tendered, it must be reducible to cash in the event of default. If it cannot be converted from its current form to cash, it is worthless as security.

The value of the security tendered is rooted in the law of bankruptcy. Bankruptcy dictates the method of distribution of assets when there are insufficient assets to pay the creditors all the money loaned. The hierarchy is as follows:

1. costs of administration
2. secured interest
3. taxes
4. wages
5. pro rata among the general creditors

An example will illustrate the distribution of a bankruptcy estate.

Example: Nerdo Well, five years ago, purchased the stock of Substantial, Inc. for $500,000. He paid $100,000 in cash at closing. The remainder of the purchase price, $400,000, was to be paid pursuant to a promissory note secured by the stock in the corporation and a second mortgage on an apartment house. Since closing, Nerdo Well has made sufficient periodic payments on the note to cover all accrued interest but has not reduced any portion of the principal. Individually, he has incurred substantial personal losses and has filed for liquidation under Chapter 7 of the Bankruptcy Act. His assets and liabilities are as follows:

ASSETS

Stock in Substantial, Inc.	$50,000.00
Cash and Marketable Securities	50,000.00
Apartment House	300,000.00
Total Assets:	$400,000.00

LIABILITIES

Note Due to Seller	$400,000.00
(Secured by a second mortgage on the apartment house and the stock of Substantial, Inc.)	
First Mortgage on Apartment House	100,000.00
General Creditors	300,000.00
Total Liabilities:	$800,000.00

As his total assets are $400,000 subject to $800,000 of liabilities, if all creditors shared pro rata, each would receive fifty cents on the dollar. Bankruptcy law dictates otherwise. Assuming that the apartment house is sold for $300,000, the first mortgagee will receive the unpaid portion of his mortgage, $100,000. The remaining $200,000 is applied to the promissory note due to the seller. The seller's promissory note is further reduced with the proceeds from the sale of the stock in Substantial, Inc. After these payments, the total unpaid promissory note becomes an unsecured claim of $100,000. The only assets remaining for distribution to the general creditors are cash and securities of $50,000. The general creditors, which include the unsecured portion of the promissory note due to the seller, receive twelve and a half cents for each dollar of debt (assets of $50,000/total unsecured credits of $400,000). Our seller under the above fact situation proved to be both a secured and unsecured creditor and received $312,500 on the unpaid portion of the promissory note for $400,000. These payments were received as follows:

$200,000 from the sale of the apartment house,

$50,000 from the sale of stock in Substantial, Inc.,

$12,500 on the unsecured portion of his note ($100,000).

If he had not properly secured the sale with the stock in the company and the second mortgage on the apartment house, he would have suffered a greater loss. Instead of receiving $312,500, he would have received $171,428 computed as follows:

Determination of funds available
to satisfy claims of general creditors

Proceeds from the sale of the apartment house in excess of first mortgage. Note: First mortgage holder gets paid in full.	$200,000
Stock in Substantial, Inc.	$ 50,000
Cash and Marketable Securities	$ 50,000
Total assets available for general creditors	$300,000
Note due to Seller	$400,000
Total Unsecured Liabilities	$700,000
Distribution to Creditors who are not secured forty-three percent (total assets divided by total liabilities)	

Obviously, the above example is simplified. There are no expenses of administration, taxes, or wages. The stock of Substantial, Inc., had a residual value that normally would not be the case when bankruptcy occurs. There were no homestead or other exempt items that would have complicated the distribution. The example is set forth solely to illustrate the general concepts and to demonstrate that if a transaction is properly secured there is a greater chance of recovering a portion or all of the unpaid principal of the promissory note in the event of either default or bankruptcy.

The question then becomes, "How much security is enough?" The answer is "There is never too much security." One of the inherent problems is the seller's and purchaser's frame of reference. There is a tendency to consider the value of the assets in the context of an operating business rather than on forced liquidation.

Example: If you were attempting to secure part of the purchase price from the sale of a men's clothing store, there would be hard assets that could be used to secure the unpaid portion of the promissory note, namely:

1. furniture and fixtures
2. inventory
3. receivables

As a going concern, the values would be significantly greater than in a forced liquidation. The furniture and fixtures valued on a going concern basis could be $75,000 (original purchase price less reasonable economic depreciation). In the event that the store faces forced liquidation, the business would probably realize only a fraction of the value. The furniture and fixtures would now have to be removed from the premises, transported, and then inserted in another location. Even inventory, which is normally valued for financial statement purposes at lower of cost or market, in the event of forced liquidation will yield substantially less than the amount listed on the balance sheet.

Note: Receivables, which would appear to be unaffected by the fact that the store is operating or is being liquidated, also have a tendency to dissipate. It is amazing how many individuals who would not hesitate to pay a bill to a going concern fail to voluntarily make payment to a business in liquidation.

You should also be aware that when a business is failing, the vultures fly. A failing business rarely will realize the full fair market value on any of its assets because there is no commercially available method to dispose of the property. The only ones left to purchase the property are those who must take a substantial risk. They are not going to purchase the assets unless the price is right (at a substantial discount). When you are looking at assets to secure the unpaid promissory note, do not look at book value or adjusted book value, but at liquidation value.

Key Idea: In the event that the business is not sold for cash, the key to security is that you can never have enough.

Key Idea: When valuing security, it is normally inappropriate to look at the value of the assets on a going-concern basis. It is important to determine the liquidation value of the assets that secure the unpaid purchase price.

It should be noted that the above discussion involves "hard assets," such as inventory, equipment, and receivables. There are obviously other hard assets that are suitable security and normally do not dissipate on forced liquidation. Some of these assets are land and buildings, motor vehicles, and marketable securities. On the other hand, soft assets such as goodwill, franchises, patents, and trademarks are extremely difficult to convert into cash and should only be used to secure a transaction as additional security or as a last resort.

HOW TO EVALUATE THE DIFFERENCE BETWEEN A SECURED AND UNSECURED PROMISSORY NOTE

It should be noted that security is only a problem if a portion or all of the purchase price is not paid in cash but is paid by the execution of an installment note or in the form of a future promise to pay such as an employment contract or covenant not-to-compete. The unpaid portion of the purchase price represented by a promissory note can either be secured or unsecured.

The Unsecured Promissory Note

This is the execution of a promissory note by the purchaser without the pledge of any specific assets. In the example on page 151, the unsecured promise is represented by the general creditors. They extended credit to Nerdo Well on the basis of his general assets. The value of the unsecured promise is dependent on the financial condition of the purchaser.

Many times the question becomes "Who is the purchaser?" Especially in an "asset purchase" it is not unusual for the purchaser to be a corporation.

Example: Widget, Inc., owned by Joe Smith, is selling its inventory, equipment, and goodwill to Widget II, Inc., for $500,000. Widget II, Inc., was just incorporated for the sole reason to accomplish the purchase. The purchase price is to be paid as follows: $100,000 in cash at closing and a $400,000 promissory note. Widget II's balance sheet before purchase was as follows:

Assets	
Cash	$100,000
Total Assets	$100,000

Liabilities and Equity	
Note Due to Shareholders	$ 80,000
Capital Stock	$ 20,000
Total Liabilities and Equity	$100,000

Its balance sheet after purchase is as follows:

Assets	
Cash	0
Inventory, Equipment, and Goodwill of Widget, Inc.	$500,000
Total Assets	$500,000

Liabilities and Equity	
Note Due to Seller	$400,000
Note Due to Stockholders	$ 80,000
Capital Stock	$ 20,000
Total Liabilities and Equity	$500,000

An unsecured promise to pay by Widget II, Inc., is not sufficient to secure the unpaid portion of the purchase price. You must at least obtain the guarantee of the stockholders of Widget II, Inc. This guarantee is equivalent to the unsecured promise by the actual purchasers of the business. Even if the individual purchasers have sufficient financial stability at that time they execute the installment note, their ability to pay at that time is not in question. The attempt to collect will occur after default when their assets have eroded.

In addition, financial statements of individuals are often exaggerated and should be reviewed with a critical eye. When the primary security is the unsecured promise of the purchaser, it is usually a good idea to have the purchaser supply you with periodic financial statements. You should also have in the sales agreement a provision that will allow you to require the pledging of additional security if financial conditions deteriorate.

Key Idea: If the sole security you are receiving for the payment of a promissory note is the general credit of either a corporation or individual, it is a good idea to have an agreement that he must provide additional security in the event that the net worth of the corporation or the individual declines.

Remember: When you have multiple purchasers, you can increase your security by having them jointly and severally guarantee the debt. When there are multiple purchasers, their financial circumstances are rarely the same. Usually one or more is substantially wealthier than the others. If you get the purchasers to jointly and severally obligate themselves for the payment of the debt, then in the event of default, you will be able to pursue those with "deep pockets." The concept of "joint and several" is that each is liable for the entire debt. The party paying has the right of contribution from his co-signors, but this is rarely a viable alternative.

Example: A, B, and C purchase a business and sign a promissory note for $300,000 "jointly and severally." They default. The seller can pursue collection entirely against "A," the "deep pocket." A must pay the entire amount but can get contribution from B and C if he can find and collect from them.

Obviously, if you are the purchaser, you want your liability limited to an undivided portion of the debt. For example, if the total liability is $300,000 and if there are three purchasers, you wish to limit your liability to one-third of the total unpaid principal balance at any time.

Key Idea: Where you have multiple purchasers of a business, attempt to have them sign the primary obligation and obligate themselves jointly and severally for its payment.

Warning: Beware of the purchaser or purchasers who will not personally obligate himself.

From time to time, the seller will request the purchaser to sign the obligations and he will be reluctant to do so. Any time the purchaser takes this position, you should be put on notice that he may not believe that the business is going to succeed and/or he is not willing to back up his belief with commitment.

Diplomatically, this is a difficult situation. Normally the best and safest way to proceed if the seller still wishes to continue with the sale is to obtain a larger downpayment.

Example: If the purchaser is willing to personally guarantee payment and if the purchase price is $500,000, a downpayment of $100,000 or $150,000 may be sufficient. If, on the other hand, he does not wish to personally obligate himself, it may behoove the seller to obtain a downpayment of no less than $200,000. Remember, cash is a form of commitment and the ultimate security.

The Secured Promissory Note

"What is it and how to perfect it?" The concept of a secured interest is the pledging of a specific asset or assets to ensure the payment of the promissory note. The promissory note is the primary obligation. The collateral may be real or personal property and, if personal, tangible or intangible. Collateral can be utilized to ensure the payment of the promissory note in the event of default by the purchaser. The collateral when converted to cash can be applied to the payment of the promissory note without regard to any other creditors if the security is perfected, up to the total amount of the unpaid note including interest. Any excess must be remitted to the owner of the collateral.

Example: A promissory note in the amount of $200,000 is secured by a first mortgage on a building. The debtor defaults and the building is sold for $300,000. The debt is satisfied and the remaining $100,000 is remitted to the debtor.

HOW THE SELLER SERVES NOTICE THAT HE HAS SECURITY INTEREST IN THE ASSETS SOLD

Perfection is the procedure that serves "legal notice" to the public and other creditors that specific collateral has been pledged for the payment of the promissory note. The most common form of perfected security interest is the recorded mortgage. In purchasing a house, the borrower signs a promissory note and places a first lien in favor of the lending institution on the property he purchases. In the event that the purchaser cannot make the payments on the promissory note, the lending institution will commence a legal action known as foreclosure. Foreclosure proceedings normally involve a court-directed sale of the property. The sale proceeds are used first to satisfy the note secured by the mortgage. Unless otherwise limited by either law or through the terms of the promissory note, in the event that the sale of the property does not produce sufficient proceeds to satisfy the promissory note, the remainder of the unpaid promise becomes an unsecured debt of the borrower. An example will illustrate this concept.

Example: Gladys buys a house for $100,000, $10,000 down, and finances the remainder of the purchase price with a lending institution. She signs a promissory note and mortgage for that amount. Unfortunately for Gladys, she subsequently loses her job and is thereafter unable to make the mortgage payments. In addition, the real estate market becomes depressed. The lending institution commences foreclosure proceedings against her. The house is sold for $75,000 while at the time the unpaid principal on the note, costs, and interest equals $95,000. The sales proceeds, $75,000, are applied against the promissory note and the remaining $20,000 is converted from a secured promise to pay to an unsecured debt of Gladys.

It is possible to perfect a security interest in both real and personal property. However, the differences between the two types of property affect the inherent usefulness of each to secure the unpaid portion of a promissory note. Normally, it is extremely difficult, even with neglect, to substantially affect the inherent value of real property. Land and buildings that have not been maintained still have inherent worth. While their value may decline through misuse, unless the economic conditions deteriorate, the property should not be seriously depreciated upon foreclosure.

It is relatively easy to perfect a security interest in real estate. The process varies from state to state but normally requires the filing of a mortgage, land contract, or other debt instrument with the Register of Deeds in the county in which the property is located. The party who receives the secured interest will request that a title search be made after the recording to ensure that his security, be it mortgage or land contract, is a perfected lien on the property. There is normally no need to refile at a later date.[1] Only upon the payment of the primary debt instrument will it be necessary to file a satisfaction of mortgage or a deed in fulfillment of land contract.

If you compare real property to the more easily dissipatible assets of receivables and inventory, the problems with securing the purchase price with personal property become evident.

Example: Sam's, a men's clothing store, was extremely successful at the time of sale. At this time, its total receivables and inventory were significantly greater than four years later when the volume of the store had decreased and it was forced to liquidate. Receivables, which are a form of intangible personal property, and inventory, which is a form of tangible personal property, both may be pledged to secure a promissory note; however, because they are readily dissipatible, their worth should be critically examined.

Key Idea: If possible, the promissory note should be secured with assets that are both readily marketable and nondissipatible. Normally, real property is preferred. However, in most sales of businesses the promissory note will also be secured by both tangible and intangible personal property.

HOW TO USE PERSONAL PROPERTY AS SECURITY

There are basically two kinds of personal property: tangible and intangible.

How to Perfect a Lien on Tangible Personal Property

Tangible personal property includes inventory, machinery, equipment, and auto. Tangible personal property can be further divided into two categories: titled and nontitled.

The most common types of titled tangible personal property, automobiles, trucks, and the like, will require the perfection of the security interest on the title itself. In Wisconsin, to perfect the interest on titled vehicles, it is necessary to file with the Department of Transportation and have the interest noted on the title to the vehicle.

---

[1]It should be noted that while virtually all states have a law that removes the mortgage as a lien against real estate after a sufficiently long period of time, even without a satisfaction of mortgage, this rarely is a problem as the promissory note calls for the entire payment prior to the expiration of this limitation period.

In other states, the appropriate method to perfect a security interest can be found in the Uniform Commercial Code adopted by that state.

Normally, the Secretary of State or the Department of Transportation can supply the forms needed to perfect the security interest in titled personal property. General filing with the Security of State in Wisconsin does not perfect the security interest in this type of property. In this case, the lien must be noted on the document of title to perfect the security interest.

Warning: It is imperative to understand how creditors' rights are established in the property and also how third party creditors are effected. In all security transactions, there are two sets of relationships that are important:

1. Debtor—Creditor
2. Creditor—Other Creditors

The relationship between the debtor and creditor can be set forth in the security agreement (see Appendix K), mortgage, land contract, and the like.

Perfection is the procedure that establishes the creditor's lien against the specific property to the exclusion of other creditors. This procedure has as its foundation notice to the other creditors. Each type of property has its own problems and therefore requires a slightly different procedure. Nontitled, tangible property, which includes virtually all tangible personal property other than vehicles, will normally require, depending on state law, the filing of a financing statement (see Appendix L) with the secretary of state or the Register of Deeds. This financing statement identifies both the debtor and creditor and indicates what property is used to secure the obligation. You will note in reviewing Appendix L that it does not reflect the terms and conditions of the agreement between the debtor and creditor. These are set forth in the security agreement mentioned above.

How to Perfect a Lien on Intangible Personal Property

Intangible personal property can also be divided into two separate categories:

1. titled intangible personal property such as stocks and bonds.

2. nontitled intangible personal property such as receivables and goodwill.

Certain types of nontitled intangible personal property such as specific accounts receivable, notes, and bonds (unregistered) can be secured in two ways.

1) One method is possession of the individual assets.
2) A second method to perfect the security interest in tangible personal property is by filing a financing statement with the secretary of state or Register of Deeds. A copy of the financing statement used in Wisconsin to perfect a security interest in all nontitled tangible and intangible personal property is attached as Appendix L.

Key Idea: In securing any promissory note, there are three goals:

1. execute a legally binding security agreement creating the creditors' rights in the property pledged.
2. perfect the security interest in the property against any and all other creditors; and
3. ensure that the property is not dissipated.

Note: The perfection of the security interest differs from state to state and the appropriate state law should be consulted to determine exactly how this interest is perfected. It should be noted that while virtually all states have adopted one form or another of the Uniform Commercial Code, the states have not developed a uniform system for perfecting security interests in personal property. Laws affecting the perfection of a security interest in real estate are also subject to a great deal of variance from one state to another.

With titled tangible and intangible personal property (titled tangible includes autos; titled intangible includes registered stocks and bonds) it is appropriate not only to execute an agreement granting a security interest in the property but also to retain the possession of the document of title. Tangible and intangible personal property that is not titled usually requires two separate and distinct documents. The financing statement set forth in Appendix L is notification to the outside world that you have a security interest in the property. The document that sets forth the rights and obligations of both the debtor and creditor is called a "security agreement." A copy of the form for the general business security agreement is attached as Appendix K.

While perfecting a security interest in real property requires a promissory note and a mortgage, the perfecting of a security interest in personal property normally requires three instruments: a promissory note, a security agreement, and a financing statement. In both real and personal property the various agreements can often be combined into one document.

Example: A land contract that could be filed with the Register of Deeds contains the provisions of both the promissory note and the security interest. A chattel security agreement can incorporate both the security agreement and promissory note in one document. In most cases, it will still be necessary to file a separate financing statement to perfect the security interest.

HOW TO USE ALTERNATIVE SECURITY

Alternative security is defined as security in addition to the purchaser's promise to pay and a pledge of the assets purchased. The need for alternative security becomes apparent when the assets sold are either not adequate or are not used to secure the sales price. The reason they could be inadequate is that they are readily dissipatible or depreciable without proper care. It could also become apparent when the fair market value of the assets sold is a small percentage of the total price. This problem is most common in the sale of service businesses in which earnings and not adjusted book value have determined the purchase price. In these cases, the assets that can be pledged are small in relation to the total purchase price. Another instance in which alternative security plays a significant role is where the purchaser does not wish to pledge the assets sold to secure the purchase price. In both of these cases, a form of alternative security becomes necessary.

If the purchaser buys all the operating assets of the business, including inventory, equipment, and receivables, the seller will normally receive as collateral for the promissory note a general security agreement and financing statement perfecting his first lien on these assets as well as the personal guarantee of the purchaser.

Warning: The sale of the corporate stock complicates the granting of a purchase money interest in the underlying assets owned by the corporation. The seller does not want only a security interest in the stock. In the event of default, the reacquisition of the stock may be a meaningless act. The equity of the shareholders represented by the stock is subordinate to all the corporate creditors. In the event of default and reacquisition by the sellers of the stock, all the equity may be lost.

Corporate and creditor law in each state will govern whether or not the corporate assets can be used to secure the personal debt of the shareholder. The legal question is, "Is it appropriate for the buyer of the corporation to place a lien against the corporate assets in favor of the seller of the stock?" Conceptually, this places general creditors of the corporation at a disadvantage by reducing the assets available in the event of default. Courts have taken differing views on the validity of these debts; however, it is a form of alternative security that should be investigated.

Example: All the stock of Fairly Successful Corporation has been sold by Joe Founder to Sam Flyer for $500,000. Sam paid $100,000 in cash and signed a promissory note secured by the stock in Fairly Successful. At the time of sale, the balance sheet of Fairly Successful was as follows:

Assets	
Cash	$1,000
Receivables and Inventory	$150,000
Equipment—net of depreciation	$349,000
Total Assets	$500,000

Liabilities and Equity	
Accounts payable	$50,000
Capital Stock	$50,000
Retained Earnings	$400,000
Total Liabilities and Equity	$500,000

Sam, instead of zooming, flopped and defaulted four years later when the balance sheet of the corporation was as follows:

Assets

Cash	$1,000
Inventory and Receivables	$80,000
Equipment	$300,000
TOTAL ASSETS	$381,000

Liabilities and Equity

Accounts Payable	$150,000
Notes Payable	$200,000
Capital Stock	$50,000
Retained Earnings	($19,000)
TOTAL LIABILITIES AND EQUITY	$381,000

The stock after reacquisition by Joe probably has little if any value. If, on the other hand, Joe had secured the promissory note with a first lien on the inventory, receivables, and equipment, although he may not have received 100 percent of the unpaid principal balance of the promissory note, he would have received his money before, not after the corporate creditors. As it was structured, he is subordinate to all creditors of the corporation. There usually is a better way, especially when the validity of this alternative security may be in doubt. An example will illustrate both the problem and one possible solution.

Example: A is buying 1,000 shares of common stock of X corporation from B for $1,000,000. The purchase price will be paid as follows: $400,000 in cash at closing and $600,000 pursuant to a promissory note. Both the purchaser and seller intend to secure the promissory note with the personal signature of B and a perfected security interest in the receivables, inventory, and equipment of X corporation. Their attorney is worried about the legality of securing a personal obligation with corporate assets.

A Better Way: In the above example, instead of A buying all the stock, he should purchase the 400 shares for $400,000 in cash at date of closing. The remaining 600 shares should be redeemed by X corporation issuing a promissory note to secure the purchase. This promissory note will be secured by a security interest in the receivables, inventories, and equipment by the personal guarantee of B. Using this particular alternative, you have avoided the question of whether or not a personal debt can be secured with corporate assets. If this is a problem within your state, the viability of this alternative should be investigated.

Warning: Before structuring the transaction as above, state corporate law should be reviewed to ensure that it is possible to accomplish the redemption of stock. States regulate the funds that can be used to redeem corporate stock. The minimum standard established by any state is to invalidate any redemption that would cause the insolvency of the corporation.

Four Types of Alternative Security

The most common types of alternative security are as follows.

Third Party Guarantee

This has been discussed earlier in Part One of this chapter. In the event that the purchaser is not an individual but a corporation formed by the individual for the purposes of purchasing the business, the personal guarantee of this individual should be obtained. It may often be possible to obtain the guarantee of additional individuals with substantial net worth: for example, father, relative, related corporation, and the like.

Other Collateral Security

At times when the downpayment is not sufficient, the seller will require security in addition to the assets being sold. The purchaser may give him a mortgage or security interest in other collateral. The most common type of collateral security is the second mortgage on a house, apartment, and the like.

Escrow Agreement

Prior to the Economic Recovery Tax Act of 1981 and the Installment Sales Act of 1980, there was substantial tax benefit in receiving the purchase price in installments over a period of years. Even before the Tax Reform Act of 1986, the tax benefits of receiving the payments in installments if not completely eliminated have been greatly reduced. With the enactment of the Tax Reform Act of 1986 and the virtual elimination of a progressive income tax structure especially for the higher basis taxpayers the goal probably will be cash receipts wherever possible. This may be the deathknell of the escrow agreement. It is easy to understand why the escrow agreement that was a tax device structured to provide 100 percent security and to allocate payments for tax purposes over a number of years had diminished even before the Tax Reform Act of 1986. However, there are still times when it is both tax wise and financially desirable to receive the payments not in cash but in installments and, in this case, the irrevocable letter of credit has replaced the escrow agreement as the device to provide the desired results.

The Irrevocable Letter of Credit

The irrevocable letter of credit noted above has supplanted the escrow agreement where additional "solid" security is desired. The purchaser may be an individual of substantial means who does not wish to encumber the selling assets with security interest or to make disclosure of his financial affairs to the seller.

A viable alternative is for the purchaser to supply an irrevocable letter of credit from his bank. The irrevocable letter of credit is nothing more than the bank's guarantee of payment of the note irrevocably in the event of default by the purchaser. In the past, sellers considered this promise "good as gold"; however, with the current financial problems of many banks, the role of the irrevocable letter of credit may be of diminished importance.

It should be noted that many times the seller is substituting the unsecured promise of the purchaser for the unsecured guarantee of the bank. Banks are interested in issuing these irrevocable letters of credit as they generate income without the need to loan funds. They normally will charge a percentage of the outstanding principal balance on a yearly basis as a fee. If the initial financed portion of the purchase price is $1,000,000, and if the bank charges one percent of the principal outstanding as a fee for the issuance of the irrevocable letter of credit, the bank has earned $10,000. This improves the return on their invested assets.

Key Idea: Alternative security should always be considered in the sale when the purchaser is an individual of substantial means who does not wish to encumber the assets purchased with a security interest or to pledge other security.

As a general rule, there is no tax problem in securing the unpaid portion of the purchase price with a secured or unsecured promise of the purchaser. Historically, the pledging of alternative security, be it in the form of additional collateral, escrow agreement, or third-party guarantee, posed tax problems. These problems have been reduced with the enactment of the Installment Sales Act of 1980.

Remember: Before receiving any form of alternative security, it is important to review the tax law to ensure that the receipt of this security will not be the equivalent of payment and therefore result in taxation before the cash payment is received. If this were the case, the seller would recognize taxable income in the year the security is pledged rather than over the term of the installment note when cash is received.

Warning: Any time that security other than the promise of the purchaser and the pledge of the assets sold is given to the seller, the law should be reviewed to ensure that the pledging of security is not considered payment, which would require the recognition of taxable income.

HOW TO MEASURE THE WORTH OF THE OFFERED SECURITY

In valuing the worth of the offered security, you should project a worst case scenario. The reason for this is you are attempting to project the value of the security in the event of default. This usually is a completely different value than exists at the time of the initial transaction. The economic climate of the business has materially changed at the time of default because:

1. the business will not be producing sufficient income to pay the note, and
2. the purchaser is unwilling or unable to make the payments from his other sources of income.

The total value of the business assets as well as their condition will in all likelihood be significantly different from that at the time of sale. How much dissipation and depreciation of the assets has occurred is always subject to conjecture. When you consider the problem from this perspective, there are three relevant factors.

1. Possibility of Dissipation—What is the lowest value of the assets that would still be owned by the business at time of default? For example, inventory and receivables fluctuate with the sales of the business. The greater the sales, the greater the value of the inventory and receivables. Accordingly, at time of default, the total value of these assets will be significantly reduced.

2. Marketability—What is the marketability of these assets? There is a great deal of difference between accounts receivable that only need to be collected and specialty equipment that has a very limited market.

3. Cost of Liquidation—What costs would be incurred to liquidate these assets? Even if an asset is marketable, it may require substantial costs to convert it to cash. To liquidate land and buildings, even if they are marketable, will be substantial. Normally, it will cost at least ten percent of the sales price to convert the land and buildings into cash.

The following is a chart that analyzes the various assets from the perspective of the creditor and considers each of the above factors' effect on pledged asset: Favorable (+), unfavorable (−), neutral or depends on the fact situation (0).

	Possibility of Dissipation	Marketability	Cost of Liquidation
1. Inventory	−	+	0
2. Machinery	+	−	−
3. Autos and Trucks	+	+	+
4. Accounts Receivable	−	+	+
5. Real Estate	+	+	−
6. Marketable Bonds and Securities	+	+	+
7. Other Assets	0	0	0

Of the four cornerstones of the negotiation process, security is obviously the key. All else is immaterial if the price negotiated is not paid. For this reason, before a binding contract is entered into, it is imperative to "role play" the worst case scenario and ascertain exactly what "you" as the seller will actually receive if all goes wrong. On the other hand, the pledging of security plays an important role (if not as important) to the purchaser because his agreement may limit his future flexibility. This may seriously hamper his chances for success in the future if he is unable at that time to obtain additional bank financing because he has no ability to pledge any further assets. The third concept "Terms," which is set forth in the next section will illustrate how to structure the payments in such a manner that it is in the best interest to both the purchaser and the seller.

PART 4

HOW TERMS CAN MAKE OR BREAK ANY SALES TRANSACTION

If a person buying or selling a business can structure the terms, price, while not immaterial, will play a small role in the overall negotiation process. Many times the easiest negotiation process to control for the purchaser is one in which the seller is myopic on price. People like the self-image of themselves as "ultimately reasonable." While certain "gliches" may occur, such as their being unreasonable on purchase price, they may easily be able to appreciate the other problems and provide "reasonable solutions" and insight that will be beneficial to the purchaser.

Warning: Don't set yourself up. If you are flexible as to the purchase price, you must be extremely flexible on terms if you wish the sales transaction to be completed. The trade-off may not be worth it. The receipt of the purchase price may result in tax disaster and the payment may not coincide with your personal needs.

THREE KEYS TO HELP STRUCTURE PROPER TERMS

There are three separate and distinct keys for evaluating the terms of the sales contract:

1. The measuring stick for all purchases of a business is cash for stock at date of closing. We set forth the various methods of discounting the purchase price on pages 139. These involve the tax ramifications as well as the time value of money.

2. The second key is that most buyers are looking to the future profits of the business purchased to pay the purchase price. Any time that the terms of the transaction are presented in such a way that it is not feasible to pay the purchase price out of the earnings of the

business (either actual or reasonably projected) the seller has placed himself in a difficult negotiating position. It is extremely important for the seller to not only consider what he wants but the ability of the purchaser to pay the remaining purchase price out of the profits of the business.

Key Idea: It is always important to consider not only the seller's financial needs, but also the actual amount that the buyer will be able to pay from the net income of the business. If the potential purchaser, in analyzing the terms presented by the seller, can show that even with a sizeable down payment, the buyer will not be able to pay the purchase price from the income of the business, he has strengthened his negotiating position. Logically, if you make a sizeable down payment, the payment of the remainder of the purchase price should be available from the net income of the business. An example will show how terms can make or break a sale.

Example: X wants to buy a business for $1,000,000. The net taxable income before payment of the purchase price and taxes is $200,000. X has $200,000 in cash for the down payment and an outside lending institution is willing to finance the transaction on the following terms:

A. interest at fourteen percent.

B. amortized in sixty equal monthly installments of principal and interest.

The financing will cost X, the purchaser, $223,376 in before-tax dollars each year. If the tax cost is considered, the total yearly financing cash outflow could exceed $305,000. This is greater than the reasonably projected income by over $100,000 per year and makes these terms unacceptable.

A Better Way: If instead of obtaining outside financing, the seller will finance the sale, the previously unacceptable cash flow can be reversed. An example of an acceptable financing package is as follows:

A. $200,000 in cash at closing

B. the remaining $800,000 paid pursuant to a promissory note:

   1. 180 equal monthly payments of principal and interest.
   2. interest at eleven percent.
   3. balloon at the end of five years.

4. yearly payments of $109,113.60.

Even if the tax effects are considered, assuming the profitability of the business is at least what it was before the sale, there should be sufficient cash flow to support the purchase. You can see how structuring the terms has changed an impossible situation to an acceptable one. Assuming the seller can obtain the proper security, this will place him in a better position than if he received all the cash at closing. The reason for this is that part of the tax impact is delayed and eleven percent interest may be more than he can safely obtain through other sources.

An Exception That Proves the Rule

As with all general rules, there are exceptions. These exceptions normally occur in those industries in which the price to be paid for the business exceeds any reasonable expectations as to a multiple of the current profits of the company. There are several reasons for the inflated and artificial price; however, usually the purchaser is not looking at the past profits to pay the future purchase price but believes that he will be able to significantly increase the total profitability of the company on purchase. In the past ten years, this concept of paying inflated prices has become apparent in certain industries. Two examples are those companies involved in high tech enterprises and the newspaper industry. Small town newspapers that are in a monopoly position have been selling at premiums over what would normally be judged as their true fair market value. The reason for this is the purchasers have been able to substantially increase the profits of the paper cutting costs and increasing advertising rates. In situations such as this, the analysis that has been discussed in this section becomes inappropriate. In these cases, the appropriate method of approach is to determine the fair market value solely from those standards set by the sale of "comparable companies." The only caveat in this particular situation is that many times the purchaser does not realize either the increased revenue or the economies that were anticipated and accordingly cash or unimpeachable security should be obtained.

3. The third, and final key is the tax ramification of the sale. Will the seller have a tax-free transaction, a sale taxed as capital gain, or a sale in which the proceeds will be taxed as ordinary income? Will the purchaser have to pay the purchase price in before- or after-tax dollars? A discussion of these alternatives will be set forth starting on

page 185. However, the implication of the recently enacted Tax Reform Act of 1986 has raised a number of questions that can only be resolved by either comprehensive regulations or future tax legislation. However, as will be seen in the discussion, while there are many more questions than answers certain techniques will be applied in an attempt to minimize the overall tax effect.

HOW TO IDENTIFY THE ELEMENTS THAT COMPRISE "TERMS"

The traditional concept of "Terms" not only includes the manner in which the purchase price is to be paid, but also the assets that are to be purchased. In addition, it includes the answer to the question of whether a portion of the purchase price will be allocated to payments other than the purchase of those assets. There are certain elements that are included within the definition of "Terms" and should be considered.

A. Down payment. Obviously, the greater the down payment, the more commitment shown by the buyer, and the less need to worry about security, or how the remainder of the purchase price will be paid. If the purchase price is $500,000 and if fifty percent is paid in cash at closing, a one percent difference in interest will result in a maximum of $2,500 per year in increased costs. If $400,000 is financed, this one percent difference in interest can result in almost $4,000 in increased interest in the first year. If the term of the note (equal monthly amortization) is ten years, in the first instance, the increase, assuming an initial interest rate in both cases of six percent, results in about $15,000 of additional payments and, in the second, the increase is about $24,500 over the entire term.

B. The interest rate. The interest rate is a creative tool within the concept of terms. Prior to the Tax Reform Act of 1986, for tax purposes, it was appropriate to negotiate a lesser interest rate.

Example: Joe was selling all of the common stock of Widgets, Inc., and has determined that he needs $50,000 a year. It is important for him to consider the difference in tax effects. The following example will illustrate the effect of terms on net cash flow prior to the Tax Reform Act of 1986.

Under Method 1, Joe was to receive a purchase price of $268,351 payable in 120 equal monthly installments at fourteen percent. In the second method, the interest rate is six percent (disregarding the tax implications of imputed interest) and the purchase price would be $375,285.59. Under both methods, the gross proceeds over this ten-year period was the same, $500,000. The difference in after-tax proceeds was substantial. For our example, we have assumed that Joe was in the fifty percent marginal tax bracket and all the principal payments resulted in capital gain.

1. Payments received under the first method:

Tax Classification	Amount Received	Applicable Tax Rate	After Tax Proceeds
Interest	$231,648.84	50%	$115,824.42
Principal	$268,351.16	20%	$214,680.93
	Total After Tax Proceeds		$330,505.35

2. Payments received under the second method $500,000:

Tax Classification	Amount Received	Applicable Tax Rate	After Tax Proceeds
Interest	$124,714.41	50%	$ 62,357.21
Principal	$375,285.59	20%	$300,228.47
	Total After Tax Proceeds		$362,585.68

The change in interest rate has increased the after-tax proceeds by about ten percent. Notwithstanding the tax benefits from designating a higher purchase price payable pursuant to a promissory note at lower interest rates, this will normally not facilitate the ultimate goal of the seller. Normally, the seller wishes to convert his promissory note into cash. In the above example, the low interest rate and high principal payment would normally dictate that the purchaser will not prepay the note. The seller should therefore consider:

a. his rate of return on other investments
b. the amount of the down payment, and accordingly, the security for the promissory note
c. whether or not he wishes to encourage the prepayment.

CHANGES BASED ON THE TAX REFORM ACT OF 1986

As noted above, prior to the Tax Reform Act of 1986, the impetus for the seller was to lower the interest rate and raise the capital gain. This always had a negative impact on the buyer if the buyer had to make the principal payments in after-tax dollars (for example, purchase of stock). However, because of the sizeable benefit to the seller from the long-term capital gain treatment, the purchaser many times was able to offset this negative with a lower interest than he would normally be able to obtain and therefore reduce his total principal and interest payments. The Tax Reform Act of 1986, which, while it does not eliminate capital gains, has in effect in 1988 taxed capital gains at the same marginal tax rate as ordinary income will change planning completely. While it is not known currently whether the Tax Reform Act of 1986 will be completely implemented in 1988 or what if any changes will be made, at least currently in a situation such as above, instead of opting for the lower interest rate, the following planning moves may be appropriate.

1. The higher interest rate will not significantly increase the tax costs to the seller and will be more beneficial to the buyer. All gain and interest will be basically taxed at the same rate and, accordingly, the seller will not care what portion of his payment is interest or capital gain. Therefore, the higher interest rate will not adversely affect him. If the interest is increased (without a total increase in cash flow) the purchaser will make a greater portion of his payments in before tax dollars. The prior beneficial provisions of Section 338 (liquidation of a wholly owned subsidiary to obtain a step up in basis at minimum tax cost) have been completely emasculated by the Tax Reform Act of 1986. Accordingly, liquidation of wholly owned subsidiaries, because they will be taxwise more costly, will become less frequent.

2. In the past, as was previously noted, consulting contracts were taxed as ordinary income and resulted in a tax of as much as thirty percent higher than capital gain payments. Accordingly, for the seller these were negotiated only as a last resort. In the above situation, it will be beneficial to the purchaser to have a greater portion classified as a consulting contract (again tax deductible) and a lesser amount to the purchase price to the stock. This will not adversely affect the seller's tax position.

Planning has completely changed under the Tax Reform Act of 1986. In the above case, instead of striving (considering only the tax ramifications) for the smallest amount allocated to interest, the largest amount to principal, and no amount being allocated to a consulting contract, the purchaser should be able to negotiate a higher interest rate and greater allocation to a consulting contract with no negative tax impact on the seller.

Caveat: Because of the far-reaching impact of the Tax Reform Act of 1986, long-term planning in this particular instance is particularly difficult. The act itself has been promulgated under the concept that it is revenue neutral. If the various "loophole closing provisions" do not produce the revenue anticipated, the ultimate savings to the individual taxpayer may not be great. We may see substantial revisions in the terms of the act even before its full implementation.

Five Ways to Structure the Interest Rate

The interest rate plays an interesting role and can be structured in many ways. Some of the possibilities are as follows.

1. The interest rate can be fixed over the entire term.
2. The term of the loan can be fixed but the interest rate may vary. For example, a ten-year amortization with the interest being fixed for the first five years and thereafter it is determined at one percent over prime.
3. The interest rate can be tied to prime over the entire term of the loan.
4. The interest rate can be tied to the rate a seller can receive on the funds he receives from the sales price. For example, one percent over the rate paid on one and one-half year C.D.s at XYZ Bank.
5. The interest rate can be tied to what the buyer must pay for money—three percent over prime.

Normally, the purchaser will be looking for fixed payments for a specific term; the purchaser may be reluctant to vary the interest rates, especially in our financial marketplace with widely varying interest rates. The seller's desire will vary according to his frame of reference which is dependent on such factors as his age, term of note, outside income, and so forth.

Consider the Terms of a Note

Normally the term of the note is dependent on the cash flow of the business, as well as the type of assets that are used to secure the purchase price. Obviously, the shorter the term, the higher the monthly, quarterly, semiannual or annual payments. Conversely, the longer the term, the smaller the payments. The length will normally be dependent on the available cash flow from the business, as well as such personal factors as the age of the seller. For example, a seller at age seventy will usually not want a fifteen-year term as his primary concern will be income during life rather than passing the unpaid portion of the obligation to his heirs.

The dilemma that can be posed by this particular situation is that a shorter term may not be financially feasible. The solution to this particular problem is a balloon payment before the note has completely amortized. For example, the unpaid principal of a fifteen-year note may be due after the fifth year. The time for the balloon payment will usually correspond to the earliest date when the business will have become established under the new owners and the obligation can be financed at the bank.

How to Structure Payments

The final question becomes "How frequent should the payments be?" The monthly payment is the most common for a number of reasons. The seller will normally need the cash flow to maintain his life style. If the buyer is having financial trouble, this is brought to the attention of the seller at a time when it may be possible to minimize his losses. Many times, if payments are made on a yearly or semiyearly basis, the seller will not realize the extent of the problem until it is too late to protect his interest. With monthly payments, the seller is at least assured of receiving some of the payments, and being informed at an early period of time as to any possibility of default. Finally, it is easier for the purchaser to schedule small more manageable monthly payments than larger annual or semiannual payments.

HOW THE ASSETS SOLD IMPACT ON THE CONCEPT OF TERMS

Included within the broad definition of terms are the assets to be purchased. There are three distinct categories of these assets:

1. the stock of the corporation
2. selected assets owned by the corporation
3. all the assets owned by the corporation

The simplest is the purchase for cash or a promissory note of all seller's stock. The alternative, a sale of a portion of the stock and a redemption of the remainder may accomplish the same goal. Stock redemption is defined as the corporation acquiring its stock from a shareholder in exchange for cash and/or other property. An example will illustrate how to utilize a redemption.

Example: A and B each own fifty percent of XYZ Corporation. B wishes to retire and it is determined for tax purposes that the best way for the sale to be accomplished is for the corporation rather than for A individually to buy B's stock. The reasons for this may be that the corporation has the available funds or that the corporate tax rates are more favorable than the individual tax rates.

Warning: While normally a complete redemption of stock in a non-family owned corporation will yield capital gain, it is particularly important to review the law and determine whether or not in a family held corporation the redemption will qualify for capital gain treatment or if the distribution will be considered dividend income. The rules are complex and beyond the scope of this book; however, before redeeming all or any portion of a family members' stock, review Internal Revenue Code Section 302.

The Tax Reform Act of 1986 again has had a significant impact on planning in this area. An example will clarify the differences in the tax treatment before and after the Tax Reform Act of 1986 and will give rise to thoughts as to future planning opportunities and possible changes in the law.

Example: A owns ten shares of Widget, Inc., which constitutes all of the authorized and issued common stock of the company. Widget, Inc., is highly profitable and it is determined that it has $100,000 of assets that are not needed in the future of the business. A, who is a taxpayer in the maximum fifty percent tax bracket prior to the enactment of the 1986 Tax Reform Act, attempts to "redeem" one share of his stock for and in consideration of the payment of $100,000 from the corporation. It is his intent that this redemption would qualify for capital gain treatment and would be subject to the maximum capital gains tax of twenty percent. His anticipation is that he will pay a capital gains tax of $20,000. The provisions of Section 302 would provide that this is not a "redemption qualifying for capital gains purposes" but is a dividend and instead of paying a $20,000 tax would be subject to a tax of $50,000.

TAX TREATMENT UNDER THE TAX REFORM ACT OF 1986

In the above situation, it would at least appear that the provisions of Section 302(b) have been unaffected by the Tax Reform Act of 1986. The tax impact has changed as it does not matter if A receives the distribution as a capital gain or as ordinary income. In each case, it will be taxed at his marginal tax rate, which should not exceed twenty-eight percent. In either case, he would pay a tax of $28,000 on the distribution.

Query: Does the lack of differentiation in tax treatment between ordinary income and capital gain mean that additional funds of a corporation now will be paid out as dividend income? Will less dollars be retained in the corporation for future expansion? Will Congress enact a more preferential capital gains tax rate? At this time, of course, the answers to these queries are unknown. However, in the near future, it would indicate that dividends will become more prevalent and there will be less need to carefully plan around the provisions of Section 302.

HOW TO COMBINE A SALE AND REDEMPTION

It is often useful to combine a sale of a substantial portion of the stock with a redemption of the remainder.

Example: Widget International, Inc., has a value of $1,000,000 as a going concern. In addition, it has cash and other liquid assets of $500,000. The prospective purchaser agrees to purchase the going business for $1,000,000 but does not need the excess liquid assets. If the purchase price is determined at $1,500,000, and there are 1,500 shares of stock outstanding, the purchaser can buy 1,000 shares at closing and immediately after closing redeem the remaining 500 shares for $500,000. In essence, the seller has sold his stock (which is his goal), and the purchaser has purchased the going concern without obligating himself to pay more than the going concern value.

Warning: This transaction is known as a Zenz transaction after the case of *Zenz vs. Quinlan* 213 F.2d914(6cir. 1954). The case dealt with the tax timing of payments received in the year of sale. The law has favorably changed since the decision in this case; however, there may still be tax traps that can catch the unwary.

ALTERNATIVES AFTER THE TAX REFORM ACT OF 1986

The above example illustrates the historical method of removing the funds in order to obtain the most favorable tax treatment prior to the enactment of the Tax Reform Act of 1986. The question that is raised is what is the impact of the Tax Reform Act of 1986? Because of the newness of this act, any definitive planning at its early stages may still be premature. However, it would appear in the above situation that there is no disadvantage to restructuring the transaction as follows:

1. Prior to the sale, have Widget International declare a dividend of $500,000.
2. Sell the 15,000 shares for $1,000,000 either in cash or a promissory note.

If the above procedure is followed, the initial distribution of $500,000 will be taxed as ordinary income if there is sufficient earnings and profits. If there is insufficient earnings and profits, part of the distribution will be considered as a tax-free return of capital and the remainder as capital gain. As a planning note, with the enactment of the Tax Reform Act of 1986, if we are contemplating a sale of a corporation with sizeable unneeded liquid assets, a dividend policy over a number of years may produce sizeable tax savings.

In the event that stock is not purchased, the question is "What assets should be purchased?" This question cannot be answered in a vacuum because of the tax ramifications of the sale which will be discussed in Part 5 of this section. The question is not only what assets should be purchased but also how should the purchase price be allocated among the various assets?

The purchaser will be looking to give as high a value as possible to depreciable personal property. This will enable the purchaser to depreciate the assets over a relatively short period.

The Tax Reform Act of 1986 has had a substantial impact on the tax ramifications for sellers. Prior to the Tax Reform Act of 1986 a sale of the assets may not have resulted in double taxation. For these purposes, double taxation is defined as a sale or liquidation that gives rise to a tax at the corporate level as well as an additional tax at the individual level. However, with the enactment of the Tax Reform Act of 1986, the tax impact on the seller, unless the sale and liquidation qualifies at both the corporate and individual level, can result in double taxation and create an adverse tax situation. Under the new act, to receive the favorable benefits, the corporate must be a small closely held corporation that has individual noncorporate shareholders who have held the stock for a period of time. A complete definition of the exception to the general rule will be discussed later in this section.

Example: A owns all of the stock in Widget, Inc. Widget, Inc. has the following balance sheet:

Cash	0
Other assets	$50,000
Total assets	$50,000
Liabilities	0
Equity	$50,000
Total Liabilities and Equity	$50,000

The true fair market value of the business is $150,000. Further assume that A has no basis for his stock. If A sells his stock for cash, he will realize $108,000 in after-tax proceeds. If, on the other hand, Widget, Inc., sells the assets in 1988 or thereafter, the resulting tax effect would be as follows:

Sale of Corporate Assets	$150,000
Less Basis	$ 50,000
Gain on Sale of Assets	$100,000
Tax on Gain	$ 24,375
Net Corporate Assets	$150,000
Less Tax	$ 24,375
Distribution to A	$125,625
Less Tax	$ 35,175
Net After-tax Proceeds to A	$ 90,450

This example illustrates that unless the seller qualifies for the closely held corporation exemption retained in the Tax Reform Act of 1986, it will be of sizeable benefit for him to sell stock and not assets. As alluded to previously, the seller can provide some relief to the purchaser by allocating a greater portion to a covenant not-to-compete or a higher interest rate. However, when an asset purchase is necessary and the small corporation exemption is not available, the seller is at an extreme tax disadvantage and in all likelihood will receive significantly less than he would have received prior to the Tax Reform Act of 1986.

With the different prospectives of the parties in mind, the different types of property that can be involved in a sale will now be reviewed.

Certain items of property will not cause valuation problems:

1. Cash and marketable securities will be valued at the date of closing.

2. Receivables will normally be valued at the actual amount less an allowance for bad debts.

3. Inventory is usually valued at lower of cost or market. There is always a fear that at closing, when an actual inventory is taken, the buyer and seller will not agree on the cost of individual items of inventory. As long as the value of the items in question is not significant, it should not pose a problem. However, where a substantial portion of the purchase price is comprised of inventory, some precaution should be taken. However, a simple way to avoid this problem is to allow the purchaser to reject a certain dollar amount or a certain percentage of the inventory if the parties cannot agree on a value without affecting the closing.

Unless the selling corporation qualifies for the benefits of the relief section available to small corporations, all gains, be they ordinary income or capital gain, will result in double taxation. The total tax effect must be considered and will be substantial. For those corporations that qualify for the small corporation exemption and who sell (or liquidate) prior to 1989, may be able to avoid a corporate tax on the capital gain portion of the sales proceeds. This table will illustrate both the tax effects on the selling corporation and on the buyer:

TYPE OF ASSET	TAX TREATMENT TO SELLING CORPORATION	TAX TREATMENT TO BUYER
Equipment	Ordinary income to corporate seller up to the amount of depreciation taken; thereafter, capital gain.	Depreciable over varying periods of time.
Goodwill	Capital gain.	Normally, buyer will not be able to amortize.
Land and Buildings	20% of the gain but not more than the depreciation taken will be ordinary income. Thereafter, capital gain except if subject to depreciation recapture (see Section 1250). A portion of the remaining capital gain will be a tax preference subject to the alternative minimum tax.	Residential buildings depreciable over 27.5 years; other buildings depreciable over 31.5 years; land not depreciable or amortizable.

Intangible Assets	Normally capital gain.	Will depend on the assets transferred. If they have an indefinite life (i.e. renewable franchise) then not subject to amortization.

The other elements included within the concept of terms include those ancillary contracts that are negotiated such as rental agreements, employment contracts, fringe benefits, and covenants not-to-compete. There are always negotiations between the purchaser and seller as to what, if any, allocation of the purchase price should apply to these agreements. There is no doubt that under the Tax Reform Act of 1986, there will be increased emphasis to allocate to either fringe benefits, or consulting or employment contracts payments that in the past would have been allocated to stock.

Observation: Unless the corporation qualifies for the beneficial small corporation exemption for exclusion of a part if not all of the taxation at the corporate level there is no doubt that the following will occur.

1. There will be fewer sales of corporate assets.
2. There will be an increased pressure to increase the interest rate.
3. There will be an increased pressure to allocate a greater portion of the purchase price to consulting contracts, covenants not-to-compete, and employment contracts.
4. There will be a greater emphasis on the continued payment of fringe benefits. This is especially true if an employment contract or consulting agreement is part of the sale and does not effect the social security receipts to the seller.
5. There will be increased problems for the seller in obtaining proper security because:
   a. a greater portion of the purchase price will be allocated to the ancillary contracts rather than the sale of assets.
   b. it is always more difficult to secure a transaction that involves the sale of stock rather than assets.

HOW TO HANDLE THE CONTINGENT SALE

It is interesting to note that specifically excluded from the definition of terms is price. However, at times terms will even encompass the purchase price. This occurs when the transaction makes sense conceptually, but the future of the business is in doubt.

In these cases, it has been impossible for both sides to agree on a purchase price because of the uncertainty. The seller may be asking a reasonable purchase price if his projections as to the future are accurate, but is completely unreasonable if the future turns out to be less than foreseen.

How to Determine the Contingent Sales Price

There are many variations as to how a contingent sales price can be determined; however, the elements of a sales agreement that establish a contingent sales price usually contain the following.

1. Fix a minimum price. Determine terms for the purchase price that are acceptable to all.
2. Determine a bonus based on earnings, gross sales, new customers, or other factors.

The determination of which of these factors should be utilized is not difficult. The parties usually can agree on the factors giving rise to insecurity as to the future profitability of the business. It may be as simple as the future purchases of a major customer of the business. In this case the additional portion of the sales price, the "kicker," could be based on the gross sales to that customer. The fear of the parties may be that in the transition of the ownership of the business, a portion of the clientele may be lost. This particular concern is well-founded, especially in the sale of service businesses.

Example: In the transfer of a CPA practice, the purchaser may be worried that the clients will not be retained by the new firm. The parties can establish a minimum purchase price and determine the "bonus" or "kicker" on the amount of retained clientele. For example, ten percent of the retained clients billings in the first year, nine percent in the second year, eight percent in the third year, and so on.

Unfortunately terms have become the stepchild of the negotiation process. Many times they are approached only as an afterthought. However, the smart negotiator will see that terms are interrelated with both price and the final concept that is set forth in Part 5. The ingenious negotiator will be able to structure the terms to accomplish that which is seemingly impossible. He will frequently pay a greater price and even bear an inordinate tax burden if the terms can be structured to make the deal economically feasible. Terms instead of the stepchild of the negotiation process should be considered as the key used to unlock transactions that otherwise may be impossible. The final key to structuring the transaction is taxes. When discussing the sale of a business, the real question should be not how much you receive or how much you pay but how much it will cost you or how much you will receive in after-tax dollars.

PART 5

HOW TO MINIMIZE TAXES ON THE SALE AT BOTH THE CORPORATE AND INDIVIDUAL LEVELS

Whether you are the purchaser or seller of a business, it is important to consider the tax effects of the sales transaction. If you are the seller, you want to structure it in such a manner that you can maximize your after-tax return. If you are the buyer, you want to structure the transaction in such a way that as much of the total purchase price as possible can be paid in before-tax dollars.

Example: X Corporation has just bought Y Corporation and must pay for the purchase price in after-tax dollars. It is in the thirty-four percent effective tax bracket. The income that Y Corporation must produce to pay for the purchase price of $200,000 is $303,030.

Income from Y Corporation	$303,030
Less:	
Tax effect	$103,030
Net after-tax proceeds	$200,000

If the $200,000 can be paid in before-tax dollars (for example, the purchase of equipment that is depreciable or the payment of a covenant not-to-compete), the gross income which needs to be earned is only $200,000.

It is important to consider not only whether or not you are purchasing in before- or after-tax dollars, but also the effective tax rate on the purchaser. In the above, if the effective tax rate of Y Corporation was only fifteen percent, the difference in before- and after-tax income would have been reduced from $103,030 to $35,294:

Income from Y Corporation	$235,294
Less:	
Tax effect	$35,294
Net after-tax proceeds	$200,000

While this discussion is not geared to make you a tax expert, it is absolutely imperative that the owner, the purchaser, and their advisors be tax knowledgeable. At least one of the advisors should be a tax expert. The obligation of determining the after-tax proceeds rests with this team member if you are the seller, and the tax cost of purchasing, if you are the buyer. It will also rest on this team member to reduce the taxes to the mutual benefit of both. Unless all parties are tax knowledgeable, they may strike a deal that is taxwise inappropriate for one or both parties. A chart such as the following can be prepared to determine the seller's after-tax proceeds.

Agreement	Owner of Property	Assets Sold	Gain on Allocable Purchase	Projected Tax Effect on Corporation	Projected Tax Effect on Sellers	Net After-Tax Proceeds
Sales Agreement	Seller	Stock	$100,000	-0-	$28,000	$72,000
Sales Agreement	Corporation	Equipment	$100,000	$34,000	$18,480	$47,520
Covenant Not-to-Compete	Seller		$100,000	-0-	$28,000	$72,000
Sales Agreement	Corporation	Land	$100,000	-0-[1]	$28,000	$72,000

The above chart has considered only federal tax and has assumed the following tax rates:

Individual Ordinary Income Tax Rate	28%
Individual Capital Gains Tax Rate	28%
Individual Ordinary Income Tax Rate	34%
Corporate Capital Gains Tax Rate	34%

[1] If the small business exception allows for the sale at the corporate level to be completely taxfree, this is the taxation that will result. If this exemption is not available, then the result will be the same as the equipment example above.

Although many assumptions have been made in this chart (for example, the various assets do not have any basis), the chart can be used to put the tax impact of the sale in perspective. A chart such as this can be prepared for each sale and it would then illustrate the tax effects on the selling shareholder individually, the tax effects on the selling corporation, and, in the event of the sale of assets, the possible double taxation, at both the corporate and individual levels.

Observation: A cursory review of the above chart shows that the most favorable tax way to receive the payment of the purchase price for the seller is through either the sale of stock or the execution of a covenant not-to-compete. The seller's strategy and goals become clearer.

The selling shareholder will receive his funds in several ways:

1. through the sale of his stock to an individual or corporation
2. through the receipt of an employment contract, covenant not-to-compete, and the like
3. through the liquidation of the corporation after the sale

Normally, on the sale of the corporate stock, or on liquidation, the receipt will be taxed at the capital gains rates. Since the Tax Reform Act of 1986, these rates are taxed at individual's marginal tax rate.

The receipt of ordinary income through a covenant not-to-compete or employment contract is taxed at the individual's marginal tax rate which, commencing in 1988, normally will not exceed twenty-eight percent. Certain brackets will be subject to a surcharge and, accordingly, the income in these brackets will have an effective tax rate of thirty-three percent. It is also possible that the sale of the stock may be accomplished through a tax-free exchange with no taxation to the individual on the sale. The following example will illustrate the difference in after-tax dollars to the selling shareholder depending on how the sale is structured.

I. Assumptions

1. Gain on sale of $1,000,000. Assume neither selling shareholder nor corporation has any basis in the assets sold.
2. Cash paid at closing.
3. The selling shareholder can earn ten percent on the net after-tax dollars.
4. All corporate ordinary income is taxed at thirty-four percent.

II. Differing tax results

A. The entire proceeds are taxed as capital gains at the shareholder level.

Prior to the Tax Reform Act of 1986, this normally occurred if the shareholder sold his stock and all of the purchase price was allocated to such sale. After the Tax Reform Act of 1986, the structure remains the same but the benefits of the long-term capital gains rates to the individual are no longer available. The result would be effectively the same if the total purchase price were either paid for the stock or allocated to a covenant not-to-compete or employment contract. The tax on the sales proceeds would be a maximum of $280,000 and the after-tax proceeds will be $720,000. The annual income to the selling shareholders will be $72,000.

NOTE: With the elimination of the favorable long-term capital gains tax rates, the maximum tax on the net long-term capital gain including the five percent surcharge can equal thirty-three percent in 1988 for individuals.

B. All of the proceeds are taxed as ordinary income to the selling shareholders.

This is not a realistic alternative, as virtually all sales will involve some allocation of the purchase price to assets or stock of the corporation and not all to an employment contract or covenant not-to-compete. Prior to the Tax Reform Act of 1986, this alternative illustrated the negative effect of having a portion if not all of the proceeds categorized as ordinary income. The tax on the receipts to the seller could have been as much as $500,000. After the Tax Reform Act of 1986, with the elimination of the beneficial tax rates for long-term capital gains commencing in 1988, the overall tax effect on the individual shareholder would be no different than if the purchase price were allocated either to the stock or to the covenant not-to-compete.

Key Idea: Because of the elimination of the beneficial capital gains rates by the Tax Reform Act of 1986 commencing in 1988, it will become more and more advantageous for the parties to allocate a significant portion of the purchase price to a covenant not-to-compete. This will have no negative effect on the seller but will have a positive impact on the buyer because he can pay a part of the purchase price in before- rather than after-tax dollars.

C. The corporate assets are sold and will be taxed at the corporate level.

This is the scenario when the closely held corporation exemption is not available or when it is available but the corporation has substantial depreciable equipment and undervalued LIFO inventory. The corporation would pay a tax of $340,000. The remaining cash of $660,000 ($1,000,000 sales price less tax of $340,000) would be subjected to an additional tax of $184,800 on liquidation. The net after-tax proceeds to the sellers would only be $457,200 and would produce an annual income of $45,720 per year.

D. The parties structure a tax-free exchange. The seller receives stock in exchange which pays an eight percent dividend.

The tax on the selling shareholder will be zero. The after-tax proceeds will be $1,000,000. The annual income will be $80,000. Please note that the stock received in the tax-free exchange retains the basis of the transferred stock. When it is sold, the tax effect will be the same as in A above; however, the tax is deferred for a period of time, and may be eliminated if the seller dies owning the stock. Under the current tax law, the estate of a decedent receives a step up in basis equivalent to the fair market value of the stock without the payment of any income tax.

Example: A incorporated Widget, Inc. many years ago with $1,000 in invested capital. The value of the stock on the date of A's death is $101,000. If A had sold the stock the day before he died, he would be liable for a capital gains tax on $100,000 of gain. If the estate sold the stock the day after A's death, there would be no capital gains tax to pay at all as the stock acquires a new basis. The basis becomes the fair market value of the stock at A's death.

WHAT THE STOCKHOLDER CAN SELL INDIVIDUALLY AND HOW THAT SALE WILL BE TAXED

The concept of determining the true value of the various components of the purchase price has been introduced. It is now time for a detailed analysis to determine their after-tax value. The individual shareholder has a limited number of options on how he can receive the purchase price.

These can be summarized as follows:[1]

What the Shareholder Can Receive	How the Shareholder Is Taxed on the Receipt	Extremely Favorable (+ +) Favorable (+) Negative(−) Unknown (0)
Sale of Stock	Capital Gain	+
Covenant not-to-compete	Ordinary Income	+
Fringe Benefits	Completely or Partially Tax-free	+ +
Employment Contract[2]	Ordinary Income	0
Lease	Ordinary Income	+

A complete description of what the shareholder can receive as well as the tax ramifications follows.

1. Stock. Almost without restriction, the sale of stock should give rise to long-term capital gain, as long as it has been held for the applicable period. This can be six months or a year, depending on when the stock is purchased and sold. This holding period is virtually never a problem. The only time that closely held stock is held less than that period of time is when the owner was the recipient of a gift. In this case, a donee assumes the holding period of the donor. Sale of stock in a closely held C Corporation will, almost invariably, give rise to long-term capital gain. The Tax Reform Act of 1986 has eliminated the advantages of the favorable capital gains rates and accordingly the individual will be taxed on the net long-term capital gain at the individual's marginal tax rate.

2. Covenant Not-to-Compete. The normal covenant not-to-compete will restrict the selling shareholders' future business activities.

[1] Please note that prior to the Tax Reform Act of 1986, the chart would have been significantly different. The reason for this would be that the sale of stock would have yielded capital gain which would have resulted in extremely favorable tax treatment. The Tax Reform Act of 1986 removed the favorable tax rate for capital gains but did retain the capital gains structure. The thinking of Congress in this case is that at a future time, capital gains may once again be taxed more favorably. If this were the case, it would once again be more favorable to sell stock than to receive any other taxable income.

[2] While generally the receipt of income under an employment contract is no more or less favorable than the receipt of any other taxable payments, there are two exceptions to this general rule: (1) if the seller is going to qualify for social security, the payments under any employment contract if he is under age seventy can reduce his social security benefits; and (2) any time employment contracts are entered into they are subject to an FICA tax up to the social security base. During 1986, the tax rate was 7.15 percent each on the employer and employee up to the taxable wages of $42,000. In addition, the employer can be subject to an unemployment tax rate as well as such other hidden costs such as workman's compensation, and the like.

These restrictions can take many forms, among which are:

a. he will not compete with the business of the seller
b. he will not contact the customers of the selling corporation
c. he will not use his prior knowledge of the business to compete unfairly, such as by becoming a consultant with a competitor

In addition to the restriction itself, there will be a period of time and a geographical area indicating when and where the restriction will apply.

Warning: All of these restrictions should be reasonable, as covenants not-to-compete are not favored in law, and depending on the state, may, if they are unreasonable, be unenforceable.

There may also be an amount paid as consideration for this covenant not-to-compete with provisions for its payment. This money is taxed as ordinary income, but is not subject to either social security tax, nor will it reduce the social security benefits of the selling shareholder. Today, with the substantial benefits to be received from Social Security as well as the fact that at least one half of the social security benefits are not taxable, it is usually a good idea to insure its uninterrupted flow.

Remember: If a part of the purchase price must be paid in a tax deductible form, and if the seller will be entitled to social security benefits, the payments should, if possible, be structured as a covenant not-to-compete rather than either an employment or consulting contract. Earned income from an employment contract or a consulting agreement will be subject to social security tax and will reduce social security benefits.

Key Idea: If an individual is entitled to social security benefits, and if it is necessary to allocate a portion of the purchase price to tax deductible payments, it is usually a good idea to consider the covenant not-to-compete, rather than an employment or consulting contract.

3. The Employment Contract. Many times an employment contract is a necessary item in the transition of the business. This type of contract, normally, will last no more than six months, and will provide reasonable compensation for the services rendered by the selling shareholder. In this case, the employment contract is independent from the purchase price. For tax purposes, it may be determined that a portion of the purchase price should be paid through an employment contract. It may or may not be anticipated that the selling

shareholder will perform substantial services. The problem with an employment contract in this case, where substantial services are not to be rendered or with an unreasonable allocation of the purchase price to a covenant not-to-compete or employment contract is that the IRS may see these payments as additional payments for stock (or assets). The question is one of form versus substance. Before and after the Tax Reform Act of 1986, the negative impact of reclassification of these agreements falls mainly on the purchaser. If the purchaser fails to sustain the reasonableness of the payments and they are disallowed as deductions, the purchaser will have to make these payments in after-tax rather than before-tax dollars.

If these agreements are structured correctly and if there are facts to support the payments, they should be able to survive IRS scrutiny. Some suggestions as to how to structure the employment contracts to pass IRS scrutiny follow.

1. Effort and task should correlate with compensation.
2. Agreements should be written.
3. Compensation paid should be viewed in light of an hourly rate.
4. Specific duties should be assigned to the employee.
    a. If possible, the employee should also be a director and should attend directors' meetings.
    b. If the employees' benefit is his special relationship with individual customers, he should sell or service these customers.
    c. If his benefit is his continuing goodwill, he should be required to attend trade conventions.
5. Whatever is contained in the written contract should be specifically adhered to by the parties. For example, if the written employment contract requires attendance at directors' meetings or conventions, he should attend regularly.

Beware: If the parties, for their own reasons, try to overallocate a part of the purchase price to a covenant not-to-compete, or to pay a salary in excess of the reasonable services rendered, the tax results will be disastrous.

Observation: If a portion of the purchase price is to be allocated to the employment contract, it may be particularly useful to maximize the fringe benefits. This will allow the payments that would normally be taxed as ordinary income to be converted into nontaxable benefits.

Warning: In the event that an employment contract is anticipated, and if the selling shareholder is otherwise eligible to receive social security benefits, he should be aware that his social security benefits will be reduced one dollar for every two dollars earned. This reduction is applicable if in 1987 he (1) earns in excess of $6,000 and is over sixty-two but less than sixty-five, or (2) earns $8,160 and is over sixty-five.

Key Idea: Earnings (in contravention to passive income) will only reduce the social security benefits until an individual has attained the age seventy. After that age, the seller can earn as much money as he wishes without reducing his social security benefits. Even in this case, if his adjusted income, as defined by Internal Revenue Code, is in excess of $35,000 if he is married ($25,000 if unmarried), up to one-half of the total benefits can be taxable.

Warning: Employment contracts normally terminate if the party dies or becomes disabled. If both the seller and purchaser contemplate the continuation of payments after these events, the agreement will be particularly susceptible to IRS scrutiny.

4. Lease of real or rental property. As long as the terms and conditions of the lease are reasonable, there should be little problems with the Internal Revenue Service. However any time the parties are concerned that the rental may be deemed unreasonable by the Internal Revenue Service, they should have in the file an appraiser's report as to valuation to sustain the terms and conditions contained in the lease.

Beware: If the lease payments are not reflective of the fair market value, the IRS may attempt to redesignate these payments. Controlled greed is what makes our society work. Uncontrolled greed can create a tax disaster.

Example: Widget International, Inc., is owned by Mary. She is the sole shareholder and chief executive officer of the corporation. She has run the corporation for many years while her husband has been a college professor. At age sixty-five, she wishes to sell. The corporation is valued at $1,000,000. The land and buildings housing the business are valued at $300,000. With the sales proceeds, Mary and her husband will have sufficient income to maintain their life styles.

Both are interested in providing a college education for their grandchildren. In this case, they may, with little or no gift tax, transfer the building to a trust for the benefit for their grandchildren.

A sale can be structured at a lesser purchase price with more favorable lease payments. This will have shifted some of the tax consequences to the grandchildren and shifted part of the purchase price to a favorable lease.

Beware: Under the Tax Reform Act of 1986, when children or grandchildren are under the age of fourteen, their income will be taxed at the marginal tax rate of their parents. Accordingly, the tax benefits of the shifting of income may not be as great as it first appears. The new emphasis under the Tax Reform Act may be the transfer of wealth rather than the transfer of income.

In transactions in which the selling parties are family members and there is no coexistence of ownership, care must be exercised. The planning opportunities are great, but these motives are also apparent to the IRS. In these cases ancillary documentation, such as appraisals or other verification from third parties to substantiate the terms and conditions, are always helpful. Self-serving documentation is not only redundant but can be counterproductive.

Key Idea: The Tax Reform Act of 1986 has provided for the elimination of the use of passive income losses against other income. Prior to the Tax Reform Act of 1986, there was little if any advantage to the taxpayer to allocate a greater amount to a lease rather than increase the salary unless there was a fear of unreasonable compensation or that the payments affect the receipt of social security. After the Tax Reform Act, it appears that all passive investments (real estate being one) will be combined and, if there is a passive income loss, its current usage against other income would either be limited or completely eliminated depending on the year in which the loss occurs, the nature of the investment, and when it was purchased. Accordingly, wherever possible, it will behoove the taxpayer with passive income losses to generate positive passive income from the lease to his closely held corporation. This will allow him to use his other passive income losses generated by tax shelters. Accordingly, it would appear the future emphasis will be to maximize the lease payments whenever possible.

Warning: The exception to this rule may be in the nonsale context. Assume an individual is to receive additional income which can reasonably be designated as rental or salary income from his closely held corporation. If he is in excess of the social security base, it may be beneficial to take the salary when the corporation has established a qualified deferred compensation plan for the benefit of its employees.

HOW TO OBTAIN TAX-FREE EXCHANGE IN THE STOCK TRANSFER

One of the cornerstones contained in our tax law is that the transfer or exchange of any two items is taxable unless there is a specific code section exempting the transaction from taxation. A tax free exchange is rooted in the concept that the shareholder has not changed his tax position and, therefore, no taxable income should result. The law, in this area, is extremely complicated, and is intertwined with related subjects such as carryover basis, continuity of interest, and the like.

A Possible Alternative to a Sale of Stock or Assets

It may be possible to exchange the stock that you own for a publicly held corporation's stock, and not pay any tax on the transfer. The *quid pro quo* for this favorable treatment is that the stock you receive retains the same basis as the stock transferred.

In a qualifying reorganization, the purchasing corporation acquires ownership of the selling corporation. The selling shareholders receive stock in the purchasing corporation or one of its subsidiaries. This obviously is an over simplification as some of the tax law sections require that only stock can be exchanged while others allow property other than stock to be received without disturbing the tax-free treatment.

As the owners of most small corporations will not have the opportunity to avail themselves of a tax-free transfer with publicly held corporations, it is inappropriate to discuss at length the prerequisites for obtaining this favorable tax treatment.

Warning: It should be noted that there are not only tax problems in a tax-free exchange, but there are also problems involving securities law if the purchasing corporation is publicly traded. The stock received is normally considered "Lettered Stock" and its subsequent sale is restricted. The restriction will provide that, for a period of time, the stock cannot be sold unless the securities are registered, which is usually not possible without substantial costs. This restriction on sale can place the shareholders fortune at the unexpected actions of the market in general and specifically at the mercy of the management of the acquiring corporation.

Example: When the conglomerates were acquiring numerous small corporations, some shareholders received what they considered exorbitant prices for their stock. They subsequently discovered that, by the time they could dispose of the conglomerate's stock, after the expiration of the SEC restriction on sale, it was only worth a fraction of the original price paid by the conglomerate. It is sufficient to note that, if one of the potential purchasers is a publicly held corporation (or the subsidiary of a publicly held corporation) and if the following factors are present, a tax-free exchange should be explored.

1. seller does not need cash at closing
2. the individual is older
3. the publicly held corporation has been paying dividends
4. the owner of the closely held corporation has a desire to pass assets on to the next generation
5. the stock in the publicly held corporation is a favorable long-term investment

Question: "Is the tax-free exchange an escape or merely a deferral of the tax liability?"

Answer: This depends on whether the individual receiving the publicly held stock is willing to hold this stock until he dies. In that case, the difference between his basis and the current fair market value of the stock is never subject to an income tax. Therefore, the older the seller and the more interested he is in passing an estate to the next generation, the more likely it is that a tax-free exchange will have viability. It is obviously not for everyone, but in specialized instances, it can produce significant tax benefits.

HOW THE CORPORATION WILL BE TAXED IF THE ASSETS AND NOT THE CORPORATE STOCK ARE SOLD

The ultimate question in the sale of corporate assets is "How much will the shareholder receive after payment of corporate and individual taxes?" In order to understand the tax ramifications of the sale of corporate assets, rather than the sale of stock, certain basic corporate tax concepts must be understood.

First, starting in 1988 there is a graduated income tax on corporate income up to $335,000. After $335,000, all income is taxed at thirty-four percent. The following are the tax rates for corporate taxable income.

0 - $50,000	15%
$50,000 - $75,000	25%
$75,000 - $100,000	34%
$100,000 - $335,000	39%
$335,000 and over	34%

Second, corporate capital gain is, after the Tax Reform Act of 1986, generally taxed in the same manner as ordinary income. In other words, it is included in income and taxed at the corporate marginal tax rate.

Third, investment credit recapture must be considered. In any case in which purchase of the asset had previously given rise to investment credit, the sale may result in a partial recapture.

Anyone who has been aware of the law prior to the Tax Reform Act of 1986 can now consider that the law at the corporate level has been completely revamped. This will require new thinking as to the best ways of accomplishing the distribution of proceeds, especially when the sale of assets has been dictated by other economic considerations. The methods available will now be discussed.

HOW TO DISTRIBUTE AFTER-SALES PROCEEDS FROM THE CORPORATION AT THE MINIMUM TAX COST

When the assets of the corporation (not the stock) are sold, the questions then become "Is there a way to mitigate the tax at the corporate level?" and "How do we most effectively get the proceeds from sale to the shareholders at the minimum tax cost?" Prior to the Tax Reform Act of 1986, there were three liquidation sections that, from time to time, were useful in maximizing the after-tax return to the shareholders. After the Tax Reform Act of 1986, these sections will only be available to certain closely held corporations that complete their liquidations before January 1, 1989. To the remainder of the corporations, the general rule has become that upon the sale of any assets at the corporate level, all gain will be realized. In the event of liquidation, gain will be recognized between the fair market value of the asset and the basis of the property. In the redemption of all or a part of the corporate stock, gain will be realized between the fair market value of the assets and its basis. In all of these cases, historically, there were limited exceptions to the realization of gain at the corporate level. The ability to avoid double taxation upon the sale and subsequent liquidation, except as pertains to certain small closely held corporations, has become a planning device of the past. Nevertheless, it is important to review the law prior to the Tax Reform Act of 1986 because it still does pertain to a vast majority of the closely held corporations until January 1, 1989 and because it will also give rise to a full understanding of the impact of the Tax Reform Act of 1986 on sale and liquidation planning.

HOW THE TAX REFORM ACT OF 1986 AFFECTS CLOSELY HELD CORPORATIONS

The Tax Reform Act has provided an exception for closely held corporations to the expensive new tax rules. A closely held corporation is eligible for the rule if its value does not exceed $10,000,000 and if more than fifty percent of the stock is owned by ten or fewer individuals who have held their stock for five years or longer. Full relief is available under this rule only if the corporation's value does not exceed $5,000,000; relief is phased out for corporations with values between $5,000,000 and $10,000,000. For the purposes of this exception, a corporation's value will be the higher of the value on August 1, 1986 and its value as of the date of the adoption of the plan of liquidation (or in the case of a nonliquidating distribution, the date of such distribution). There are also rules that relate to affiliated corporations and if an individual, or group of individuals, owns more than one corporation and wishes to liquidate only one, they should review the new law. The prior law utilized three separate Sections that can still be utilized by these closely held corporations. The most common was Section 337 which will be discussed in full. This particular liquidation section will still be available for small corporations with a value of under $5,000,000 if they liquidate before January 1, 1989. When the full impact of the Tax Reform Act is implemented, small corporations, as well as other corporations, will find the sale and liquidation of a business costly taxwise.

Key Idea: If a small corporation is contemplating selling and liquidating, it will be beneficial taxwise to elect Section 337 and liquidate before January 1, 1989.

In addition, as will be noted later in the chapter, Section 331 and 333 will, in specialized situations, provide relief. It appears that the beneficial provisions of Section 333 will be available to closely held corporations that qualify until January 1, 1989. In addition to the possible liquidation of the corporation after the sale, there are other planning tools. The most common are retaining the corporation as a holding company, converting it into an "S" corporation, accomplishing a partial liquidation, or obtaining a tax-free spinoff prior to sale. All of these nonliquidation alternatives will also be discussed in this chapter.

The best way to compare the advantages and disadvantages of liquidating under Section 337 with selling the corporate assets and retaining the corporation as a personal holding company are illustrated in the following example.

Example: Facts: Widget International's balance sheet is as follows:

	Original cost	Book value		Fair market value
Cash		0		0
Receivables		$200,000		$200,000
Inventory		$300,000		$300,000
Equipment		$300,000		$500,000
Goodwill				$200,000
Land and Buildings	$300,000		$500,000	
Depreciation to Date	($200,000)	$100,000	($200,000)	$300,000
Total Assets		$900,000		$1,500,000
Liabilities		$500,000		$500,000
Common Stock		$ 50,000		$50,000
Retained Earnings		$450,000		$450,000
Unrealized Appreciation		______		$600,000
Total Liabilities and Equity		$900,000		$1,500,000

The shareholders of Widget International, who have no basis in the stock, have received an offer to purchase all the assets in the corporation for $1,500,000 free and clear of any liabilities.

Method One: Liquidation Under Section 337

The simplest and many times the most advantageous method to proceed is to elect under Section 337. A full discussion of the requirements and consequences of this election will be set forth later in the chapter.

The provisions of Section 337 provide that the assets that are sold and give rise to capital gain will not be taxed at the corporate level if the requirements of this Section are satisfied. In our example of Widgets International, goodwill has been determined at $200,000. This amount would not be taxed. A majority of the $200,000 gain allocated to land and buildings will not be taxed at the corporate level unless its sale results in Section 1250 recapture. Even if the corporation qualifies for the exemption and makes the proper election under Section 337, the following ordinary income will be taxable upon the sale:

Gain of Sale of Equipment (ordinary income by reason of Section 1245)	$200,000
Ordinary Income on the Sale of Land and Buildings	$40,000
Total Income to the Corporation	$240,000
Income Tax at 34%	$81,600

Assuming that the entire proceeds were received in cash, the corporation would liquidate and distribute to the shareholders the proceeds of $918,400, which is determined as follows:

Sales Proceeds		$1,500,000
Less Income Tax	$ 81,600	
Liabilities	$500,000	$ 581,600
Net Proceeds After Sale		$ 918,400

Upon distribution to the shareholders, an additional capital gains tax of no more than twenty-eight percent would result (unless the five percent surcharge is applicable). From the original sale of $1,500,000, there are net after-tax proceeds of $661,248. This is the law that will apply to closely held corporations before January 1, 1989, and to all other corporations before January 1, 1987. It should be noted that by qualifying under Section 337, the corporation has saved the following tax.

Taxable Gain on Sale

Goodwill	$200,000
Equipment	$200,000
Land and Buildings	$200,000

Total Gain	$600,000
Corporate Tax Assumed at 34%	$204,000
Corporate Tax Applicable if a Corporation Qualified under Section 337	$ 81,600
Tax Saved by Electing under Section 337	$122,400

Key Idea: When the purchaser is adamant about purchasing the assets of the business, rather than the corporate stock, it is a good idea to analyze the tax effects on the corporation and shareholders, assuming that the corporation properly elects to liquidate under Section 337.

Key Idea: Please note that small corporations will still receive the benefits of Section 337 if they liquidate prior to January 1, 1989. Accordingly, this Section should be utilized by these corporations in the near future to eliminate an excessive tax burden.

Key Idea: It would appear after January 1, 1989, for small corporations and beginning in 1987 for all other corporations, the tax burden that would be occasioned by the sale of assets would be heavy. Sale of stock not assets will be the most viable alternative. In our above example, the effective total tax rate would appear to exceed fifty-three percent. The tax ramifications of the sale of assets versus the sale of stock will have to be watched closely in the future. The tax law and probably not economic ramifications will play a larger role in all future decision making.

Method Two: Converting to a Personal Holding Company

The second method is the payment of tax at the corporate level and conversion of the corporation after sale to a personal holding company. If a majority of the assets after sale are invested in common or preferred stock, there would be no burdensome penalty taxes to make this approach inappropriate. The advisability of using this method depends on the total amount of the assets after corporate tax. The advantage of this method is the savings of the tax on liquidation of the corporation.

While prior to the Tax Reform Act of 1986, this was a little used technique because of the availability of Section 337, with the total elimination of the tax benefits of Section 337 beginning in 1989, the personal holding company may have increased applicability.

In the above example, after December 31, 1988, the tax at the corporate level of approximately $204,000 cannot be reduced by electing under Section 337. It therefore may behoove the taxpayers not to liquidate and while this does not reduce the tax at the corporate level, it will save the tax upon liquidation of over $220,000. If the corporation is not liquidated but converted to a personal holding company, the funds are locked in. To liquidate before death of the shareholder will produce a tax at the individual level.

Note: Even a short period of time when the corporation is operated as a personal holding company may produce favorable tax benefits. A simple example will illustrate the viability of this planning tool.

Example: XYZ corporation was forced to sell all of its assets for various reasons. The net assets after the payment of all taxes is $215,700. The corporation is owned by A and B, husband and wife. The question becomes "Should they liquidate all in one year and pay the tax?" or "Receive these liquidations in equal amounts of $71,900 over the next three years?" Assume they have no basis in the stock of the corporation and that their other income equals their itemized deductions and exemptions. If they receive a distribution in 1988, their tax liability will be over $60,000. If they receive three equal distributions, their tax liability would only be $48,794. This is a savings of approximately $11,000, which must be counterbalanced by the amount of additional tax that would be paid at the corporate level.

Note: The payment in three tax years can be accomplished in just over twelve months.

Example:

Payment 1— December 31, 1988
Payment 2— January 1, 1989
Payment 3— January 1, 1990

In the above example, the advantages of the personal holding company become even more evident if we change the facts so the $200,000 value of goodwill is added to inventory for both book value and fair market value purposes and the book value of the equipment is equal to its fair market value. The remaining corporate assets could be sold at their fair market value resulting in a $200,000 gain. The tax at the corporate level would not exceed $68,000. The corporation would have $932,000 in after-tax funds. This is determined as follows:

Total fair market value of assets		$1,500,000.00
Less liabilities	$500,000.00	
Less corporate income tax	$ 68,000.00	
		$568,000.00
Net proceeds to the corporation		$932,000.00

This amount should be counterbalanced with what the after-tax proceeds to the individual shareholder would be after an election under Section 337 even if the closely held corporation exemption is available. This can be determined as follows:

Total fair market value of assets		$1,500,000.00
Less liabilities	$500,000.00	
Less corporate tax	$ 6,000.00	
		$506,000.00
Distribution to shareholders		$994,000.00
Tax on Liquidation		$278,320.00
Net after-tax distribution to shareholders		$715,680.00

A full discussion of the utilization of the personal holding company as well as its advantages and disadvantages is beyond the scope of this book. However, whenever there is a seller who is older and does not need the after-tax funds for his personal use, a personal holding company should be considered.

Also, it should be considered that with the elimination of the favorable benefits of the liquidation distributions being treated as capital gains, the periodic partial liquidations of personal holding companies can yield significant tax results. Further discussion of how this can be utilized will be investigated later in this chapter.

The eventual decision as to whether to elect under Section 337 or convert the corporation into a personal holding company will be made at the time of sale based on the existing tax laws and investment possibilities at that date. The most obvious consideration is the tax saved by not liquidating the corporation after sale. However, an analysis used in determining which method should be chosen would have to include the following.

1. The dividend rates that can be earned on investment. A personal holding company to be effectively utilized will invest a substantial portion of its portfolio in common and preferred stock paying dividend income. The reason for this is that eighty percent of the dividends are excludable from income subject to taxation at the corporate level.

2. The amount of income tax and maintenance costs that must be paid by the personal holding company.

3. Any further benefits that can be obtained by maintaining a personal holding company. These include medical insurance, maintenance of an office, payment of reasonable salary, and the like.

4. Age of the principals at the time of sale. If the shareholders at the time of sale are fifty-five and younger, it is probable that the corporation will be in existence for a long period of time. Remember, one of the objects of a personal holding company is to eliminate the tax upon liquidation of the corporation. This can be obtained at the shareholder's death. At that time, the estate obtains a step up in basis without the payment of an individual capital gains tax.

Example: Joe dies and the value of the personal holding companies stock that he owns at the time of his death is $500,000. He originally paid $100,000 for this stock. $400,000 escapes tax as capital gains. The older the individual is, the more viable a personal holding company becomes.

5. The outside income of the selling shareholder.
6. The personal financial needs of the shareholder.
7. The shareholder's estate planning goals.
8. Whether the selling shareholders have considered utilizing the net corporate proceeds to purchase a new business.

IS IT EVER POSSIBLE TO ELECT AS AN S CORPORATION TO PREVENT DOUBLE TAXATION?

The entity designated as the Subchapter S corporation or the small business corporation has become an integral part of the tax law since its creation in 1958. In 1982, a substantial revision in the tax laws was accomplished by the Subchapter S Revision Act of 1982. This act has had a substantial impact on planning as it affects S corporations. The S corporation is a hybrid means of doing business. For state purposes, it is treated as a corporation and therefore all the nontax advantages of incorporating are available. For tax purposes, it is really nothing more than an incorporated partnership.

Beware: This is an oversimplification and there are differences in tax treatment. Some of these will be explored in this section.

With this background in mind, some possible positive planning characteristics utilizing the S corporation become apparent.

A review of the example set forth under Method One on page 199 illustrates that a substantial portion of the tax incurred was not as a result of the liquidation of the corporation but from the sale of the assets at the corporate level. The tax at the corporate level is significant. The question then becomes "Could we use the S corporation to reduce the overall tax impact?" or "What is the possibility of using the following scenario?":

1. Widgets International, Inc. is anticipating selling.
2. It elects S corporation status prior to sale.
3. It sells its assets after the Subchapter S election becomes effective. The ordinary income and capital gain that need to be reported are reported individually.
4. A distribution of the earnings is made that year.
5. The next year the corporation is liquidated and a tax is paid by the shareholder.

The benefit in this particular instance is that the corporate tax of $68,000 that resulted from the gain of $200,000 from depreciation recapture is eliminated. The shareholder in this instance would only receive $86,400 from the sale of this equipment. This would be calculated as follows:

Gain on depreciation recapture		$200,000
Less:		
Corporate tax on gain	$ 68,000	
Less individual tax	$ 36,960	
Total tax		$104,960
Net to the individual shareholder		$ 95,040

The above calculation illustrates the worst possible scenario as the figures are based on the corporation and individual being in the highest marginal tax bracket. The effective tax rate is in excess of fifty-two percent. Under the law prior to the enactment of the Tax Reform Act of 1986, it was necessary to balance the individual's marginal tax rate with the combined corporate and individual capital gains rates to determine the optimum tax result. Under the 1986 Tax Reform Act, it is hard to envision a case where the prior election under Subchapter S where a major portion of the assets is going to be sold would not be appropriate; if the corporate tax can be eliminated. Congress foresaw the positive planning that the S corporation could provide and engrafted the concept of taxation of an S corporation on its net unrealized "built-in gain." Ramifications of this new provision will now be discussed.

The S Corporation Is Generally Subject to a Corporate Tax upon Sale of its Assets which Have Built-in Gains

In the above example of Widgets International this planning alternative would not have been viable for two reasons.

1. There is an exception to the general rule that income and losses are divided among its shareholders and retain their characteristics without any imposition of a tax at the corporate level. This exception is that an existing C Corporation that elects to be taxed as an S Corporation may be subject to tax at the corporate level on its net unrealized built-in gain. A corporate level tax is imposed on any gain that arose prior to the conversion (built-in gain) and is recognized by the S corporation upon the sale or distribution of said asset within ten years after the date on which the S election took effect. This gain is limited to the net built-in gain of the corporation at the time of conversion. The built-in gain will be taxed at the maximum corporate rate applicable to the particular type of income. There are two exceptions to the general rule:

   a. corporations that elected S corporation status prior to December 31, 1986;[1] and
   b. corporations that have always been S corporations.

2. Even if it were possible to avoid the tax resulting from the sale of assets at the corporate level, another problem would prohibit its usage.

This problem involves excess passive income. For simplification, passive income for S corporation purposes is defined as normal

[1]The new law generally came into effect for S Corporations on January 1, 1987. However, a qualified corporation is allowed to avoid the full impact of this act if it elects sub S status prior to January 1, 1989. A qualified corporation includes any corporation if, on August 1, 1986, and at all times, thereafter, more than fifty percent (by value) of its stock is held by ten or fewer qualified persons and the applicable value of the corporation does not exceed $10,000,000. Full relief is allowed only for corporations with a value not in excess of $5,000,000.

investment income less allocable deductions. To determine how much of the passive income is excess net passive income, you must multiply the corporation's net passive income by a fraction. The numerator of the fraction is the corporation's passive income for the year that exceeds twenty-five percent of the gross receipts and the denominator of which is the corporation's passive investment income for the year.

Example: Assume that during a taxable year, a Subchapter S corporation has $200,000 of gross receipts, passive income of $75,000 and expenses attributable to passive income of $10,000. As a result, its net passive income is $65,000 ($75,000 investment income minus $10,000 of expenses) and the amount by which its passive income for the taxable year exceeds twenty-five percent of the gross receipts is $25,000 ($75,000 passive income minus $50,000 ($200,000 gross receipts times twenty-five percent)). The income subject to the tax is determined as follows:

$65,000 times $25,000 divided by $75,000 = $21,666.67

Observe: The net passive income has two negative effects. If a corporation has earnings and profits as an ordinary C corporation at the end of three consecutive taxable years, and more than twenty-five percent of its gross receipts for each of those years is from passive income, the Subchapter S election would be terminated. In addition, the amount of net passive income (the $21,666.67 in the example above) is taxed at the maximum corporate tax rate which is thirty-four percent in 1988.

HOW THE TAX REFORM ACT OF 1986 AFFECTS THE FUTURE OF S CORPORATIONS

With prior planning, the S corporation can provide sizeable benefits. Prior to the Tax Reform Act of 1986, because of the ability to use the favorable provisions of Section 333 and Section 337 as well as the higher individual tax rates and favorable capital gains rates for individuals, the S corporation rarely played a major planning role in the sale of a business. However, with the reduction of individual tax rates (from a maximum of fifty percent to a maximum of 28 percent) without a corresponding reduction in the corporate rate (from forty-six percent to thirty-four percent), the S corporation will be more frequently used as a tool through which assets are sold. It would appear that an increasing number of corporations which in the past for tax reasons would have elected as C corporations will now elect as

S corporations. In the past, the retention of funds by a C corporation could provide on the first $50,000 of income a benefit of as much as $16,750 of tax savings (maximum individual tax rate fifty percent less average tax rate for corporations on $50,000 of income of 16.5% × $50,000). The post Tax Reform Act of 1986 benefits for retention of the $50,000 has been reduced to $6,500. When you counterbalance this marginal benefit versus the increased possibility of double taxation, more and more corporations will initially elect as S corporations or convert to S status.

Key Idea: Whenever a corporation is anticipating the possible sale of its business, it is a good idea to elect S corporation status at the earliest possible time.

Key Idea: When all other factors are equal, there will be increased pressure to elect as an S corporation even though sale is not imminent.

With the above background, it is easy to see that while the passive income rules and taxation on unrealized built-in gain may provide some problems, S corporations are going to play a more significant role in future tax planning.

HOW CODE PROVISIONS FOR LIQUIDATION CAN BE USED TO REDUCE TAXES UPON SALE

The ultimate question for the selling shareholders is "What are the net after-tax proceeds to me?" We have discussed the ramifications of an individual sale of stock solely and in conjunction with the receipt of additional payments from an employment contract, covenant not-to-compete, consulting contract, and the like.

The alternative to a stock sale is the sale of assets. Once the assets are sold, the corporation usually must liquidate in order to transfer the proceeds of sale to the stockholders. The most commonly utilized liquidation Section of the Internal Revenue Code involving the sale of a business by a corporation prior to the Tax Reform Act of 1986 was Section 337. The benefits and continuing applicability of this Section have been discussed earlier. There are three other Code Sections that can provide some relief when a sale of the business and liquidation of the corporation are involved. These Code Sections can be summarized as follows:

1. Section 333—The liquidation of a corporation with no tax to either the shareholder or corporation. Again, this Section is no longer

available to other than closely held corporations but it is still available to those closely held corporations liquidating before January 1, 1989.

2. Section 331—The Code Section to be utilized when no other Section is applicable to minimize taxes.

3. The partial liquidation of the corporation pursuant to Code Section 302(e).

In all asset sales, it is extremely important to realize that there are two separate entities that can be affected by taxes upon the liquidation of a corporation.

1. the corporation itself
2. the individual

The Tax Reform Act has substantially altered the taxation to the corporation upon liquidation. Generally in all cases upon liquidation where there is appreciated property, the corporation will have to pay a tax on this liquidation. The sole exception was referred to on page 197. It is liquidation of small closely held corporations prior to January 1, 1989. In addition, except in very limited situations, the taxation of the individual shareholder will not depend on whether or not the receipt is categorized as ordinary income or capital gain. Because of the vast changes made as to both the taxation to the individual and to the corporation as well as the unknown implications of the Tax Reform Act, a complete discussion of all the ramifications of the liquidation procedure is beyond the scope of this book. Notwithstanding this, I will attempt to structure a discussion of each of the possible planning opportunities as follows.

1. an overview of the provisions of each section
2. an illustration of the utilization of the section
3. the taxation upon the individual and the corporation
4. some general comments as to the advantages and disadvantages of proceeding under each Code Section

Method 1: How to Use Section 333

An unusual relief provision in the code is included in Section 333 and is known as the "one-month liquidation." This was originally enacted in 1938 to allow personal holding companies an opportunity to liquidate in order to escape the personal holding tax that was enacted in that year.

These provisions and their uses are far broader than the original purpose for which they were enacted. The purpose of these provisions is to allow the shareholders to defer all or part of the gain on liquidation until they dispose of the property in a taxable transaction. However, the scope of this relief provision is rather narrow and to obtain its beneficial tax effect the provisions of the Code Section must be strictly complied with. If a corporation that is going to sell its assets has the following characteristics, the provisions of Section 333 should be investigated:

1. the corporation has little or no accumulated earnings and profits; and
2. a major portion of the corporate assets are capital assets or assets used in a trade or business that will qualify for capital gain if and when sold. If these assets (upon sale) would result in both capital gain and recapture (depreciation and LIFO recapture), the benefits may be lost. The otherwise tax free liquidation can be converted into a transaction that will result in dividend income.
3. The corporation is a closely held corporation as explained earlier and the liquidation will occur prior to January 1, 1989.

An example will illustrate the ability to utilize Section 333 in a sales context.

Example: ABC Corporation has been in existence for many years. Its sole shareholder, Joe, has managed the corporation for his own personal benefit during the past ten years. He has received a comprehensive compensation package including salary, fringe benefits, and a pension plan that has allocated all the company's earnings to him rather than retaining them in the corporation. He is now contemplating the sale of the business and has been offered $280,000 for the operating assets. The purchaser has neither sufficient cash nor the desire to purchase the land and buildings. However, as part of the purchase price, Joe has required the purchaser to enter into a five-year lease. ABC Corporation has the balance sheet shown on the next page. Because the book value and fair market value of the equipment and inventory are the same, no gain or loss will be recognized by the corporation on the sale. The cash realized from the sale, $280,000 plus $10,000 in cash, would be used to reduce the accounts payable. The sole asset for distribution would be the real estate. If the shareholder's basis in the stock was $60,000 and no election was made under Section 333, the shareholders would realize a gain of $440,000 (fair

Assets

		Book Value		Fair Market Value
Cash		$ 10,000		$ 10,000
Receivables		$100,000		$100,000
Inventory		$150,000		$150,000
Equipment		$ 30,000		$ 30,000
Land and	$500,000		$900,000	
Buildings	($400,000)	$100,000	($400,000)	$500,000
TOTAL ASSETS		$390,000		$790,000

Liabilities and Stockholders Equity

	Book Value	Fair Market Value
Accounts Payable	$290,000	$290,000
Common Stock	$100,000	$100,000
Retained Earnings	0	0
Unrealized Appreciation	______	$400,000
Total Liabilities and Equity	$390,000	$790,000

market of value of building $500,000 less basis in stock $60,000) upon liquidation. On the other hand, if Section 333 is elected, $40,000 of ordinary income will be realized to the corporation. In addition, $34,000 of ordinary income dividend will be realized on the distribution to the shareholder of the land and building. The basis of the land and building in the shareholder's hands will be $100,000. It should be noted that the corporation could have been liquidated under Section 333 and then the shareholder could have sold the receivables, inventory, and equipment. The tax result would have been the same.

The requirements for a Section 333 liquidation are as follows:

1. Adoption of liquidation resolution and liquidation within one calendar month.

2. A distribution to qualifying individual and corporate shareholders. Basically, any individual shareholder will be a qualifying shareholder if:

a. he owns stock in the liquidating corporation at the time the liquidation is adopted
b. he files an election to be governed under Section 333; or

c. if said election is filed by eighty percent of the total combined voting power of all cases of stock entitled to vote.

The qualifications for corporate shareholders are more complicated and should be reviewed if the benefits of a Section 333 liquidation are contemplated and there are corporate shareholders.

Qualifying electing shareholders under Section 333 will be able to limit their taxable portion of the gain upon liquidation to the greater of:

a. the shareholder's pro rata share of the earnings and profits; or
b. the sum of money received by the shareholders plus fair market value of stock and securities acquired after 1953.

The noncorporate shareholder will report his taxable gain as dividend income to the extent of the pro rata portion of the earnings and profits. If the cash distribution exceeds the pro rata portion of the earnings and profits, the remainder of the cash and securities will be taxed as capital gains.

Example: ABC Corporation adopts a Section 333 liquidation and distributes to Joe cash and securities in addition to the other property as hereinafter set forth. If Joe has a basis of $5,000 in the stock of ABC, what will be the tax ramifications to him:

A. If $10,000 in cash is distributed to Joe and if ABC Corporation had earnings and profits of $15,000, he would be taxed on $15,000 of dividend income.

B. If $15,000 in cash is distributed to Joe and if ABC Corporation had earnings and profits of $10,000, he would be taxed on $10,000 of dividend income and $5,000 of capital gains.

Warning: Beware of taxation to the corporation upon liquidation pursuant to Section 333. There are three exceptions to the general rule that no gain will be realized to the corporation upon liquidation. They are the distribution of (1) installment obligations; (2) property subject to depreciation and investment credit recapture; and (3) appreciated LIFO inventory. Taxable income created by the distribution of these three types of property in liquidation will not only result in taxable income to the corporation, but will also increase the earnings and profits. This in turn could increase the amount of dividend income attributable to the individual shareholder upon liquidation.

When It Is Advantageous to Use Section 333 Liquidation

1. When a substantial portion of the property has appreciated in value but is not subject to depreciation recapture.
2. The earnings and profits of the corporation are relatively small in relation to the potential gain the shareholders will receive on liquidation.
3. The shareholders have no intention of selling a portion of the substantially appreciated assets.
4. A majority of the shareholders gain on liquidation is attributable to nondepreciable property or LIFO inventory and the sellers do not want to pay the entire gain on liquidation.

When It Is Not Advantageous to Use Section 333

1. When the earnings and profits are high in relation to the potential capital gain to the shareholders.
2. When a large portion of assets to be distributed will be cash, stock, or securities.
3. When the shareholders intend to sell the appreciated assets for cash soon after liquidation.
4. When the corporation holds depreciable property that has appreciated and the shareholders can readily pay a capital gain tax in exchange for a step up in basis.

Key Idea: Even if a corporation is not contemplating selling in the near future, if it qualifies under the small closely held corporation exemption, it may be beneficial to liquidate under Section 333 prior to January 1, 1989.

The above is a summary of the possible utilization of Section 333. The Section itself is complicated with tax traps for the unwary. The major ones are set forth in the WARNING on page 212. In summary, if a corporation has small earnings and profits, little possibility of recapture and is not going to sell all of its assets, Section 333 should be investigated as an alternative to either Section 337 or Section 331.

Method 2: How to Use Section 337

Prior to the Tax Reform Act of 1986, all corporations were eligible to elect under Section 337. Section 337 provided that if a corporation adopts a plan of complete liquidation and within twelve months thereafter distributes all of its assets to its shareholders, it will recognize no gain or loss on the property during the twelve-month period. The benefits and utilization of the 337 liquidation have been illustrated in the example beginning on page 199.

After the Tax Reform Act of 1986 only small corporations that have the following characteristics and that liquidate prior to January 1, 1989, will qualify for these favorable characteristics:

1. Corporation is eligible for this rule if its value does not exceed $10,000,000.
2. More than fifty percent of its stock is owned by ten or fewer shareholders.
3. Said shareholders have held the stock for five years or longer.

Full relief is available under this Section only if the corporation does not exceed $5,000,000 and relief is phased out for corporations between $5,000,000 and $10,000,000.

Section 337 requires the directors to adopt a plan of complete liquidation. The date of its adoption is particularly critical because it triggers the commencement of the twelve-month period. A problem can occur if any assets are inadvertently sold prior to the adoption of the plan. In this case, the corporation will recognize income on the sale of those assets. On the other hand, if the liquidation distribution is not completed within the twelve-month period, the entire income realized by the corporation will be taxable income. Section 337 applies only to a gain or loss recognized by a corporation in liquidation of its business and not from the gain resulting from sales in the ordinary course of business. The general rule that all other sales or distributions after the adoption of the liquidation resolution are tax free is subject to the following exceptions:

1. The sale of stock in trade or other property that is normally included in inventory at the year end, or property held primarily for sale in the ordinary course of business will result in taxable income. However, if there is a bulk sale of the inventory items to a nonrelated party, this will not be considered a sale in the ordinary course of business and will be excluded from any taxability.

2. A distribution of any installment obligation received as a result of a sale or exchange of property will be taxable upon distribution if the sale occurred prior to the date of the adoption of the plan for complete liquidation.

3. A liquidation will be considered a sale and income resulting from recapture under Sections 1245 and 1250 will be realized. The

investment credit recapture provisions are also applicable on either sale or distribution of property in liquidation.

4. If a corporation distributes LIFO inventory in liquidation, it realizes a gain in the amount of the excess of the value of the LIFO inventory over the value of the inventory determined under the FIFO method.

5. In addition to the above statutory restrictions, there are also certain court imposed exceptions that usually involve the assignment of income or tax benefit doctrines.

Prior to the Installment Sales Act of 1980 any distribution of installment obligations from a corporation in liquidation under Section 337, were included in taxable income of the shareholder upon liquidation of the corporation. The Installment Sales Act of 1980 changed this and allowed for a reporting by the shareholders of the installment obligations entered into after the adoption of the Section 337 election as cash is received. An example will clarify this.

Example: A is the sole shareholder of X Corporation. His basis in the stock is $14,250. X Corporation owns the following assets free and clear of any liabilities:

	Book Value	Fair Market Value
Cash	$ 1,000	$ 1,000
Other Property giving rise to capital gain (no depreciation recapture)	$10,000	$110,000

The purchaser is willing to pay for the assets of the corporation as follows:

Purchase price	$110,000
Down payment	$ 20,000
Balance Due	$ 90,000

The balance due of $90,000 will be paid pursuant to a promissory note payable as follows:

a. 120 equal monthly installments of $1,291.24; and

b. interest on the unpaid principal balance at the rate of twelve percent.

Before the enactment of the Installment Sales Act of 1980, if the corporation elected under Section 337, this sale would have been tax free to the corporation. However, upon distribution of the installment note, the shareholder would have had to report the entire gain in the year of distribution. In other words, A would have received $111,000 in assets comprising cash of $21,000 and an installment note of $90,000. This would have resulted in a capital gain of $96,750 (total proceeds received—$111,000 less basis in stock of $14,250).

Under the Installment Sales Act of 1980, only the cash and other property received will have to be reported in the year of distribution. In this particular example, only $18,304 of gain will be reported to the shareholder upon distribution. The income to be realized is determined by multiplying the cash received in the year of sale by the fraction the numerator of which is the total gain and the denominator of which is the total proceeds ($21,000 times $96,750 divided by $111,000). The remainder of the gain will be reported as the principal is received under the terms of the installment note. This relieves the shareholder from current taxation on a distribution of the installment note.

Warning: Effective for installment sales after June 6, 1984, the entire amount of depreciation recapture must be included in taxable year income in the year of sale. This rule applies even if no cash is received in the year of sale. If the down payment is inadequate, a transaction can generate more tax liability than cash in the year of sale. In situations with the potential of substantial depreciation recapture, installment sales will now be a less effective income averaging technique.

Warning: The Tax Reform Act of 1984 changed the rules relative to interest that should be charged on installment sales pursuant to Section 483. In order to not give rise to imputed interest, a safe harbor has been engrafted in the act. As long as interest is 110 percent of the applicable federal rate, there will not be any imputed interest. If it is not 110 percent of the applicable federal rate, the imputed interest rate will be 120 percent of the applicable federal rate.

The applicable federal rate each month is based on the average yield for marketable U.S. obligations during a preceding one-month period. For debt instruments with a term of three years or less, the short-term federal rates are used. If the term of the installment debt is over three years but less than nine years, the midterm rates are used. Long-term applicable federal rates must be used when the term of the debt instrument is over nine years. For example, for December, 1986, the applicable federal rate, interest payable annually, ranged from 6.18 percent for short-term to 7.71 percent for long-term.

Key Idea: At any time that a sale is contemplated under the installment method and the parties wish to set the interest at lower than the applicable federal rate, the exceptions to Section 483 should be reviewed. These exceptions include the sale or exchange of land between the family members. In this case, a six percent interest rate can be applied if the sale does not exceed $500,000. It is also possible to use nine percent for sales of real property and used personal property under $2,800,000.

The benefits and attractiveness of Section 337 are self-evident. The possibility of eliminating a capital gains tax at the corporate level is particularly attractive. At any time that you have a small closely held corporation and there is a sale of the assets contemplated that gives rise to capital gains with little or no depreciation recapture, benefits under Section 337 should be analyzed. This benefit, unless Congress takes some action, will terminate on January 1, 1989.

Method 3: How to Use Section 331

Sections 333 and 337 are sections that provide extraordinary relief. In a vast portion of cases, it may be that the special provisions provided for in these two sections will not be applicable to your particular fact situation. In these cases, you will utilize Section 331. While on its face Section 331 does not seem to provide any tax relief, if it is properly utilized, there can be substantial benefits. There is usually substantial benefit in liquidating over a number of years. An example will illustrate how this can be applied.

Example: Contracting Corporation has been in the business of constructing various properties for sale to municipalities and private individuals. At the time liquidation is contemplated, the corporation has several projects in various stages of completion. In addition, it owns parcels of real estate that will be disposed of within a year. It is impossible to tell how long it will take the other properties, including the equipment, to be sold. The equipment can only be disposed of after the last project is completed. The founding father has retired and is interested in receiving cash over the next several years. He is the sole shareholder and has left his chief assistants to accomplish the liquidation.

It is anticipated that upon complete liquidation of all properties, there will be $359,500 in cash to be distributed after payment of all expenses. If the corporation accumulates the cash during the five years and then distributes it, it will be necessary to realize $359,500 of gain in one year. Assuming the founding father owns 100 percent of the stock, is married, has no basis for the corporate stock, and his other income equals his exemptions and deductions, the tax in the year of liquidation would be at least $100,660. If, on the other hand, a partial liquidation distribution of $71,900 is made each year, the yearly tax could be as low as $16,264.50. This would result in a total tax savings over the five-year period of just under $20,000.

There is no definite time schedule that must be followed in a complete liquidation. The Internal Revenue Service has announced that it will ordinarily not issue advance rulings or determination letters on the tax effects of a complete liquidation where the liquidation distributions are to be made over a period of time greater than three years. However, the courts have been more lenient and have permitted liquidations that have extended up to twenty-three years. It is a prerequisite that every reasonable effort be made to dispose of the properties and liquidate within the shortest period of time. If taxes are the sole reason for maintaining the corporate entity, the liquidation will not be able to extend over the desired period. In the cases where tax motivation has been the primary reason, the courts have imposed a constructive liquidation dividend prior to the date of actual distribution.

When a corporation distributes all of its cash and other assets to its shareholders in a complete liquidation, the tax law treats the transaction as a sale or exchange of its assets for and in consideration of the stock. The shareholders report any gain or loss that may result by ascertaining the value of the assets received versus the basis of their stock in the corporation.

Example: XYZ Corporation liquidates under Section 331 and distributes to its sole shareholder, A, whose basis in the stock is $10,000, the following assets.

Assets	Corporate Book Value	Fair Market Value	Basis After Liquidation
Cash	$50,000	$ 50,000	$ 50,000
Land	$20,000	$ 60,000	$ 60,000
	$70,000	$110,000	$110,000

A must report a gain of $100,000: the fair market value of the assets received ($110,000) less his basis in the stock ($10,000). His basis in the land has now increased to $60,000. Unless the corporation in this case were a small corporation as previously described in the discussion on Section 337, it would realize taxable income on the difference between the value of the land and the book value or $40,000. If the small corporation exception applies, the corporation would realize no taxable income in this case. However, there are exceptions even to this rule. If the corporation liquidates and distributes any of the following types of property, it will realize income: installment obligations, property that would result in depreciation or investment recapture if sold, and LIFO inventory. There are also specialized situations that could create taxable income to the corporation upon liquidation.

If Section 331 is used, the entire gain will be taxable to the shareholders in the year of actual distribution. Distributions in complete liquidations are treated as a sale or exchange which will normally result in capital transactions. If a distribution is not considered a distribution in complete or partial liquidation of the corporation, these distributions will be taxed as ordinary income if the corporation has earnings and profits. The difference between a transaction being taxed as a capital gain or dividend income has been mitigated by the Tax Reform Act of 1986. The difference still has certain ramifications.

1. In the event that it is classified as dividend income, the basis will not be subtracted from the distribution to determine the applicable taxable gain.

2. In the case of an installment redemption of a shareholder's interest, if the payment were designated as a dividend, the interest paid by the corporation would probably not be deductible. On the other hand, if it is a capital transaction, the interest could be used to reduce the corporation's taxable income.

The requirements for a complete liquidation under Section 331 are relatively easy to satisfy. In order for Section 331 to apply, a status of liquidation must exist at the time the first distribution is made. However, neither the code nor the regulations define what the term "complete liquidation" means. Whether the corporation at the time that this distribution is made is in the "status of liquidation" involves a factual determination. Neither the retention of the corporate charter to protect the corporate name nor the retention of sufficient assets to satisfy any contingent liabilities would disqualify the liquidation.

Where retention of any assets is contemplated or any business transaction is transacted after the adoption of liquidation resolutions, a complete analysis should be made to ensure that Section 331 is being complied with. A failure to comply could result in dividend distributions. Proper documentation setting forth the resolutions in the minutes, while it may not be required by law, is useful in establishing the format which gives rise to favorable tax results.

The utilization of Section 331 usually occurs where the beneficial provisions of Section 337 or Section 333 do not apply. The ability to maximize the benefits to the individual shareholders through the utilization of Section 331 should not be overlooked. Even if it is hard to justify a distribution period over many years, a distribution over fourteen months can in effect provide for payments in three separate years.

Example: X Corporation is owned by A. It is in the process of liquidation and plans to distribute $215,700 in proceeds after taxes and expenses. X Corporation is a calendar year corporation. The sale will occur in December of 1988. It is possible to distribute $71,900 to A in 1988, $71,900 to A in 1989, and the final $71,900 to him on January 1, 1990. The tax savings by this maneuver for a married taxpayer would be in excess of $11,000, less any additional corporate tax that may be incurred.

The tax to be saved depends on such factors as the marginal tax rate of the shareholder, the size of the distribution, and the taxpayers other income and exemptions. Prior to the Tax Reform Act of 1986, the benefits of timing the liquidation distribution over a number of years were counterbalanced by the threat of the determination that either the distributions were dividend income or that a constructive distribution had occurred. After the Tax Reform Act of 1986, these negatives are definitely reduced and tax planning will probably call for longer periods of liquidation even if the corporation will be classified as a personal holding company during a portion of the time.

Key Idea: Use of Section 331 to liquidate a corporation over a long period of time may produce significant tax savings at minimum risk in the future.

Method 4: How to Use Partial Liquidation to Extract Money or Property from the Corporation

While a partial liquidation has a good deal of utilization in tax planning, its impact is less important in transactions involving the sale of a business. Usually where the purchase of an individual shareholder's stock by the corporation is contemplated, the transaction will qualify not as a partial liquidation but as a redemption. A detailed discussion of the differences between a redemption and partial liquidation as well as the tax ramifications of redemptions is beyond the scope of this book. However, the concepts and major differences will be alluded to later in this section. The area where the partial liquidation can be effectively utilized involves the sale of one of the multiple businesses owned by a corporation. In this case, the alternative approach of electing Sub S status should be considered.

Example: Multiple Corporation operates two separate businesses: the manufacture, distribution, and sale of widgets; and a string of franchise restaurants located throughout the Midwest. The officers of Multiple Corporation have decided to concentrate their future efforts in the widget industry and wish to dispose of the string of franchise restaurants. If these restaurants are sold there are two questions, "What will be the tax to the corporation?" and "What will be the tax to the shareholders if the after-tax corporate proceeds are distributed to them?"

Prior to the Tax Reform Act of 1986, it was important to have a distribution qualify as a partial liquidation (not dividend income) because of the favorable capital gains rates at the shareholder level. For example, prior to the act, if the sale resulted in a gain of $1,000,000 that was taxed at the corporate level, assuming a marginal tax rate of fifty percent, the corporation would pay a $500,000 tax. The remaining $500,000 would then be distributed to the shareholder. If the shareholder was taxed on the distribution as dividend income, at a fifty percent marginal tax bracket, he would incur an additional $250,000 of tax. Accordingly the total tax burden on the $1,000,000 gain could be $750,000. If the distribution qualified as a partial liquidation, the tax at the corporate level would remain the same; however, on the $500,000 distribution to the shareholders it would be taxed at a maximum of $100,000 and the after-tax proceeds would be $400,000. The Tax Reform Act of 1986 alters the prior differences. As the corporate rates have been reduced and as there are no longer any major favorable tax implications to have the distribution taxed as a long-term capital gain, the above transaction, whether it would be a partial liquidation or dividend distribution, would be taxed as follows:

Gain on sale	$1,000,000
Less corporate tax	$ 340,000
After-tax proceeds at corporate level	$ 660,000

Tax upon distribution whether or not it is capital gain or dividend	$ 137,280
Net after-tax proceeds	$ 422,270

Accordingly, in a sales context, the prior benefits of obtaining capital gains treatment on partial liquidations if not eliminated is greatly reduced.

HOW TO PLAN PARTIAL LIQUIDATIONS PRIOR TO JANUARY 1, 1989

The small closely held corporations previously defined on pages 198 and 208 have limited planning opportunities for distributing appreciated property prior to January 1, 1989. In the event that a small corporation owns appreciated capital gain property, it well may behoove them to distribute same to the shareholders prior to January 1, 1989. An example will illustrate the planning opportunities.

Example: XYZ Corporation owns two manufacturing plants, one in Appleton and one in Oshkosh. It wishes to distribute the Oshkosh factory in partial liquidation.

Value	Book Value	Fair Market
Equipment, inventory, and receivables	$100,000	$100,000
Goodwill	0	$200,000
Total assets	$100,000	$300,000
Accounts payable	$ 50,000	$ 50,000

After January 1, 1989, this will result in corporate taxable income of $200,000 and individual shareholder income of $250,000. Before that time, it appears that if the distribution qualifies as a partial liquidation and the corporation qualifies for the positive benefits of a closely held corporation, it will not be subject to the $200,000 of taxable income.

REQUIREMENTS FOR A PARTIAL LIQUIDATION

Section 346(a)(2) of the Internal Revenue Code was amended by the Tax Equity and Fiscal Responsibility Act of 1982 and is now reincorporated within Section 302. While there was a substantial change in the law, the definition of partial liquidations was continued. Basically, a distribution shall be treated as a partial liquidation if:

1. the distribution is not essentially equivalent to a dividend; and
2. the distribution is pursuant to a plan and occurs within the taxable year in which the plan is adopted or the succeeding taxable year.

A distribution is not essentially equivalent to a dividend if it is attributable to the distribution of a qualified trade or business. The question revolves around what is a qualified trade or business. A business will qualify if:

1. the trade or business was actively conducted throughout the five-year period preceding the date of distribution;
2. said trade or business was not acquired by the distributing corporation within that period of time in a taxable distribution.

Section 302(e) states that whether or not a redemption meets the requirements of a partial liquidation shall be determined without regard to whether or not the redemption is pro rata with respect to the shareholders of the corporation. Accordingly, a pro rata distribution may still qualify for a partial liquidation.

The law as to the possibility of creating taxable income at the corporate level on the distribution of appreciated property in a partial liquidation is virtually the same as involving corporate liquidations, which was discussed under Method 3. While there are similarities between a partial liquidation and a redemption, it is imperative that the distribution be considered a partial liquidation if you wish to distribute appreciated property to an individual shareholder in a partial liquidation without resulting in income to the corporation. Obviously the goal in the above example was in the not too distant future to sell the Oshkosh factory. This may be an opportunity even if the Oshkosh factory is not sold by January 1, 1989, to remove it from the corporate umbrella if the shareholders are willing to pay a tax on the distribution.

Key Idea: Any small corporation that operates two businesses may consider utilizing the partial liquidation provisions prior to January 1, 1989.

Why is it necessary in various cases to have a distribution to a shareholder considered as a qualifying redemption for capital gains purposes? It would appear that there are still some instances where the redemption should qualify under Section 302 rather than as dividend income. These cases involve the installment redemption of the stock of a shareholder.

Example: A and B each own fifty percent of the stock in a corporation valued at $100,000. If all of the stock of A is redeemed in sixty equal monthly installments at ten percent, the total payments over that period of time would equal $63,741.60. While $50,000 would be paid in after-tax dollars, the remaining $13,741.60 will qualify as deductible interest. If, on the other hand, the transaction is considered not as a redemption but as dividend income, it would appear that all $63,741.60 must be paid in after-tax income.

The rules under Section 302 are complicated and planning in this area will have to go through substantial rethinking in light of the Tax Reform Act of 1986.

HOW TO DIVIDE THE CORPORATION INTO SEPARATE PARTS AND REDUCE TAXATION

The positive planning that can be accomplished by a division of the corporation into separate entities occurs when the owners of the corporation are contemplating the sale of one of the two or more businesses owned by the corporation. The division process, depending on the method utilized, is variously described as a spin-off, split up, or split-off. In all cases, the techniques involve either a pro rata or non-pro rata distribution of the business. The key is to divide the corporation tax free into two or more corporations. A pro rata division of the corporation envisions the ownership of the two succeeding businesses in the same proportion as the current stock ownership.

Example: A and B each own fifty percent of XYZ Corporation, which conducts two businesses—a men's retail sales store in Appleton, Wisconsin, and a men's retail sales store in Oshkosh, Wisconsin. In a pro rata distribution after the division, A and B will each own one-half of the stock of XYZ-1, which operates the men's retail store in Appleton, and one-half of the ownership of XYZ-2, which operates the men's retail store in Oshkosh.

A non-pro rata division of the corporation envisions the ownership of the two succeeding businesses in a different proportion.

Example: In the above example, if XYZ Corporation were divided into two new corporations XYZ-1 and XYZ-2, A may end up owning all of XYZ-1, which operates the Appleton store, and none of XYZ-2. B, on the other hand, would own all the common stock of XYZ-2, which operates the Oshkosh store, and none of XYZ-1.

In all cases, the prerequisite to accomplishing a division of the business that is either pro rata or non-pro rata is that it qualify for the tax-free division of the business pursuant to the provisions of Section 355. The IRS, realizing the positive planning characteristics of a pro rata distribution, has attempted to treat whenever possible these as taxable transactions especially when there is a sale after the division. On the other hand, a non-pro rata distribution, even if one of the parties eventually sells his stock, may yield positive planning opportunities. Prior to the Tax Reform Act of 1986, the benefits of a tax-free spin-off had to be counterbalanced with the possibility that the distribution would be dividend income instead of tax-free. An example will show why there may be increased usefulness of the spin-off after the Tax Reform Act of 1986, especially where a corporation owns two businesses.

Example: In the above example of XYZ-1 and XYZ-2, assume that XYZ-2 was a wholly owned subsidiary of XYZ-1. The stock of XYZ-2 was to be sold by XYZ-1 for $200,000. XYZ-1 has no basis for XYZ-2's stock. Further assume XYZ-1 is in the thirty-four percent marginal tax bracket. Prior to the Tax Reform Act of 1986, if a partial liquidation could be accomplished through the distribution of XYZ-2's stock to the shareholders of XYZ-1, they would realize a capital gain upon distribution. This would result in a maximum tax of $40,000. However, when they resold XYZ-1's stock there would be no further gain. Accordingly, they would net $160,000 in after-tax proceeds. This of course assumes that the partial liquidation qualified and did not result in a tax to the corporation upon liquidation. If it did not qualify, the corporation would also have to realize a tax on distribution.

The alternative before the Tax Reform Act of 1986 was a tax-free spin-off. This would be the transfer of the stock of XYZ-2 tax free to XYZ-1's shareholders. There would be no gain at the corporate level but XYZ-1's shareholders would realize a capital gain on the sale. Spin-offs always contained the prohibition against the subsequent sale by the shareholders of XYZ-1 of XYZ-2's stock. Accordingly, if the transaction could have qualified as a partial liquidation, this route was followed. The goal was not to recognize any gain at the corporate level. The tax-free spin-off normally without a prior ruling created too great a risk. If the spin-off was not considered as a tax-free distribution but as a taxable transaction it would not have been capital gain but ordinary dividend income and could have been subject to a tax of as much as fifty percent.

Under the rules promulgated by the Tax Reform Act of 1986, the distribution, assuming that the small corporation exemption is not met, would result in taxable income at the corporate level ($68,000 of tax) as well as income at the individual level (again $56,000 of tax). Accordingly, the division of businesses tax free before sale may provide positive planning opportunities.

Key Idea: Family owned corporations that conduct multiple businesses should consider pro rata tax-free divisions especially where sale is not imminent.

BUYING A CORPORATION WITH A NET OPERATING LOSS OR OTHER CORPORATION WITH FAVORABLE TAX ATTRIBUTES

A corporation may have positive tax characteristics that the buyer wishes to utilize. These include a net operating loss carry forward, an investment credit carry forward, jobs credit carry over, or book value in excess of fair market value. The caveat in this particular instance is that any time a purchase of a corporation is made by third parties, the prior tax attributes of the corporation could be disturbed. Accordingly, the tax law at that time should be reviewed. This is an extremely complicated area, especially after the Tax Reform Act of 1986, and care should be exercised. On the other hand, in special situations, if not all, some of the positive tax characteristics can be carried forward against the future income of the corporation.

A SUMMARY OF THE PSTT CONCEPT

It is important to consider the relationship of all factors when negotiating the sale of a business. The basic concepts can be summarized as follows:

1. The measuring stick of the purchase price is cash for stock at date of closing.
2. No taxation at the corporate level upon sale to the seller.

3. The shareholder is taxed on all his proceeds from his stock. Any ordinary income that he receives through an employment contract, lease, and the like, is not part of the purchase price but is appropriate compensation for the services rendered or a proper payment for the property leased.

4. Without proper security, the remainder of the sales process is meaningless. Payment of the purchase price is all-important.

5. While terms and taxes should play a subordinate role (only a vehicle for the payment of the purchase price), many times these factors must be maneuvered and manipulated to provide for a successful sales transaction. In these instances, creativity and inventiveness become the key to success. The Tax Reform Act of 1986 has made planning more complicated and reduced or eliminated many of the prior planning techniques. It has changed the frame of reference of the tax practitioners and has also caused them to rethink and restructure sales and transfers.

6. It is easy during the negotiation process to become lost in the complexity of the terms of the sales or security agreements, the provisions of the Internal Revenue Code, and the concept of discounting; however, the four keys (the PSTT Concept) should be firmly entrenched in your thinking so that at all times during the sales process you know what is and what is not negotiable.

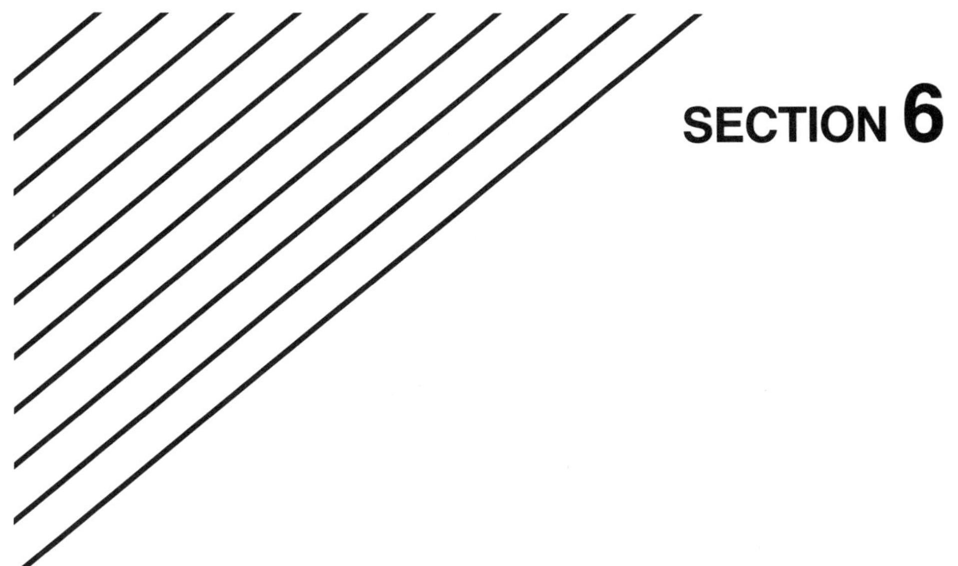

SECTION 6

HOW TO FOLLOW UP AFTER CLOSING THE SALE

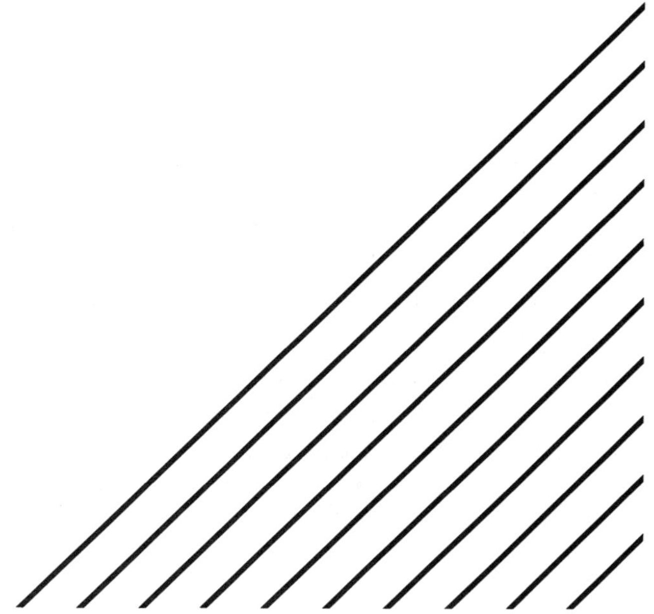

WHEN MANDATORY FOLLOW-UP IS NECESSARY

Any time that the seller has any vested interest in the success of the purchaser, provision for follow-up after closing should be included in the sales agreement. An investment in the future success of the purchaser can come in many forms including the following:

1. A portion of the purchase price is represented by a promissory note.
2. The purchaser owes a continuing financial commitment to the sellers under a covenant not-to-compete or employment contract.
3. The purchaser may have leased real or personal property from the selling shareholders.
4. A portion of the purchase price may be contingent on the performance of the purchaser.

In all of the above, some follow-up should be provided for in the sales agreement. Another situation that is not as obvious is when the seller remains contingently liable on corporate obligations. The bank, at the time of making the original corporate obligation, may have required the selling shareholder's personal guarantee. At the time of sale, the bank may have been unwilling to release the seller from the contingent liability under the guarantee. The seller may also have some continuing personal obligations in the form of guarantees to trade creditors, or through the signature on a performance bond. In any of these events, it is necessary to provide a continuing review of the performance of the purchaser.

Warning: The ability to obtain the proper financial information after the sale must be provided in the sales agreement and the enabling documents. If these documents do not provide a mandatory obligation on the purchaser to provide this financial information, no obligation exists.

WHAT TYPES OF FOLLOW-UP SHOULD BE PROVIDED IN THE SALES AGREEMENT

There are several different types of direct and indirect documentation that can be provided to the seller. The obligation to provide this documentation must be included in the original sales agreement and other ancillary agreements such as the mortgage or security agreement. These documents will allow the seller to review the success or failure of the business and to anticipate and plan for problems rather than only to react to the default of the purchaser. The various types of direct information that can be required in these documents take many forms.

One of the most common are management prepared statements. These statements are prepared by the purchaser and will be supplied to the seller on a monthly, quarterly, or annual basis. Obviously, the greater the investment in the success of the purchaser, the more frequent the need for these statements. It is a good idea for the seller to compare the statements that he is receiving to the statements from comparable prior periods. This provides the seller with a frame of reference as to performance both before and after the sale. The goal in all these cases is to anticipate problems before they occur. Unfortunately, most individuals, once they have sold the business, consider it an "old problem" and do not wish to take the time or effort necessary to review the performance of the purchaser. This is analogous to the ostrich putting his head in the sand.

The second source of information that could be required of the purchaser is an independent review of the assets by the seller. This may be particularly important if the main assets securing the unpaid portion of the sales price are those that can be easily dissipated, such as inventory or receivables. In these cases, the seller can require a physical inventory be taken by the purchaser and the seller on an annual, semiannual, or quarterly basis. This will ensure that on a "periodic basis" the inventory of the business is being properly reported. If this information is utilized in conjunction with the financial statements that have been prepared, it will be possible for the seller to spot any irregularities.

Another common way to monitor the business after the sale is to supply the seller with financial statements prepared by an independent certified public accountant. There are three different classifications of these statements. It is important to know what each does and does not do. The amount of reliance that a seller can place on these statements depends on the representations made by the CPA.

The first type of representation is contained in a compilation statement. A compilation statement is nothing more than the financial information prepared by management that is put into a form that is recognized by accountants. There are no affirmative checks performed by the CPA. There may be some obligation on the CPA not to prepare a compilation if he knows or has reason to believe that the information is inaccurate. This is of small comfort to the seller.

The second type is the audit. In an audit, the independent certified public accountant represents that he has performed certain tests on the correctness of the inventory and the receivables, and has further performed a review of the internal accounting procedures of the corporation. After performing these tests, the CPA prepares statements that are in conformity with generally accepted accounting standards.

The certified audit is sometimes misconstrued as an indication that the statements are "true and correct." This is a misstatement. What it does indicate is that the independent accountant has verified the method of taking receivables and inventory and has performed other auditing procedures to determine whether or not there are any deviations from standard practices. This is a relatively sophisticated procedure and involves applying numerous audit techniques.

A certified audit conducted by a competent CPA is usually a good indication of the results of operation and the financial condition of the corporation for the relevant period. The problem with the certified audit is twofold. The first is cost. The man-hours necessary to verify inventory and receivables and perform the other auditing functions carry a high cost. In addition, the purchaser may not want to give up the flexibility of reporting the financial information as he deems appropriate. Accordingly, the purchaser may be hesitant to obligate himself to supplying a certified audit.

In between the compilation and certified audit is the third type or review. The review is more than a compilation but less than an audit. It does not require the active participation by the independent CPA in taking the inventory or checking the receivables; however, it does provide for certain positive audit functions. Many times this is mutually acceptable to the seller and to the purchaser.

In addition to the requirement for the supplying of information, there is an indirect method to ensure that the information being received is true and correct. It is so obvious that many times it is overlooked. This is for the seller to remain an employee in a sensitive financial position with the purchaser. In the proper situation, this can smooth over many problems.

> **Example:** Two sisters and a brother owned a corporation. One sister was active and was the chief executive officer. She had three children who were in the business. One sister was an inactive shareholder. The unmarried brother was the treasurer of the corporation. The children wished to purchase the business. The oldest sister, who was the chief executive officer, wished to sell.
>
> As it was impossible to purchase all the stock of the individual shareholders for cash, a portion of the purchase price was to be financed with long term installment notes. The problem in this particular case was that the brother felt insecure as to the future of the business in the hands of "his sisters' children." His reluctance was a stumbling block in the negotiation process. Once the real reason for his reluctance was ascertained, the solution became obvious. He signed an employment contract with the corporation which guaranteed that he would retain his position as treasurer for five years. He felt that if they operated the business successfully for five years, they would succeed. The indirect check solved the stalemate that had developed. An additional bonus was that the expertise of the seller became available to the purchasers.

GUIDELINES FOR DETERMINING WHEN FOLLOW-UP IS NEEDED

Not all transactions are clean. A clean transaction for this purpose is defined as a transaction that encompasses all the assets of the selling business. For example, there may be the operating corporate assets as well as the land and buildings owned by the individual shareholders. The purchasers may have sufficient capital to purchase the operating assets but do not wish to become encumbered with an obligation to also purchase the land and buildings. The two most obvious reasons for their hesitancy are:

1. It is not the best usage of their money.
2. They may at a later date wish to move the business to another location.

As it is usually in the seller's best interest to sell all the assets whenever possible, the lines of communication should be kept open. If there is no continuing obligation other than to "tie up these loose ends," many opportunities to sell these remaining assets may be lost.

The reason the seller is interested in selling all of the assets and does not want to retain the land and building is that normally they are not readily marketable to other parties. The highest and best use may be the continuation of the operating business on the property. Also, older individuals have no real desire to continue as landlords after they have disposed of their operating businesses.

The second reason that some follow-up may be suggested is to maintain the goodwill of the purchaser. This usually occurs where only one segment of the business is sold. In these situations, some sort of continuing contact may be beneficial. The extent and type of this contact will depend on the particular facts arising from the sale.

WHEN FOLLOW-UP MAY BE NOT ONLY MEANINGLESS BUT COUNTERPRODUCTIVE

It is extremely difficult for an individual who has run a business for a long time to turn over that business to someone else, particularly in a family situation. Normally, the father or mother has run the show for many years and the next generation "will never run it right." They may be more or less successful depending on the individual facts and circumstances but usually the older generation is uncomfortable with any changes they don't initiate. When the business is being transferred between relatives, the continuation of the retiring individual as an officer or through an employment contract often is counterproductive and leads to family problems. It is usually better in these instances to supply the information on a yearly, semiyearly, or quarterly basis and to have it reviewed in a passive manner rather than active participation.

The same type of problem can occur in a non-family transaction when the portion of the business is sold to a competitor. In this case, if you have adequate security and require additional financial information, the purchaser may not believe that it is for the obvious reason of ensuring payment. In this case, it may be possible to obtain the necessary information from outside sources.

If you have received all your purchase price for cash and the remaining payments to be received by you are a small covenant not-to-compete, the supplying of detailed information may be inappropriate. In these cases, the information that you need may be inexpensively obtained through a Dun and Bradstreet report or some other source that would not necessitate the seller's "meddling into the purchaser's business."

Accordingly, the need for follow-up and the type of follow-up that is appropriate depends on the facts in each individual instance. However, it should be kept in mind that if there is a need, it should not be as an afterthought as there is no inherent obligation on the purchaser to supply the seller with financial or other information even though he may owe money to the seller. All requirements must be set forth in the sales agreement or enabling documentation.

Obviously, the sale or purchase of a corporation is relatively simple once you are initiated into the mechanics of the sales procedure. It is imperative that the owner of the business be schooled to recognize the "appropriate time" to sell. When the time is right, you must guide the entire sales process, from the first step to the "follow-up" discussed in this chapter. The "initiated" and "knowledgable" owner can maximize his return on investment. As with all business decisions, the more you know, the greater the chance for positive results. This book and the following appendices have been designed to provide the "tools for success."

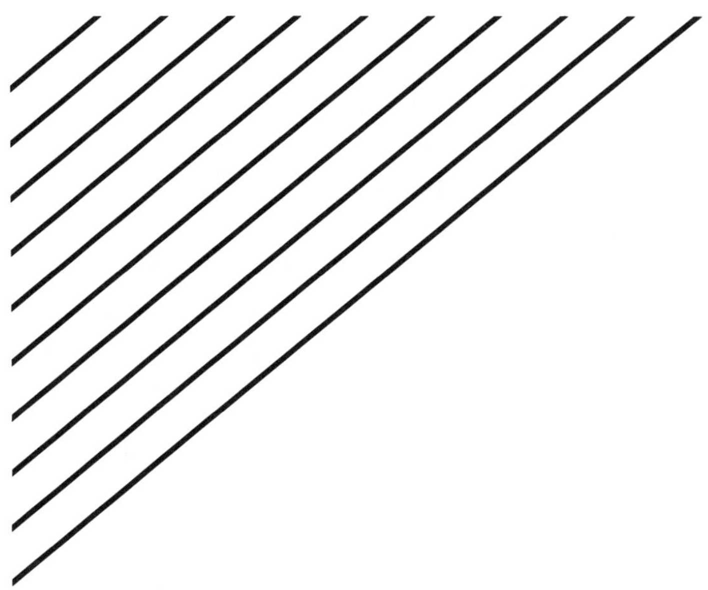

APPENDICES

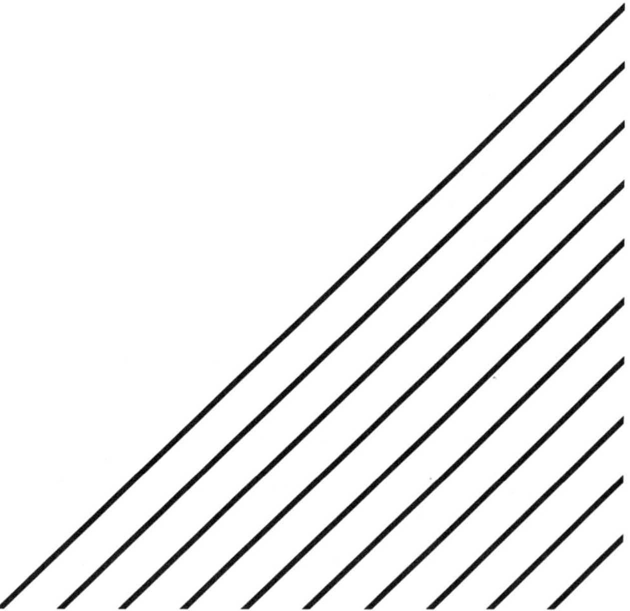

LIST OF APPENDICES

1. Appendix A—Valuation Letter—used to establish a "high reasonable value" for the stock of a minority shareholder.
2. Appendix B—Valuation Letter—setting the highest possible value of the company. The 100 percent owner will use this as a negotiating tool. The prior years low earnings are explained away by stating "the company has turned the corner."
3. Appendix C—Form used to help determine after-tax income both before and after the sale.
4. Appendix D—Annuity Tables determining monthly annuity payments for a single purchase annuity. I have been informed that these are standard tables and that insurance companies will negotiate the rates when substantial sums of money are involved.
5. Appendix E—Tickler Letter. This letter is a response to an inquiry from an outsider. However, it could easily be altered for distribution to potential purchasers. It includes the three basic elements of a tickler letter: (1) explanation of business; (2) summary of financial information; and (3) requested purchase price and terms.
6. Appendix F—Nondisclosure Agreement—indicating the requested information will be used solely to determine whether or not the parties should purchase the business.
7. Appendix G—Letter requesting detailed specific information about the company for sale.
8. Appendix H—Nonbinding Letter of Intent.
9. Appendix I—Letter of Intent that is both legally binding and comprehensive.
10. Appendix J—Comprehensive Sales Agreement for Purchase of Assets.
11. Appendix K—Selective Business Security Agreement
12. Appendix L—Uniform Commercial Code Financing Statement
13. Appendix M—Agreement Not-to-Compete

APPENDIX A

Joe Jones
321 Washington
Anywhere, U.S.A.

RE: Worldwide Widgets

Dear Joe:

Pursuant to our conversation of August 1, 1985, I have reviewed the financial statements you have supplied me relative to Worldwide Widgets, hereinafter referred to as "WWW".

This review and analysis is not an in-depth appraisal, nor do I represent myself as an appraiser of businesses such as WWW. I have made assumptions throughout that could, if incorrect, materially affect the value. However, I have attempted to analyze this company's fair market value in light of not only the intrinsic factors which affect the value of the corporation, but also the extrinsic factors that are present. You should be aware that I am not at all familiar with either the products or operations of WWW, and accordingly, I have been unable to add additional insight that could add increased validity to the analysis enclosed.

In addition, I have operating statements and balance sheets in my possession for only the years 1981 through 1984 (see Schedule I). In valuing a corporation, the earnings of the corporation in the current year have the greatest impact on its value, and these figures, even on a monthly basis, have not been submitted to me. For the calculations contained herein, I have utilized the information supplied to you that sales and the gross profits are reduced by about 30%, and the net income will be approximately 50% of what it was in 1984. If the actual accounting data indicates different gross sales and net profits, this could again materially affect the stock's fair market value.

I am sure that you do not need me to tell you that WWW is an extremely profitable and financially well-situated manufacturing company. For the period 1981 through 1984, the gross sales of the company have increased, compounded at a rate greater than 10%, and the net after-tax income of the corporation has also increased, compounded by just less than 10%. In addition, the dividend payments have increased by over 265% in that period. In all cases, I would assume that the current operations for 1985, as reflected on their statements, would materially affect the extremely favorable picture that was portrayed for the period 1981 through 1984. During this entire period, there was uninterrupted growth, except for the year 1983. I do not know the reason for this interruption, but I am sure that you have this information available.

The current market situation appears to be at best unsettled. Manufacturing companies generally have been depressed, and the historical basis for valuing corporations as a multiple of earnings has gone under complete reappraisal for two reasons. Firstly, few are pure manufacturing corporations. Secondly, those that fall into that category are extremely depressed and may have little or no earnings. Accordingly, the market place, according to the stockbrokers that I have talked to, has been valuing the manufacturing companies on anticipated earnings rather than actual earnings. To have a corporation such as WWW, which has substantial real earnings during 1985, is somewhat of an anomaly.

There are certain factors that become readily apparent:

1. Book value must be adjusted for certain factors. The assumptions that I have made in determining these adjustments are set forth on Schedule III. Both the assumptions and method may be subject to question.

2. The book income should be adjusted to reflect certain tax-oriented decisions that were made by the corporation which materially distorted the actual income on the financial statements. The major adjustment is the LIFO inventory adjustment. LIFO has a tendency to undervalue the net income of the corporation and also undervalue its book value. An analysis of the correct book income is set forth on Schedule II.

3. For the period 1981 through 1984, as indicated above, the corporation has been growing at a compounded rate of approximately 10% per year. During 1985, there has been a significant decrease in both gross sales and net profit. Accordingly, in ascertaining the fair market value of the company using an earnings approach, it is necessary to weight the later years heavier than the first. An analysis of this procedure is set forth on Schedule IV.

4. Usually, in valuing a corporation, a multiple of dividends is an appropriate tool. However, because of the nature of a closely held corporation wherein dividends are used only as a last resort, I did not feel this was appropriate. However, you should be aware that for a corporation of this size with the earnings capacity as shown, the payment of just under 25% of its earnings as dividends is a substantial bonus.

5. The only sales that have occurred during the period 1981 through 1984 were your and your brother's sale of approximately

1,000 shares for $175 per share and the purchase by the company in 1984 of 425 shares for $200 per share. Because of the small number of shares that have been purchased and because the sale of these shares may be dictated a great deal by personal motivation rather than actual market valuation, I have disregarded them in this analysis.

The next step in the analysis is to attempt to ascertain a comparable company so that the current price earnings ratio of the company can be applied to the average earnings adjusted as ascertained for WWW. In my research, the only truly comparable, publicly traded company is a corporation known as The Better Widget based in Burbank, California. There are currently three broker/dealers making a market in this company, and it currently is trading between $240 and $260 per share. However, I have attempted, through both stock brokerage houses and directly, to obtain financial information on this corporation, and they have refused to supply it. I will continue in my endeavors to obtain this information, but at this time I will have to proceed in valuing the corporation without the benefit of the financial information of Better Widget Company. Currently the composite Standard & Poor's is between 7½ and 8 times earnings. Those manufacturing corporations that have had a sustained earnings record in the past, even though current earnings have been adversely affected by the economic recession that the country had been selling at a price earnings of between 10 and 11. Accordingly, I have chosen 10 as a proper price earnings ratio to apply (see Schedule IV).

Because you are selling a minority interest and because a vast percentage of the 1,543 shares of stock that are being sold by you is nonvoting stock, I considered that it was necessary to apply both a minority discount and a discount representing the fact that the shares were nonvoting. Accordingly, a total 20% discount was applied on Schedule IV to the value once arrived.

I would appreciate your reviewing the analysis that I have undertaken, pursuant to your conversation, and review the sum and substance of both the assumptions made in my analysis to coordinate same with your own thinking. After said review, please contact me with your further thoughts.

Sincerely,

Lawrence C. Silton

LCS:sjw
Enclosures

ANALYSIS OF WORLDWIDE WIDGETS STOCK AS OF THE END OF DECEMBER 31, 1984, BASED ON INFORMATION CONTAINED IN FINANCIAL STATEMENTS OF WORLDWIDE WIDGETS AND 1985 INFORMATION AS SUPPLIED BY OFFICERS

Summary of Financial Information of WorldWide Widgets for the Period of 1981 through 1985.

	1981	1982	1983	1984	1985
Sales	$129,590,444.00	$143,978,258.00	$142,813,647.00	$176,227,724.00	$123,200,000.00 (est.)
Gross Profit	25,478,452.00	26,977,649.00	23,272,772.00	28,381,541.00	(unknown)
Gross Profit Percentage	19%	18%	16%	16%	(unknown)
Net Income (After Tax)	7,983,835.00	8,647,772.00	6,704,050.00	8,498,376.00	4,200,000.00 (est.)
Income per Share	39.25	42.65	33.12	42.06	21.00
Dividends per Share (approx.)	4.50	6.50	8.00	10.00	(unknown)
Outstanding Shares (End of Year)	203,397.00	202,397.00	202,397.00	201,972.00	201,972.00

Schedule I

ANALYSIS OF THE EARNINGS OF WORLDWIDE WIDGETS
FOR THE YEARS 1978 THROUGH 1982—ADJUSTED

	1981	1982	1983	1984	1985 (est.)
Net Income (After Tax)	$7,983,835.00	$8,647,772.00	$6,704,050.00	$8,498,376.00	$4,200,000.00
Add					
LIFO Inventory Adjustment*	898,000.00	1,670,000.00	2,401,000.00	2,035,000.00	
Other Adjustments	6,458.00	–0–	(410,000.00)		
Gross Adjustments:	904,458.00	1,670,000.00	1,991,000.00		
Less:					
Tax Effect (50%)	452,229.00	835,000.00	995,500.00	1,017,500.00	
Net Income Increase or (Decrease)	452,229.00	835,000.00	995,500.00	1,017,500.00	
Adjusted Net Income (After Tax)	8,436,064.00	9,482,772.00	7,699,550.00	9,515,876.00	4,200,000.00
Adjusted Net Income per Share	41.48	46.74	38.04	47.07	21.00

*LIFO Inventory does not properly match expenses to income, and accordingly, adjustment should be made to properly reflect the income for each and every year. LIFO Inventory has a tendency to depress income and depress the real value of a corporation.

Schedule II

CURRENT BOOK VALUE ADJUSTED FOR THE FAIR MARKET VALUE OF THE ASSETS

ASSUMPTIONS:

1. That the inventory valued at LIFO must be revalued at lower of cost or market FIFO to adequately reflect the true market value.

2. Much of the plant and equipment has increased in value at current replacement cost. Accordingly, assume that the current cost (fair market value of new equipment depreciated for use) would be the current net value of the plant and equipment plus the depreciation to date.

Book Value as of 12/31/84	$47,705,749.00
Additions:	
LIFO Inventory Increase	10,965,000.00
Plant and Equipment	6,604,430.00
Adjusted Book Value as of 12/31/84	$65,275,179.00
Adjusted Book Value per Share 12/31/84	$ 323.19
Plus Income Earned During 1985	21.00
Anticipated Book Value as of 12/31/85	$ 344.19

SCHEDULE III

FAIR MARKET COMPUTATION

COMPUTATION:

Year Ended December 31	*Earnings Per Share*	*Weight*	*Total*
1985	$ 21.00	5	$105.00
1984	47.07	4	188.28
1983	38.04	3	114.12
1982	46.74	2	93.48
1981	41.48	1	41.48
			$542.36

$542.36 divided by 15 = $36.16 = Weighted Average Earnings
Weighted Average Earnings of $36.16 × P/E Ratio of 10 = $361.60

WEIGHTING OF EARNING VALUE AND BOOK VALUE PER SHARE:

Earning Value of 10 P/E Ratio:	$361.60 × 5 =	$1,808.00
Book Value at 12/31/79: Adjusted	$344.19 × 1/6 =	344.19
		$2,152.19
Computed Value:	$2,152.19 divided by 6 =	$ 358.70
Discount:		
Marketability and Nonvoting Stock Discount		(71.74)
Price per Share:		$ 286.96
Number of Shares Owned by Joe Jones:		
1543 of Class A and Class B		
Fair Market Value of Joe's Stock Considering All Factors:		$442,779.28

SCHEDULE IV

APPENDIX B

Joe Owner
Widget Inc.
111 Main Street
Anywhere, USA

RE: Widget Inc.

Dear Joe:

Pursuant to our prior conversations, I have reviewed the financial statements you have supplied me with relative to Widget Inc., an Illinois corporation hereinafter referred to as Widget.

This review and analysis is not an in-depth appraisal, nor do I represent myself as an appraiser of businesses such as Widget. I have made assumptions throughout that could, if incorrect, materially affect the value. However, I have attempted to analyze this company's fair market value in light of not only the intrinsic factors which affect the value of the corporation, but also the extrinsic factors that are present.

You should be aware that while I am familiar with the products manufactured by your company as well as its methods of distribution of its merchandise, your company is substantially different than other corporations in the widget industry. This factor makes obtaining a reasonable fair market value of the corporation extremely difficult.

In addition, I have been informed by you that there has been a substantial turnaround in the operating income and profits of the corporation. You indicated to me that currently approximately 40 percent of the equipment owned by Widget Inc., is not on location. In addition, during the past three or four years substantial accounts of the company have either gone out of business or redirected their merchandising in such a way that they no longer use your machines. Both factors have had a tendency to depress the income and profits for the years 1981 and 1982.

During 1984, new accounts have been obtained, and there is reason to believe that the current machines owned by the company, which are currently being refurbished, can be placed on location within the next year without incurring substantial additional costs.

Since you have further indicated to me that the profits of the company are derived not so much from the sales of the manufacturing equipment, but from the sale of merchandise, it will be possible to increase your income substantially without incurring any further manufacturing cost.

The ability to project exactly how greatly this will affect the profitability is, of course, purely conjecture since it is dependent upon many factors unknown at this time, among which are: who will lease the widgets, how much cost will be incurred in leasing them, the profitability of each and every location. Therefore, I was placed in a dilemma. If I valued the corporation solely on the past financial data for the years 1980 through 1984, the value would probably be substantially less than Widget's fair market value. On the other hand, in using projected financial information based upon assumption not fully grounded in financial history, a value could be arrived at that was inappropriate.

In discussing this dilemma with you, I indicated it was my own personal feeling that a valuation at this time can only result in an approximation of the fair market value of Widget. Since you indicated to me, notwithstanding my concern in this matter, that you wished me to proceed, I tried to develop a value based on both the prior financial information and the current projections. The manner of accomplishing this was to utilize the actual financial data for the years 1981 through 1984 and to annualize the March 31, 1985, financial information. As far as I have been informed, the annualization should be appropriate since normally your company's quarters are not cyclical.

The current market situation appears to be at best unsettled. The vending companies in the past have been subjects to acquisition and during 1984 there appeared to be only two companies that were anywhere comparable to Widget. These companies were ABC International and Widgets Forever. Later in this letter I will discuss how the valuation of Widget is affected by these two companies.

However, before discussing the applicability of comparing these companies, I think there are certain factors that become readily apparent:

1. Book value must be adjusted for certain factors. The assumptions that I have made in determining these adjustments are set forth on Schedule III. The biggest single adjustment relative to the book value also impacts upon the book income. The method of accounting in the past has had a tendency to expense rather than capitalize manufacturing costs. Therefore, the widgets owned by the company have been substantially undervalued. In expensing cost that probably should have been capitalized, the book income has been understated. Accordingly, an adjustment has been made to the book

value for the difference between the depreciated book value and the replacement costs of these widgets. Also, it has been the practice of Widget to expense parts, and work in progress. The officers of the company have informed me that the approximate fair market value using lower of cost or market is $250,000 for these items. The final adjustment made to book value was represented by the net effect of the deferred income account that is represented on the March 31, 1985, balance sheet at $328,758. This represents the unrealized portion of the installment gain on various items of equipment. In presenting the actual book value of the corporation, it would appear that 70 percent of this deferred income account or $230,130 should be added to the book value. It should also be noted that the adjusted book value is based on a going concern basis. There is no realistic way to determine a liquidation value for Widget. Both the assumptions and the method may be subject to question.

2. The book income should be adjusted to reflect certain tax-oriented decisions that were made by the corporation which materially distorted the actual income on the financial statements. The major adjustments are as follows:

a) It has been estimated that certain costs and expenses could be saved by a purchaser of the business. These costs and expenses are in the form of fringe benefits for the officers of the corporation.

b) As indicated above, the method of accounting has been to expense certain manufacturing costs that probably should have been capitalized. This has resulted in additional expenses during the years in question. For the purposes of simplification this has been characterized as "book depreciation over economic depreciation." In reality this probably should have been categorized as "book expenses that should have been capitalized."

c) An analysis of the correct book income is set forth on Schedule II.

3. Historically, it has been appropriate to weight in determining a value, based upon the earnings approach, the current year's earnings over prior earnings. This is appropriate in a case such as yours where your business had been in the dulldrums for a number of years. The reason for the dulldrums, as I understand it, was the changing nature of your business, the need to find new accounts, and the adverse impact that your business suffered because of the increased cost of distribution. It would appear that time has eliminated or mitigated the impact of many of the negative factors. Accordingly, in ascertaining the fair market value of Widget using an earnings approach, I have weighted the later years heavier than the

first, and in addition, have included projected earnings for the year 1985. An analysis of this procedure is set forth on Schedule IV.

The next step in the analysis is to attempt to ascertain a comparable company so that the current price earnings ratio of the company can be applied to the average earnings adjusted as ascertained for widget. In my research, the only semi-comparable companies were ABC International and Widgets Forever. For your information, ABC International was purchased through a leveraged buy out at the end of 1984 based on approximately 15 times its earnings. Currently, Widgets Forever is selling at 11½ or 60 times its price earnings ratio. Obviously the widget industry has received increased attention from the public, which is reflected in its high PE ratio. With the instability of the current market place and the lack of truly comparable companies, I was pressed to determine an appropriate price earnings ratio. Accordingly, I chose a price earnings ratio of 15 to determine the value of Widget (see Schedule IV).

I would appreciate your reviewing this analysis and the assumptions that I have made to see if any of them are inappropriate. At the risk of being repetitive, I truly believe that a determination of value at this time is both difficult and probably not in the shareholders of Widget's best interest.

As indicated, in order to attempt to determine a fair market value that is realistic, I have had to work with projected figures, which is not the historical method of valuing corporations. In addition, it is always in the selling shareholder's best interest to sell a corporation at the top of its earnings curve. Everything that you have indicated would lead me to believe that the corporation is currently in a turnaround situation. The projected earnings without the expenditure of any substantial sum of money should substantially increase in the next two to three years. The sole positive benefit of attempting to sell currently for the selling shareholders, is that the market is currently valuing vending companies at substantial premiums. Obviously, they are anticipating that not only is your company in a turnaround situation, but the entire vending industry is in an upswing, and the future profits should be substantially above the current profits.

After you have had an opportunity to review this, I would appreciate your contacting me.

Sincerely,

Lawrence C. Silton

LCS:sjw
Enclosures

ANALYSIS OF WIDGETS, INC. STOCK AS OF JULY 31, 1985
BASED ON INFORMATION CONTAINED IN FINANCIAL STATEMENTS OF WIDGET, INC.
AND 1985 INFORMATION AS SUPPLIED BY OFFICERS

Summary of Financial Information of Widgets, Inc. for the Period 1981 through Projections for the Year 1985.

	1981	1982	1983	1984	Projected 1985
Sales	$1,696,618.00	$1,514,817.00	$1,327,065.00	$1,293,477.00	$1,486,452.00
Gross Profit	803,519.00	683,069.00	620,656.00	755,416.00	825,580.00
Gross Profit Percentage	47.90%	45.90%	47.00%	58.40%	56.90%
Net Income (or Loss) After Tax	(45,926.00)	(48,714.00)	2,378.00	3,142.00	124,600.00 **
Income (Loss) Per Share*	(183.70)	(194.86)	9.51	12.57	498.40

* During the entire period in question there were 250 shares of Common Stock outstanding.

** For the projections in 1985, I assumed an effective Federal and State Tax rate of 30 percent. The corporation does have an investment credit carryover.

Schedule I

ANALYSIS OF THE EARNINGS OF WIDGETS, INC.
FOR THE YEARS 1981 THROUGH 1985 PROJECTED—ADJUSTED

	1981	1982	1983	1984	1985 (est.)
Net Income (or Loss) After Tax	($45,926.00)	($48,714.00)	$62,378.00	$83,142.00	$124,600.00
Add					
Expenses that Can be Eliminated by Purchaser	55,000.00	55,000.00	65,000.00	75,000.00	75,000.00
Excess of Book Depreciation Over Economic Depreciation	68,642.00	30,404.00	38,301.00	42,000.00	42,000.00
Tax Effect	(17,836.00)	(5,854.00)	(30,990.00)	(35,100.00)	(35,100.00)
Net Income Increase or (Decrease)	105,806.00	79,550.00	72,311.00	81,900.00	81,900.00
Adjusted Net Income (After Tax)	59,880.00	30,836.00	134,669.00	165,042.00	206,500.00
Adjusted Net Income Per Share	239.52	123.34	538.75	660.17	826.00

Schedule II

CURRENT BOOK VALUE ADJUSTED FOR THE FAIR MARKET VALUE OF THE ASSETS

ASSUMPTIONS:

1. Management considers that the receivables set forth on the balance sheet are all collectible except as set forth on the Financial Statement. However, the amount due from the franchisee may contain bad debts, and accordingly 10 percent has been deducted to reflect possible uncollectibles.
2. The fair market value of the vending machines owned are substantially greater than the depreciated book value shown on the books. Management estimates that the current manufacturing cost of a No. 400 vending machine is $800. The current cost of a robot is $1,200, and the current cost of the revolving valet is $80. The company owns 951 No. 400 widget vending machines, 618 robot widgets, and 224 revolving valet widgets. Accordingly, the total replacement costs of the vending equipment is $1,536,320. This is $1,290,514 in excess of book value, and accordingly the fair market value for the corporation should be adjusted for that factor.

Book Value as of 3/31/85	$ 479,926.00
Reduction in Value by Reason of Possible Uncollectible Debts	(54,355.00)
Additions	
Equipment Owned by Corporation in Excess of Book Value	1,290,514.00
Inventory of Parts, Work in Process, and Other Items Previously Expensed	250,000.00
Net After-tax Effect of Deferred Gain	230,130.00
Adjusted Book Value as of 3/31/85	$2,196,235.00
Adjusted Book Value per Share 3/31/85	$ 8,784.94

Schedule III

FAIR MARKET COMPUTATION

COMPUTATION:

Year Ended December 31	*Earnings per Share*	*Weight*	*Total*
Projected 1985	$826.00	5	$4,130.00
1984	660.17	4	2,640.68
1983	538.75	3	1,616.25
1982	123.34	2	246.68
1981	239.52	1	239.52
			$8,873.13

$8,873.13 divided by 15 = $591.54 = Weighted Average Earnings

Weighted Average Earnings of $580.13 × P/E Ratio of 15 = $ 8,873.13

WEIGHTING OF EARNING VALUE AND BOOK VALUE PER SHARE:

Earning Value of 15 P/E Ratio:	$8,873.13 × 5 =	$44,365.50
Book Value at 3/31/85: Adjusted	$8,784.94 × 1 =	8,784.94
		$53,150.44
Computed Value:	$53,150.44 divided by 6 =	$ 8,858.41
Computed per Share Value shall be multiplied by the 250 shares currently issued and oustanding		× 250.00
Fair Market Value of All The Authorized and Issued Common Stock of Widgets, Inc. Considering All Factors:		$2,214,602.50

SCHEDULE IV

APPENDIX C

	Presale Income	Post-Sale Income
Salary		
Interest (1)		
Dividends		
Rental Property Income (Cash Flow)		
Profit Sharing Plan (Joint and Survivor)		
Individual Retirement Account (Joint and Survivor)		
Pension Plan		
Social Security Benefits		
Other Income		
Total Income Before Tax		
Tax Impact		
Net After-tax Income		

NOTE (1): In preparing this particular schedule I would utilize a return of 8 percent on all interest bearing assets even though this may be unreasonably low. In addition, the post-sale income should include the net after-tax funds at 8 percent. For example, if the sales price is $1,000,000 in cash and $200,000 of tax is anticipated, the post-sale income would include $64,000 of additional interest (800,000 × .08).

APPENDIX D

ANNUITY PAYOUT PER $1000 NET AMOUNT
JOINT ANNUITY WITH 100% TO THE SURVIVOR

FOR UNISEX RATES
ASSUME THAT THE YOUNGEST AGE IS FEMALE

	FEMALE AGE							
MALE AGE	10 YRS. LESS	8 YRS. LESS	6 YRS. LESS	4 YRS. LESS	2 YRS. LESS	SAME AGE	2 YRS. MORE	4 YRS. MORE
50	6.98	7.00	7.02	7.05	7.07	7.10	7.13	7.16
51	6.99	7.02	7.04	7.07	7.10	7.13	7.16	7.20
52	7.01	7.04	7.06	7.09	7.12	7.16	7.19	7.23
53	7.03	7.05	7.08	7.12	7.15	7.19	7.23	7.27
54	7.05	7.08	7.11	7.14	7.18	7.22	7.26	7.31
55	7.07	7.10	7.13	7.17	7.21	7.26	7.30	7.35
56	7.09	7.13	7.16	7.20	7.25	7.30	7.34	7.40
57	7.11	7.15	7.19	7.24	7.29	7.34	7.39	7.45
58	7.14	7.18	7.23	7.28	7.33	7.38	7.44	7.50
59	7.17	7.22	7.26	7.32	7.37	7.43	7.50	7.56
60	7.20	7.25	7.30	7.36	7.42	7.49	7.56	7.63
61	7.24	7.29	7.35	7.41	7.48	7.55	7.62	7.70
62	7.27	7.33	7.39	7.46	7.53	7.61	7.69	7.78
63	7.31	7.38	7.44	7.52	7.60	7.68	7.77	7.86
64	7.36	7.42	7.50	7.58	7.67	7.76	7.86	7.96
65	7.40	7.48	7.56	7.65	7.74	7.84	7.95	8.06
66	7.45	7.54	7.63	7.72	7.83	7.93	8.05	8.17
67	7.51	7.60	7.70	7.80	7.91	8.03	8.16	8.29
68	7.57	7.67	7.77	7.89	8.01	8.14	8.28	8.42
69	7.64	7.74	7.86	7.98	8.12	8.26	8.41	8.56
70	7.71	7.82	7.95	8.08	8.23	8.39	8.55	8.72
71	7.78	7.91	7.05	8.20	8.36	8.53	8.70	8.89
72	7.87	8.01	8.15	8.32	8.49	8.68	8.87	9.07
73	7.96	8.11	8.27	8.45	8.64	8.84	9.06	9.27
74	8.06	8.22	8.40	8.59	8.80	9.02	9.25	9.49

ANNUITY PAYOUT PER $1000 NET AMOUNT
JOINT ANNUITY WITH ⅔ TO THE SURVIVOR

FOR UNISEX RATES
ASSUME THAT THE YOUNGEST AGE IS FEMALE

	FEMALE AGE							
MALE AGE	10 YRS. LESS	8 YRS. LESS	6 YRS. LESS	4 YRS. LESS	2 YRS. LESS	SAME AGE	2 YRS. MORE	4 YRS. MORE
50	7.24	7.27	7.29	7.32	7.35	7.39	7.43	7.47
51	7.27	7.30	7.33	7.36	7.39	7.43	7.47	7.52
52	7.30	7.33	7.36	7.40	7.43	7.48	7.52	7.58
53	7.34	7.37	7.40	7.44	7.48	7.52	7.57	7.63
54	7.38	7.41	7.44	7.48	7.53	7.58	7.63	7.69
55	7.42	7.45	7.49	7.53	7.58	7.63	7.69	7.76
56	7.46	7.50	7.54	7.58	7.63	7.69	7.76	7.83
57	7.50	7.54	7.59	7.64	7.69	7.76	7.82	7.90
58	7.55	7.60	7.64	7.70	7.76	7.83	7.90	7.98
59	7.61	7.65	7.70	7.76	7.83	7.90	7.98	8.07
60	7.66	7.71	7.77	7.83	7.90	7.98	8.07	8.17
61	7.72	7.78	7.84	7.91	7.99	8.07	8.17	8.27
62	7.79	7.85	7.92	7.99	8.07	8.17	8.27	8.39
63	7.86	7.93	8.00	8.08	8.17	8.27	8.38	8.51
64	7.94	8.01	8.09	8.18	8.27	8.38	8.51	8.64
65	8.02	8.10	8.18	8.28	8.39	8.51	8.64	8.78
66	8.11	8.19	8.29	8.39	8.51	8.64	8.78	8.94
67	8.20	8.29	8.40	8.51	8.64	8.78	8.93	9.11
68	8.31	8.40	8.52	8.64	8.78	8.93	9.10	9.29
69	8.41	8.52	8.64	8.78	8.93	9.10	9.28	9.49
70	8.53	8.65	8.78	8.93	9.09	9.28	9.48	9.71
71	8.66	8.78	8.93	9.09	9.27	9.47	9.69	9.94
72	8.79	8.93	9.09	9.26	9.46	9.68	9.92	10.19
73	8.93	9.09	9.26	9.45	9.67	9.91	10.17	10.46
74	9.09	9.25	9.44	9.65	9.89	10.15	10.44	10.76

ANNUITY PAYOUT PER $1000 NET AMOUNT
JOINT ANNUITY WITH 10 YR. CERT.
WITH 100% TO THE SURVIVOR

FOR UNISEX RATES
ASSUME THAT THE YOUNGEST AGE IS FEMALE

	FEMALE AGE							
MALE AGE	10 YRS. LESS	8 YRS. LESS	6 YRS. LESS	4 YRS. LESS	2 YRS. LESS	SAME AGE	2 YRS. MORE	4 YRS. MORE
50	6.98	7.00	7.02	7.05	7.07	7.10	7.13	7.16
51	6.99	7.02	7.04	7.07	7.10	7.13	7.16	7.20
52	7.01	7.04	7.06	7.09	7.12	7.16	7.19	7.23
53	7.03	7.05	7.08	7.12	7.15	7.19	7.23	7.27
54	7.05	7.08	7.11	7.14	7.18	7.22	7.26	7.31
55	7.07	7.10	7.13	7.17	7.21	7.26	7.30	7.35
56	7.09	7.13	7.16	7.20	7.25	7.29	7.34	7.39
57	7.11	7.15	7.19	7.24	7.29	7.34	7.39	7.44
58	7.14	7.18	7.23	7.28	7.33	7.38	7.44	7.50
59	7.17	7.21	7.26	7.32	7.37	7.43	7.49	7.56
60	7.20	7.25	7.30	7.36	7.42	7.48	7.55	7.62
61	7.23	7.29	7.34	7.41	7.48	7.54	7.61	7.69
62	7.27	7.33	7.39	7.46	7.53	7.60	7.68	7.76
63	7.31	7.37	7.44	7.51	7.59	7.67	7.76	7.85
64	7.35	7.42	7.49	7.57	7.66	7.75	7.84	7.93
65	7.40	7.47	7.55	7.64	7.73	7.82	7.92	8.03
66	7.45	7.53	7.62	7.71	7.81	7.91	8.02	8.13
67	7.50	7.59	7.68	7.78	7.89	8.00	8.12	8.24
68	7.56	7.65	7.75	7.86	7.98	8.10	8.23	8.36
69	7.62	7.72	7.83	7.95	8.08	8.21	8.35	8.48
70	7.69	7.80	7.92	8.05	8.18	8.32	8.47	8.62
71	7.76	7.88	8.01	8.15	8.29	8.45	8.60	8.76
72	7.84	7.97	8.11	8.26	8.42	8.58	8.74	8.90
73	7.92	8.06	8.21	8.37	8.54	8.72	8.89	9.06
74	8.01	8.16	8.33	8.50	8.68	8.86	9.05	9.22

ANNUITY PAYOUT PER $1000 NET AMOUNT
JOINT ANNUITY WITH 10 YR. CERT.
WITH ⅔ TO THE SURVIVOR

FOR UNISEX RATES
ASSUME THAT THE YOUNGEST AGE IS FEMALE

	FEMALE AGE							
MALE AGE	10 YRS. LESS	8 YRS. LESS	6 YRS. LESS	4 YRS. LESS	2 YRS. LESS	SAME AGE	2 YRS. MORE	4 YRS. MORE
50	7.21	7.23	7.25	7.28	7.31	7.34	7.38	7.42
51	7.24	7.26	7.28	7.31	7.35	7.38	7.42	7.47
52	7.26	7.29	7.32	7.35	7.38	7.42	7.46	7.51
53	7.30	7.32	7.35	7.39	7.42	7.46	7.51	7.56
54	7.33	7.36	7.39	7.43	7.47	7.51	7.56	7.61
55	7.36	7.39	7.43	7.47	7.51	7.56	7.61	7.67
56	7.40	7.43	7.47	7.51	7.56	7.61	7.67	7.73
57	7.44	7.48	7.52	7.56	7.61	7.67	7.73	7.80
58	7.48	7.52	7.57	7.62	7.67	7.73	7.80	7.87
59	7.53	7.57	7.62	7.67	7.73	7.79	7.87	7.94
60	7.58	7.62	7.68	7.73	7.79	7.86	7.94	8.02
61	7.63	7.68	7.73	7.80	7.86	7.94	8.02	8.11
62	7.69	7.74	7.80	7.86	7.94	8.02	8.10	8.20
63	7.74	7.80	7.87	7.94	8.02	8.10	8.20	8.30
64	7.81	7.87	7.94	8.01	8.10	8.19	8.29	8.40
65	7.87	7.94	8.01	8.10	8.19	8.29	8.39	8.51
66	7.94	8.01	8.10	8.18	8.28	8.39	8.50	8.62
67	8.02	8.09	8.18	8.28	8.38	8.50	8.62	8.75
68	8.09	8.18	8.27	8.37	8.49	8.61	8.74	8.87
69	8.17	8.27	8.37	8.48	8.60	8.73	8.87	9.01
70	8.26	8.36	8.47	8.59	8.71	8.85	9.00	9.15
71	8.35	8.46	8.57	8.70	8.84	8.98	9.14	9.29
72	8.44	8.56	8.68	8.82	8.97	9.12	9.28	9.44
73	8.54	8.67	8.80	8.95	9.10	9.26	9.43	9.59
74	8.65	8.78	8.92	9.08	9.24	9.41	9.58	9.75

PAYOUTS PER $1,000 NET AMOUNT
SINGLE LIFE ANNUITY RATES
FOR UNISEX RATES USE THE FEMALE RATES

	LIFE ONLY		LIFE 5 Y.C.		LIFE 10 Y.C.		LIFE 15 Y.C.		LIFE 20 Y.C.		CASH REFUND		INST REFUND	
AGE	MALE	FEMALE	MALE	FEMALE	MALE	FEMALE	MALE	FEMALE	MALE	FEMALE	MALE	FEMALE	MALE	FEMALE
50	7.70	7.39	7.67	7.38	7.60	7.34	7.51	7.30	7.41	7.25	7.54	7.31	7.59	7.34
51	7.76	7.43	7.73	7.42	7.65	7.38	7.55	7.33	7.44	7.28	7.59	7.35	7.64	7.37
52	7.82	7.48	7.79	7.46	7.70	7.42	7.59	7.37	7.47	7.31	7.64	7.39	7.69	7.41
53	7.89	7.53	7.85	7.51	7.76	7.47	7.64	7.41	7.51	7.34	7.69	7.43	7.75	7.46
54	7.96	7.58	7.92	7.56	7.82	7.51	7.69	7.45	7.54	7.37	7.75	7.47	7.81	7.50
55	8.04	7.64	8.00	7.62	7.89	7.57	7.74	7.49	7.58	7.40	7.81	7.52	7.87	7.55
56	8.12	7.70	8.07	7.68	7.95	7.62	7.80	7.54	7.62	7.44	7.88	7.57	7.94	7.61
57	8.21	7.77	8.16	7.74	8.03	7.68	7.85	7.59	7.66	7.48	7.95	7.63	8.02	7.66
58	8.31	7.84	8.25	7.81	8.10	7.74	7.91	7.64	7.70	7.52	8.02	7.68	8.10	7.73
59	8.41	7.92	8.35	7.89	8.19	7.80	7.97	7.69	7.74	7.56	8.10	7.75	8.18	7.79
60	8.53	8.00	8.46	7.97	8.27	7.87	8.04	7.75	7.78	7.60	8.19	7.81	8.27	7.86
61	8.65	8.09	8.57	8.05	8.37	7.95	8.10	7.81	7.82	7.64	8.28	7.88	8.37	7.94
62	8.79	8.19	8.69	8.14	8.47	8.03	8.17	7.87	7.86	7.69	8.38	7.96	8.48	8.02
63	8.93	8.29	8.83	8.24	8.57	8.11	8.24	7.94	7.90	7.73	8.48	8.04	8.59	8.11
64	9.09	8.41	8.97	8.35	8.68	8.20	8.31	8.01	7.93	7.78	8.59	8.13	8.71	8.20
65	9.26	8.53	9.12	8.47	8.79	8.30	8.38	8.08	7.97	7.82	8.70	8.23	8.84	8.30
66	9.44	8.66	9.28	8.59	8.91	8.40	8.45	8.15	8.01	7.87	8.82	8.33	8.97	8.41
67	9.64	8.81	9.46	8.73	9.03	8.51	8.52	8.23	8.04	7.91	8.95	8.44	9.12	8.53
68	9.85	8.97	9.64	8.87	9.16	8.63	8.59	8.31	8.07	7.95	9.09	8.55	9.27	8.65
69	10.07	9.14	9.84	9.03	9.29	8.75	8.66	8.38	8.10	7.99	9.23	8.68	9.43	8.79
70	10.32	9.32	10.04	9.20	9.42	8.88	8.73	8.46	8.13	8.03	9.39	8.81	9.60	8.93
71	10.58	9.53	10.26	9.38	9.56	9.02	8.80	8.55	8.15	8.07	9.55	8.95	9.78	9.09
72	10.86	9.75	10.49	9.58	9.70	9.16	8.86	8.63	8.17	8.10	9.72	9.11	9.98	9.26
73	11.16	9.99	10.73	9.79	9.83	9.31	8.92	8.70	8.19	8.13	9.89	9.27	10.18	9.44
74	11.48	10.26	10.99	10.02	9.97	9.46	8.98	8.78	8.21	8.16	10.08	9.45	10.40	9.63
75	11.83	10.55	11.26	10.27	10.11	9.61	9.03	8.85	8.22	8.18	10.28	9.63	10.63	9.84

APPENDIX E

December 10, 1985

Mr. William Smith
Consultants to Management
123 Main Street
Houston, TX

Dear Mr. Smith:

Your letter dated August 8, 1985, directed to Joe Seller, president of Bambi Blasters, Inc., has been forwarded to me for response. You should be aware that the business conducted by Bambi Blasters, Inc., is currently not being offered for sale. However, in discussing your letter with the principals, if an appropriate purchase price and terms of sale could be arrived at, they would be interested in selling.

One reason this particular business is not currently for sale is that the principals firmly believe that the full potential of the business will not be realized for a period of between three and five years and accordingly, to sell the business at this time would be premature. To illustrate the prior financial history and the projections, I have enclosed herein excerpts of financial information for the periods ending June 30, 1982, through June 30, 1985, and projected information for the years ended June 30, 1986, and June 30, 1987.

You should be aware that as of January 1, 1985, Bambi Blasters, Inc., went on the national newsstand. Currently, management is anticipating that there will be little gross profit generated directly from newsstand sale; however, the newsstand sales have had the following positive effects:

1. There have been an additional 15,000 new subscriptions generated by the newsstand for the current year. Management has been informed by its outside consultants that the subsequent increase in home-paid subscriptions will not be as significant; however, they still anticipate an increase in home-paid subscriptions of between ten and twelve thousand per year.

2. The increase in readership indicates that they will be able to successfully raise their advertising rates. These rates currently are the lowest in market among competitors. They anticipate that these will be substantially increased in the next couple years. Accordingly, in projecting gross profits for the years 1986 and 1987, the question is whether the increased revenues from advertising will offset the

reduced gross profit from newsstand sales. The answer at this time is not clear; however, to present the financial data on a conservative basis, the gross profit has been reduced. Exhibit B sets forth the home-paid and newsstand sales for the prior three years as well as projections for the years ended June 30, 1986, and June 30, 1987.

Upon review of this financial information, I believe you will agree that this is an extremely successful publication whose full potential has yet to be realized. Accordingly, my clients have determined that they would be interested in a sale only upon the following terms and conditions:

1. A purchase price of $1,750,000.
2. Assets to be sold—all the common stock of Bambi Blasters, Inc.
3. Terms of sale—cash is preferred at closing; however, if this is not possible, a minimum of 30% down must be paid at closing with the remainder to be paid over a term of not more than ten years with appropriate interest and security.
4. Employment contract—my clients realize that the smooth transition of a business such as theirs requires the continuity of management for a period of time. Accordingly, they would be willing to continue to be employed for as long as the purchaser deems necessary as long as they receive adequate compensation.

If your client is interested in pursuing a purchase such as contemplated above, please feel free to contact me. We realize that in addition to the information supplied in this letter, you will need substantial other information. Because of the competitive nature of the industry and because of the sensitivity of the information that we are sure that you will need, prior to the disclosure of any other information, the following will be required:

1. The name of your client.
2. Financial information about your client indicating the capability to purchase my client's business.
3. An agreement that the information supplied is solely for the purpose of purchasing my client's business and will not be used to its competitive disadvantage.

If I can be of any further assistance, please feel free to contact me.

Sincerely,

Lawrence C. Silton

LCS:sjw
Enclosures

EXHIBIT A

	6/30/83	6/30/84	6/30/85	Projected (1) 6/30/86	Projected (1) 6/30/87
Sales	464,149.00	599,729.00	878,634.00	1,783,326.00	2,232,486.00
Gross Profit Percentage	277,013.00	356,870.00	514,589.00	976,684.00	1,211,811.00
Gross Profit	60.90	60.90	59.90	55.90	54.90
Expense without Principals Salaries and Fringe Benefits	101,060.00	197,722.00	326,658.00	375,657.00	432,006.00
Net Income Before Taxes, Principals Salaries and Fringe Benefits	175,953.00	159,148.00	187,931.00	601,027.00	779,805.00

(1) In January of 1985, Bambi Blasters, Inc., went on the national newsstands. This has had a positive effect on both direct sales at the newsstand plus additional sales from home-paid subscriptions.

EXHIBIT B

	6/30/83	6/30/84	6/30/85	Projected (1) 6/30/86	Projected (1) 6/30/87
Home-paid Subscriptions	30,000.00	37,000.00	47,000.00	75,000.00	87,000.00
Newsstand	5,000.00	8,000.00	18,000.00	30,000.00	40,000.00

APPENDIX F

January 10, 1986

Mr. Lawrence C. Silton
PATTERSON, JENSEN, WYLIE,
SILTON & SEIFERT, S.C.
331 East Washington Street
Appleton, WI 54911

Dear Mr. Silton:

Your letter (see Appendix G) dated December 10, 1985, requesting financial and other information relative to WWW of USA, Inc., has been forwarded to me by the company's president, Mr. Jonathon Smith, for response. As I am sure you are aware, your client's company and my client's company are competitors. The detailed information which you have requested in this letter is definitely needed by you if you are to intelligently proceed in making a determination of whether your client is interested in purchasing the agricultural division of my client's business. However, before supplying said documentation certain restrictions must be placed:

1. You and your client acknowledge that the information to be supplied here is confidential and shall not be copied, reproduced, summarized for your purposes or disseminated to any other party.

2. In the event that the purchase is not consumated all documentation supplied to you will be returned and any records that you may have regarding summaries, projections, etc., will be destroyed.

3. The information supplied hereunder will solely be used for the purpose of determining whether or not to purchase my client's business. This information will in no way be utilized to the detriment of my client.

If the above conditions are acceptable to you and your client, I would appreciate his acknowledging acceptance by signing below and returning to me a copy of this letter. Upon receipt of a signed copy, the information requested in your December 10, 1985, letter will be forwarded to you.

Sincerely,

John Q. Attorney

The above conditions are accepted and approved.

WWW of USA, Inc.

BY: ______________________________
Jonathon Smith, President

APPENDIX G

December 10, 1985

Mr. Jonathon Smith
WWW of USA, Inc.
100 Main Street
Anywhere, USA 12345

Dear Mr. Smith:

Our office represents Acquisition, Inc., and during a recent conversation with its president, Mr. B. Dealer, I was informed that your Agricultural Division is for sale. It is my client's understanding that the current properties for sale are the business operated under the name Agricultural Widgets located in Sheboygan, Wisconsin; the business operated under the name Agricultural Widgets of the Southwest located in Fort Worth, Texas; and your Widget Importers Division. These businesses are obviously complimentary to Acquisition, Inc.'s business, and a combination of the two companies would on its face appear to be an appropriate extension of my client's current operation. Accordingly, we discussed the best method to proceed. My client has several alternative methods to approach this acquisition. One would envision Acquisition, Inc., and a lender accomplishing the purchase, and another would be to have Acquisition, Inc., participate in a joint venture with another investor.

My suggestion to Mr. Dealer was that prior to approaching the bank or another investor, we obtain the information hereinafter set forth and have our company accountant, as well as Acquisition, Inc.'s, independent Certified Public Accountants, determine whether or not a combination of the two companies would produce the savings and increase the overall profitability in order to justify the purchase. I realize that my client and your Agricultural Division are competitors, and my client has informed me that all the information that you supply will be used solely for the purpose of purchase and will not be used to your company's competitive disadvantage. If you have prepared an offering circular which contains virtually all the information that I have requested, please supply same. If not, we would appreciate the following information being supplied at the first convenient opportunity:

1. The financial statements for each of the above businesses for the prior five fiscal years, as well as the most current financial statement.

2. A complete description of the assets which are to be part of the sale. If there are any intangible assets that may not be on the books, such as export/import licenses, trademarks, etc., we would appreciate a complete description of these assets.

3. If any of the businesses to be sold own appreciated real or personal property and if an analysis has been made as to its fair market value in excess of book value, a detailed analysis of these assets.

4. A copy of any and all employment contracts between the company and its employees.

5. We have been informed that there currently is no union representing the employees at any of the businesses. If there is a union or if there are any certification proceedings now underway or if you have any indication that any organizational activities have been undertaken, a complete description of the current activity.

6. A list of any and all contingent liabilities which are to be assumed by the purchaser.

7. A list and description of any and all lawsuits or possible claims involving the company which will not be indemnified by the seller.

8. A list of any and all contracts, leases and other documents which may be material and will be assumed by the purchaser.

9. If any customer amounts to more than five percent of your sales, please apprise us of this fact.

10. A statement of whether or not your unemployment compensation fund is positive or negative and the applicable rate at this time.

11. A description of your sales force; how many are full-time employees and how many are manufacturers' representatives. If any of the sales force are not full-time employees of any of the businesses, a description as to how you contemplate their future relationship.

12. Please describe all intercompany sales and/or other transactions, such as leases, purchases, etc.

13. A description of the current corporate financing, including name of bank, terms of repayment, interest rate, security for the loan, and ability to assume these obligations.

14. Payroll records for management employees for the prior five years.

15. A detailed explanation of all fringe benefits available to any and all officers of the company, including, but not limited to, any deferred compensation plans, insurance programs, stock option plans, use of company property, etc.

16. If you are willing to finance any portion of the purchase price, an indication of the terms of financing, including appropriate interest rate, amount to be financed, repayment terms, and security.

17. It is my client's understanding that the businesses are offered as a package and cannot be purchased separately. If that is not the case, please indicate the cost of each of the divisions separately.

18. If the sold businesses and agricultural's are to enter into any additional contracts for the supply of goods or services, please indicate the terms and conditions of these contracts.

Thank you in advance for your prompt attention to this matter.

Sincerely,

Lawrence C. Silton

LCS:sjw
cc: Mr. B. Dealer

APPENDIX H

November 11, 1985

Mr. Steve White
P.O. Box 1111
Oshkosh, WI 54901

RE: Wisconsin Fireworks, Ltd.

Dear Steve:

Pursuant to a conversation I had with Joe Brown, I will attempt in this letter to set forth the sum and substance of any agreement whereby my client would be willing to purchase all the authorized and issued common stock of Wisconsin Fireworks, Ltd., hereinafter referred to as the "Company," from you and your wife, hereinafter collectively referred to as "Seller." If the agreement as outlined herein would be acceptable to you, I would appreciate your signifying your acceptance by signing below where indicated. This will not result in a legally binding agreement; however, it will signify that you have in principle accepted the format by which this sale could be accomplished.

Before a legally binding contract could be entered into, certain matters still must be resolved. Two of the most important are:

1. An amount to be allocated to goodwill. For the purposes of this letter, I will use $10,000; however, this has not been accepted by either you or my client.

2. A fair market value for the furniture and fixtures which, for the purposes of this letter, will be established at $10,000. This figure has not been approved by either party.

The basic method will be an installment sale of the common stock currently owned by you and your wife. At the date of closing, financial statements will be prepared for the Company reflecting the financial condition of the Company at that date. These statements will be prepared according to generally accepted accounting principals utilizing the accrual method of accounting; however, certain adjustments will be made for the purposes of this agreement. The net book value after these adjustments will be referred to as "adjusted book value." The adjustments contemplated are as follows:

1. Inventory will be valued at current market value, distributor cost.

2. A liability will be established for estimated income tax due. This tax liability will be based on federal and state income taxes applicable to the Company's income. The income to the date of closing will be annualized and calculated as a regular corporation and not a Subchapter S corporation. This annualized income shall take into consideration any prepaid or unpaid expense.

3. Goodwill will be reflected.

4. Furniture and fixtures will be reflected at fair market value, not cost.

I. SALE OF STOCK AND COMPUTATION OF PURCHASE PRICE

All the common stock of the company will be sold to Joe Brown, hereinafter referred to as the "Purchaser," for a purchase price to be determined at the "adjusted book value." I have prepared a balance sheet based upon the figures that you have supplied me as the current value of the inventory. I have also utilized the compiled financial statements in my possession as of September 30, 1985, under the assumption that all current liabilities and accruals will be paid by you prior to the date of closing and will be reflected in total under the heading "Note Due to Steve White."

BALANCE SHEET
December 31, 1985

ASSETS:	
Cash	$ 100.00
Accounts Receivable	10,000.00
Inventory	107,500.00
Goodwill	10,000.00
Furniture, Fixtures and Office Supplies	12,400.00
TOTAL ASSETS:	$140,000.00
LIABILITIES AND SHAREHOLDER'S EQUITY:	
Current Liabilities and Accruals	$ 0.00
Note Due to Steve White	100,000.00
Accrued Tax Liability	20,000.00
Adjusted Book Value of Capital Stock:	20,000.00
TOTAL LIABILITIES AND EQUITY:	$140,000.00

The purchase price in our example of $20,000 would be paid as follows:

1. $5,000 in cash at closing;

2. The execution of a promissory note for the remainder of the purchase price payable as follows: Interest at 10% payable in equal monthly installments over a period of nine years.

3. The promissory note due to Steve White by the Company in the approximate amount of $100,000 shall be payable as follows:

i. No money down;
ii. Amortized in one hundred twenty equal monthly installments with interest thereon at the rate of 10% per annum.
iii. This promissory note will be secured by a security agreement covering the inventory, receivables and furniture and fixtures of the Company and the personal signature of Joe Brown. Seller will agree to subordinate his security to a lending institution as long as Purchaser is not in default and the amount of the loan does not exceed $20,000.

II. REPRESENTATIONS AND WARRANTIES BY SELLER

The Seller will make the following representations and warranties relative to the Company:

A. The Company is in good standing.

B. There are no outstanding liens or encumbrances, save and except for the money due to the Seller.

C. There are no contingent liabilities.

D. That the sale or transfer of the stock will not accelerate or terminate any current agreements of the Company including, but not limited to, the warehouse and distributor contracts and lease agreement by and between the Company and third parties.

E. That all taxes have been paid, except those accrued on the Balance Sheet.

F. That the financial statements in the possession of the Purchaser for the Company truly reflect the profitability and financial condition of the Company for the period covered in said statements.

G. All accounts receivable of the Company are good and collectible.

III. MISCELLANEOUS OTHER TERMS AND CONDITIONS

A. Seller agrees that neither he nor any other related party nor the Company in which he has any interest will compete with the business of the Company for a period of five years from the date of closing; however, this will not preclude Seller from continuing his current businesses in the same manner and scope they are currently being operated.

B. Seller shall have the right to purchase any and all inventory of the Company at jobber's rates for the period of time from the date of closing until all monies due to Seller are paid in full.

C. Seller will jointly and severally indemnify the Purchaser from any cost and damages arising from any breach of representation or warranty in the agreement.

D. Seller will make available all corporate and financial documents for inspection by the Purchaser or his legal representative.

E. Closing of this transaction shall take place on or before January 4, 1986.

F. Notwithstanding anything to the contrary, no legally binding or enforceable contract or agreement between the parties shall arise until a definitive agreement has been executed.

If the above sets forth the general terms and conditions by which you would be willing to sell all the shares of stock in the Company to Joe Brown, I would appreciate your executing a copy of this letter and returning the same to me. At that date, it would behoove you and Joe to negotiate those remaining unresolved areas, and after that is done, I will draft a legally binding agreement to be signed by all parties. If you have any questions or comments or in the event that I have misinterpreted the intent of the parties, do not hesitate to contact me.

Sincerely,

Lawrence C. Silton

CS:sjw

ACKNOWLEDGED AND APPROVED:

____________________________ ____________________________

Steve White Mary White

____

Joe Brown

APPENDIX I

Mr. Joe Buyer
One Wiaway Court
Anywhere, MN

Dear Joe:

I have reviewed the terms and conditions of the offer you tendered to me, a copy of which is attached hereto and made a part hereof, and am willing to enter into an agreement for the purchase of my stock in Worldwide Printing by you and your assigns which would specifically include a qualified Employee Stock Ownership Plan ("ESOP") to be established by Worldwide Printing, Inc., on behalf of its employees. Nothing contained herein shall in any way indicate that this agreement is contingent upon the formation of the ESOP. While terms and conditions upon which I am willing to sell my stock are set forth herein and upon the execution of this agreement by both of us, it will be considered a legally binding agreement, it does contemplate the entry into subsequent additional legal documents, including but not limited to a covenant not-to-compete, security agreement, promissory note, bill of sale, etc. The terms and conditions upon which I am willing to sell my stock in Worldwide Printing, Inc., hereinafter referred to as Worldwide, are as follows:

1. Property to be sold: 600 shares of the Common Stock of Worldwide which represent one-half of its authorized and issued Common Stock.
2. Purchasers: You will purchase three shares of the Common Stock, and either you or your assigns (including but not limited to the "ESOP") will purchase the remaining 597 shares which I own.
3. Sales price: The purchase price of each share of stock of Worldwide transferred hereunder shall be $1,666.67.
4. Payment of purchase price:
    a. The three shares which you will be purchasing will be purchased for cash at closing.
    b. The 597 shares of stock that will be purchased either by yourself, your assigns, or the ESOP shall be paid as follows:
        (1) $200,000.00 in cash at date of closing.
        (2) The balance of the purchase price shall be paid pursuant to a promissory note in the amount of $795,000 containing the following terms and conditions:

(a) One hundred and twenty level monthly payments of principal and interest sufficient to fully amortize the debt.
(b) Interest on the unpaid principal balance at 10%.
(c) In the event of default in the payment provisions or in the security agreement, the promissor shall have thirty days after written notice to correct default. Failure to correct said default shall cause the entire unpaid principal balance to become due and payable.
(d) Prepayment may be made at any time without penalty.

5. Security: The security for the promissory note set forth in paragraph 4.b.(2) will be:
   a. All the stock which you own, as well as all the stock purchased by your assigns, shall be pledged as security for repayment. A security agreement properly securing the pledge of stock shall be executed which will incorporate among other provisions (usual and normal in said agreements) those set forth in paragraphs 6, 9, 10, and 11 of this agreement. In the event that one of the assigns of the ESOP, partial release of the collateral will be made as the promissory note is paid. For each $1,666.66 I receive in principal reduction of the promissory note set forth in paragraph 4.b.(2) above, I will release one of the shares of stock pledged by the ESOP as security for the repayment of the note.
   b. Worldwide will guarantee the payment to me of the promissory note set forth in paragraph 4.b.(2). This guarantee shall be unsecured.
6. Prohibition against sale or transfer of stock by you and your assigns and a partial prohibition against sale of assets by Worldwide during the period of time any portion of the promissory note is still due me.
   a. Neither you nor your assigns shall sell, assign, encumber or in any way transfer the shares of stock in Worldwide. Specifically excluded from this prohibition is any of the shares of stock released as set forth in paragraph 5(a).
   b. The non-cash assets of Worldwide shall not be sold or transferred unless the proceeds are used to reduce the indebtedness due me. This shall not be construed as limiting the company's right and privilege to replace real or personal property with real or personal property of the same or greater value. This shall not preclude the normal retirement of assets.
7. Conditions precedent to closing: As you are well aware, I currently have a binding agreement with Messrs. Johnson and Field. The

terms and conditions of this agreement have previously been communicated to you. Nothing in this agreement shall be construed as indicating that I will fail to proceed with the closing of said agreement upon the terms and conditions originally contracted for. Therefore, my agreement with you is contingent upon: (1) Messrs. Field and Johnson failing to purchase the shares of stock I own in Worldwide. (2) Messrs. Field and Johnson releasing me from any further obligations under their contract without cost to me. If both conditions are not met or waived by me on or before February 24, 1984, the terms and conditions of this agreement shall be null, void and of no effect.

8. Covenants not-to-compete: At closing you will enter into a covenant not-to-compete that will prohibit you from directly or indirectly competing with Worldwide in the printing business for the earlier of a period of three years from the termination of your employment with Worldwide or the payment of the indebtedness in paragraph 4.b(2) within a geographical area of 150 mile radius of its current plant. I agree at closing to also enter into a covenant not-to-compete that will prohibit me from competing directly or indirectly with Worldwide in the printing business for a period of three years within a geographical area of 150 mile radius of its current plant.
9. Negative covenants: You and Worldwide agree that during the period of time any portion of the principal note set forth in paragraph 4.b(2) remains outstanding, that without my prior consent, you will not:
    a. Issue any additional stock in Worldwide. Nothing herein shall preclude Worldwide from declaring a stock split which does not affect proportional stock ownership.
    b. Increase the outstanding liabilities of Worldwide to an amount greater than $1-million or 75% of the stock equity whichever is greater; provided, however, that outstanding liabilities shall increase over $650,000 (to a maximum of $1,000,000) only for capital asset acquisitions and not for operating funds. If for any reason Worldwide sells its real property at 100 Milton Road, Den, Minnesota, the total amount of indebtedness permitted above shall be reduced by the then outstanding indebtedness on said real property. Notwithstanding the preceding, this provision is limited for a period commencing at closing and ending five years thereafter. Worldwide's obligation to me shall not be a liability for this purpose.
    c. Allow Worldwide to pay you a salary in any one year which exceeds the greater of:

(1) Base income, or

(2) Base income plus a bonus determined at 25% of the earnings as determined on the tax return for Worldwide excluding from the expenses the following:

(a) ESOP payment,

(b) income taxes.

However, the payment of this bonus is contingent upon the fact that after payment of the bonus, the ESOP and income taxes the corporation still would report a positive income.

The base income shall be $165,000 and shall increase 8% per year providing that the prior fiscal year was profitable after all payments (including ESOP, taxes and all salaries including bonuses). For the purposes of this determination, the base year shall be the fiscal year ended March 31, 1985.

d. Will not enter into any leasing agreement for the lease of real or personal property with you or any of your family members.

10. Affirmative representations: You and Worldwide agree to take the following actions during the period of time any portion of the promissory note due me remains outstanding:

(a) Worldwide will maintain life insurance on your life, Worldwide being the named beneficiary, in an amount sufficient to pay any indebtedness due me under paragraph 4.b(2) and all proceeds will be used to pay the indebtedness.

(b) Worldwide will deliver to me quarterly and year-end statements within a reasonable time after the close of the appropriate period.

(c) You will devote your full time and effort as an employee of Worldwide to its successful operation. Notwithstanding this prohibition, nothing will preclude you from spending a reasonable amount of time on your personal investment endeavors.

(d) That while these representations are made by you, you will vote your stock and act as an officer and director to insure that Worldwide, the ESOP and any other appropriate party complies with the terms and conditions set forth in this agreement.

11. Profitability of Worldwide: In the event that Worldwide shows a fiscal year loss and two consecutive loss quarters in the next fiscal year or Worldwide shows a cumulative loss for the last consecutive eight quarters after all expenses, including but not limited to ESOP payments, income taxes, salaries including

bonuses, Worldwide will pledge sufficient security to cover the total unpaid balance of the promissory note set forth in paragraph 4.b(2). Due to original contributions to the ESOP, etc., in the fiscal year ending March 31, 1984, this provision will apply only for fiscal years beginning on April 1, 1984.

12. Closing: The closing shall occur within three weeks after the notification by me that the contingencies set forth in paragraph 7 have been fulfilled but no later than March 16, 1984.
13. Survival of representations and warranties: All representatives and warranties contained in this agreement shall survive the execution of this agreement and the closing of the transactions contemplated by the agreement.
14. Rights to bonus and termination of employment: Upon closing I will resign as an officer and director of the corporation. At that date I shall only be entitled to any accrued but unpaid vacation pay. I will waive any and all right I have to a bonus that may be due me by reason of my employment during the current fiscal year.
15. Binding effect: This agreement shall be binding upon the parties hereto, their heirs, executors and assigns.

If the above sets forth terms and conditions upon which you and your assigns would be willing to purchase all the shares of stock I own in Worldwide, please signify your acceptance by signing two copies below where indicated and returning a completely executed copy to me.

Sincerely,

Frank Seller

Accepted:

Joe Buyer

APPENDIX J

SALES AGREEMENT

THIS AGREEMENT entered into this ______ day of May, 1984, by and between SELL-RIGHT, INC., a Wisconsin corporation, hereinafter referred to as "SELLER," and WORLDWIDE FABRICATING, INC., a Wisconsin corporation, hereinafter referred to as "PURCHASER."

WHEREAS, Seller is willing to sell, and Purchaser is willing to purchase, a majority of the tangible and intangible personal property, used in conducting the metal fabricating business owned by Seller under the name of Sell-Right, on the following terms and conditions:

IT IS HEREBY AGREED AS FOLLOWS:

1. *Assets to be Sold.* Seller agrees to convey to Purchaser the then existing assets which pertain to, or are a part of, the operation of the metal fabricating business of Seller conducted under its own name consisting of the following:

(A) Personal Property:

(i) Tangible Property: Machinery and equipment. A detailed list of which is attached hereto and made a part hereof as Exhibit "A".

(ii) Inventory consisting of all the merchandise, work in process and other supplies and goods on the premises of the Seller. See Paragraph (2) (B) for method of taking inventory, pricing and the right of Purchaser to reject a portion of the inventory owned by Seller.

(iii) Name, telephone number, and listing. Seller makes no representation or warranty as to any proprietary rights it may have to the use or ownership of the name of Sell-Right or derivations thereof. However, any and all rights to use said name or trade name which Seller has will be conveyed to Purchaser as well as its listing in the telephone books and directories and good will connected with the Seller's business operation.

(B) Excepted Property: The parties hereto acknowledge that the following property is not included in this sale:

(i) Any and all cash and receivables.

(ii) All vehicles owned by Sell-Right.

(iii) Office furniture and fixtures and miscellaneous other items such as prepaid expenses and prepaid income taxes.

(iv) Leasehold improvements.

(v) Miscellaneous assets not sold pursuant to this Agreement.

2. *Purchase Price.* The total purchase price shall be determined as follows:

(A) Machinery and equipment set forth on Exhibit "A" attached hereto and made a part hereof, $433,479.46, which has been determined at ninety (90%) percent of the original cost. The original cost of the various items purchased will be subject to verification as a part of the accountants' review as set forth in Paragraph (22).

(B) Inventory: The purchase price for the inventory will be determined according to a method utilizing the lower of cost or market in accordance with the methods historically utilized by Seller, consistently applied. Physical inventory shall be taken by both parties on June 1, 1984. If the parties hereto cannot arrive at the value for specific items of inventory, the Purchaser at its sole option shall have the right to reject up to ten percent (10%) of the total cost of the inventory without affecting the obligations hereto. If the Purchaser rejects more than ten percent (10%), then the Seller at its option shall have the right to terminate this contract without further obligation to either party. All property that is not purchased shall remain the property of Seller, and the Seller shall have the complete power to dispose of said property without limitation. Notwithstanding the preceding, in the event that the inventory to be purchased hereunder is greater than $700,000, the Purchaser has the right to reject anything over said $700,000 without affecting the obligation of the parties to this agreement.

(C) Goodwill and going concern value, $10,000.

3. *Payment of Purchase Price.* The purchase price due hereunder plus or minus appropriate prorations shall be paid as follows:

(A) $5,000 in cash as earnest money at the time of execution of this agreement.

(B) $400,000 pursuant to a promissory note containing the following terms and conditions:

(i) Interest at the rate of nine percent (9%).

(ii) $6,436 on the 1st day of July, 1984, and $6,436 on the 1st day of every month thereafter until fully paid.

(iii) The security for said promissory note shall be:

a. A Wisconsin Banker's Association Security Agreement and Financing Statement on all accounts receivable, inventory, equipment, furniture and other tangible personal property used in the metal fabricating business purchased hereunder.

If requested, Seller shall subordinate his security interest to a bank in an amount not to exceed $400,000. The total indebtedness shall not, during the term of the loan, exceed the depreciated value of the equipment, plus inventory at the lower of cost or market, and receivables. In the event the total indebtedness does exceed the sum of the above, Purchaser will pledge sufficient additional security within ten (10) days of notification by Seller. A failure to pledge sufficient additional security will allow the Seller, at its option, to call the promissory note immediately due and payable.

b. The signature of the Purchaser.

(C) The remainder of the purchase price in cash at closing.

4. *Lease.* The Seller and Purchaser shall enter into a lease for real and personal property upon the terms and conditions set forth hereunder:

(A) Property to be Leased: The Purchaser will lease the personal property set forth on Exhibit "B" attached hereto and made a part thereof. In addition, the Purchaser shall lease the real property consisting of the office space, warehouse and manufacturing space, a description of which is set forth on Exhibit "C" attached hereto and made a part hereof.

(B) The term of this lease shall commence upon the date of closing and will terminate two (2) years thereafter unless terminated sooner as set forth in Paragraph (4) (E) below.

(C) For all the property leased hereunder, the Lessee shall pay a total monthly rental of $3,100 to be allocated as agreed.

(D) In addition thereto, the Lessee shall bear the cost of all the utilities in the manufacturing and warehouse space. The Lessor shall bear the cost of all the insurance (save and except for contents insurance), real estate taxes on all the property leased hereunder and utilities for the entire office space.

(E) The Lessor shall have the right to terminate on six (6) months' notice in the event that it wishes to sell the leased premises or obtains a favorable long term lease on said premises.

5. *Employment Contract.* The Purchaser and Joe Jones, the chief executive officer of the Seller, will enter into an employment contract for a period of two (2) years.

(A) The terms and conditions of the first year are as follows:

(i) Salary: $52,000.

(ii) Purchaser to pay all medical insurance and three (3) weeks paid vacation. No other fringe benefits will be borne by the Purchaser.

(iii) The Purchaser shall pay on a monthly basis as a car allowance to Joe Jones $250 and will reimburse Joe Jones for any and all direct expenses incurred in the Purchaser's business.

(iv) Joe Jones will devote his full time and efforts to the operation of the metal fabricating business sold hereunder. Notwithstanding the preceding, he will be allowed to devote up to thirty percent (30%) of his working time to other business ventures.

(B) The terms and conditions for the second year and succeeding period is summarized on Exhibit "D" attached hereto and made a part hereof.

6. *Consulting Agreement After the End of the Employment Agreement.* It is contemplated, but there is no obligation on either of the parties, that some form of Employment Contract or independent representative's agreement will be entered into by and between the Purchaser and Joe Jones after the termination of the Employment Contract set forth in Paragraph (5). In addition to any agreement which may be entered into by the Purchaser and Joe Jones, Joe Jones for the years three (3) through five (5) will serve as a consultant for the Purchaser. The terms and conditions of said Consulting Agreement shall be as follows:

(A) Yearly compensation, $4,000 (to be paid in twelve (12) equal monthly installments).

(B) Joe Jones will devote one (1) day per month for and in pursuit of the Purchaser's business.

(C) In the event that it is necessary to travel, all direct costs of said travel will be reimbursed to Joe Jones.

(D) In the event that Purchaser does not utilize Joe Jones' service in any one (1) month, it will be allowed to accumulate up to five (5) days to be used in a future period. However, in no event shall any more than five (5) days be carried from year to year.

7. *Covenant Not-to-Compete.*

(A) In consideration of the payment of the purchase price and $5,000 in cash, the Seller and Joe Jones (collectively and individually) agree that they will not, either directly or indirectly, for themselves or through officers, employees, or agents, compete with the Purchaser in the conduct of the business purchased from Seller or in any other business that could be in direct or indirect competition to the business currently operated by the Purchaser for a period of five (5) years from the closing date, within the geographical area set forth on Exhibit "E". Nor will Seller and Joe Jones (collectively and individually) extend direct or indirect financial assistance to, manage, operate or participate in the ownership, management, operation or control of, any person, firm or corporation during such period which competes, directly or indirectly, with the business purchased hereunder or the current business operated by the Purchaser within such geographical area. Notwithstanding the preceding, nothing contained herein shall prohibit the Seller, its officers and directors from selling trim coil which requires no conversion, save and except for painting.

(B) In the event of breach or threatened breach of this paragraph, the Purchaser shall be entitled to an injunction restraining such breach or threatened breach. This shall not prohibit the Purchaser from pursuing any other remedies available to it including the recovery of damages for such breach.

(C) The waiver by the Purchaser of a breach of this section shall not operate or be construed as a waiver of any subsequent breach.

(D) The cash payment of $5,000 shall be paid in five (5) equal installments of $1,000; $1,000 at closing and $1,000 on the anniversary date of the closing for every year thereafter until fully paid.

8. *Assumption of Lease Obligations of Seller.* The Seller has represented that it is currently the Lessee of certain long term truck leases. A complete description of these is set forth in Exhibit "F" attached hereto and made a part hereof. The Seller will assign and the Purchaser agrees to assume the obligations under the terms and conditions of said leases. Save and except for the assumption of the obligations specifically set forth on Exhibit "F", the Purchaser will assume no further obligations of any kind of Seller.

9. *Time and Place of Closing.* The closing shall occur not later than June 4, 1984, at 10:00 A.M., at the offices of Patterson, Jensen, Wylie, Silton & Seifert, S.C., 331 East Washington Street, Appleton, Wisconsin.

10. *Transfer of Assets.* Seller shall convey all property and assets of the business to be sold to Purchaser by delivering to Purchaser warranting bills of sale and assignments with all necessary documentary tax stamps affixed at Seller's expense, as follows:

(A) A bill or bills of sale warranting Seller to be the owner of and conveying all machinery, equipment, tools, parts, and inventory of completed work and work in process, raw materials, supplies, trade name, telephone number and listings, good will and all other personal property being sold.

(B) Assignments of all truck leases (including insurance policies) to be assigned to Purchaser with consents from third parties as may be required for the assignment and transfer to Purchaser of any of the Seller's leases and other agreements which cannot be transferred to Purchaser without consent of third parties.

11. *Indemnification.* This transaction is intended to be a purchase and sale of the assets of the metal fabricating business conducted under the name of Sell-Right free and clear of all liabilities and obligations of Seller except as set forth herein. Seller and Joe Jones, jointly and severally, indemnify and agree to hold Purchaser harmless from claims of any and all creditors of Seller existing on the date of closing, whether determined or contingent. If any amount is determined to be due under this Agreement, it shall reduce the promissory note due to Seller from Purchaser.

12. *Possession.* Legal and physical possession of the property shall be delivered to Purchaser at the date of closing.

13. *Purchaser's Default.* Should Purchaser fail to carry out this agreement, all money paid hereunder shall be forfeited as liquidated damages.

14. *Seller's Default.* Should Seller fail to carry out the terms of this agreement, the Purchaser, at its option, may request that all money paid hereunder shall be returned to Purchaser, or in lieu thereof may demand performance under the terms of this agreement by way of a suit for specific performance.

15. *Prorations.* At closing, the following items will be prorated:

(A) Prepaid insurance.

(B) Utilities.

(C) All accrued income and expenses, including taxes, shall accrue to Seller.

(D) Telephone bills and listing.

(E) Leases for equipment.

(F) All other properly proratable items.

16. *Lack of Sales Commission.* The parties hereto acknowledge that there is no sales commission due by reason of this sale.

17. *Miscellaneous Provisions.*

(A) Business Records: The Seller shall make available to Purchaser and allow Purchaser to copy for the use in his business any records relating to the metal fabricating business sold hereunder, including but not limited to customer lists, amount of previous sales by customer during the last five (5) years and any and all other business records that Purchaser may deem reasonably necessary to review for purposes of his continuing conduct of the business of Sell-Right.

(B) Sales Tax: Any and all sales tax and other transfer tax which may be due upon the transfer of assets shall be borne by Seller.

(C) Bulk Sales: While it is not anticipated, Purchaser shall have the right to request that the parties comply with the provisions of the Bulk Sales Act of the State of Wisconsin. Notwithstanding this fact, the Seller hereby agrees to indemnify Purchaser by reason of not complying with the provisions of said Act.

(D) Survival of Representations, Warranties, and Agreements: All representations, warranties, and agreements made by Seller shall survive the consummation of this agreement and any investigation made at any time by and on behalf of Purchaser.

(E) Assigment and Successors: This agreement shall be binding upon, and inure to the benefit of, the heirs, legal representatives, successors, and assigns of Seller and Purchaser. Purchaser is given the right to assign the rights and obligations under this agreement to a corporation in which Purchaser owns at least seventy-five percent (75%) of the authorized and issued common stock of said corporation, as long as Purchaser guarantees the performance of all obligations set forth herein.

(F) Severability: The invalidity of any provision of this agreement shall not impair the validity of any other provision of this agreement. If any provision of this agreement is determined by a court of competent jurisdiction to be unenforceable, that provision shall be deemed severable and the agreement may be enforced with that provision severed or as modified by the court.

(G) Entire Agreement and Modification: This agreement sets forth the entire understanding of the parties. It may be amended, modified, or terminated only by an instrument signed by all the parties.

(H) Damage to Property to be Transferred: If prior to closing, a portion or all of the property transferred herein is destroyed or materially damaged by fire or other casualty, the Purchaser, at its option, shall have the right to terminate this contract.

(I) Notices: All notices shall be in writing and delivered in person, or sent by certified mail, return receipt requested, if for Seller addressed to:

Joe Jones
Sell-Right, Inc.
P.O. Box 000
Appleton, WI 54911

and if for Purchaser addressed to:

Sam Smith
Worldwide Fabricating, Inc.
P.O. Box 001
Appleton, WI 54911

and

Lawrence C. Silton
PATTERSON, JENSEN, WYLIE, SILTON & SEIFERT, S.C.
Attorneys at Law
331 East Washington Street
Appleton, WI 54911

or at such other address as stated in a written notice given in compliance under this paragraph.

(J) Paragraph Headings: Paragraph headings are inserted herein solely for convenience, and if they conflict with the text in the construction of this agreement, the text shall control.

(K) Applicable Law: This agreement shall be construed and enforced in accordance with the laws of the State of Wisconsin.

18. *Documents at Closing.*

(A) At closing, the Purchaser shall deliver to the Seller:

(i) A check in the amount of the cash portion of the purchase price set forth in Paragraph (2) less the earnest money deposit.

(ii) A promissory note in the amount of $400,000.

(iii) Security Agreement and Financing Statement.

(iv) An opinion of the Purchaser's attorneys, dated the date of closing, to the effect that:

a. The Purchaser is a corporation duly organized, validly existing and in good standing under the laws of the State of Wisconsin.

b. This agreement and all documents connected herewith signed by the Purchaser, are valid and binding undertakings of the Purchaser enforceable against the Purchaser in accordance with their terms, and that all corporate action necessary for the authorization of the execution of this agreement and all other such documents and the transactions contemplated thereby has been taken, and neither they nor the consummation of this agreement violates or will violate the Purchaser's Articles of Incorporation, by-laws or any order or statute applicable to the Purchaser nor any agreement to which the Purchaser is a party.

(B) At closing, the Seller shall deliver to the Purchaser:

(i) Its Bill of Sale for all personal property transferred hereby, in a form preapproved by the Purchaser, which Bill of Sale shall convey title free and clear of all liens and encumbrances, and by which the Seller shall indemnify the Purchaser and hold it harmless against any and all claims against said title.

(ii) Certificates of Title to transferred property, if any, properly endorsed for transfer to the Purchaser, along with all documentation and information necessary for registration of transferred vehicles.

(iii) An opinion of the Seller's attorneys, dated the date of closing, to the effect that:

a. Sell-Right, Inc. is a corporation duly organized, validly existing and in good standing under the laws of the State of Wisconsin.

b. This agreement and all documents connected herewith signed by the Seller, are valid and binding undertakings of the Seller enforceable against the Seller in accordance with their terms, and that all corporate action necessary for the authorization of the execution of this agreement and all other such documents and the transactions contemplated thereby has been taken, and neither they nor the consummation of this agreement violates or will violate the Seller's Articles of Incorporation, by-laws or any order or statute applicable to the Seller nor any agreement to which the Seller is a party.

(iv) Document preapproved by the Purchaser, signed by the Seller and Stockholder indemnifying and holding harmless the Purchaser from and against any and all transferee liability as a result of this agreement including, but not limited to transferee liability which may arise under the Bulk Sales Law as adopted in Wisconsin.

(v) An assignment of all truck leases.

(C) At closing, the Seller and Purchaser will jointly execute and deliver the following documents:

(i) An Employment Contract by and between the Purchaser and Joe Jones. The terms and conditions of which are set forth in Paragraph (5).

(ii) A Consulting Agreement by and between the Purchaser and Joe Jones. The terms and conditions of which are set forth in Paragraph (6).

(iii) A Lease for certain real and personal property by and between the Seller and Purchaser. The terms and conditions of which are set forth in Paragraph (4).

(iv) A Covenant Not-to-Compete by and between various parties. The terms and conditions of which are set forth in Paragraph (7).

19. *Conduct of Business Pending Closing and Transition of Business.*

(A) Between the date of this agreement and the closing date, the Seller shall conduct the business in the ordinary course and in a commercially reasonable manner. The Seller shall not incur any obligations between the date of this agreement and the closing date except such obligations as are ordinarily incurred in the normal course and conduct of the business. The Seller shall not sell or encumber any of the business assets except such sales as are normally made in the ordinary course of the business. The Seller agrees that it will not remove or cause to be removed from the premises, without the Purchaser's express written consent, any items of property of the type to be sold hereunder, except as may be required in the ordinary course of business up to the date of closing.

During said period, the Seller shall maintain at its expense all present insurance covering the premises and the business, and shall promptly provide the Purchaser with certificates evidencing said insurance upon the Purchaser's request.

(B) The Stockholders of Seller, Seller, and the Purchaser agree to consult and cooperate with each other as to the timing and content of announcements of this transaction to the general public and to employees, customers and suppliers. The Stockholders of Seller and the Seller agree to cooperate fully and completely in the introduction of Purchaser to Seller's customers and the transition of the customers' business to Purchaser.

20. *Representations of the Seller and Stockholders of Seller.* The Stockholders of Seller and Seller, jointly and severally, represent that as of the date of closing:

(A) Seller is a corporation duly organized, validly existing and in good standing under the laws of the State of Wisconsin, is qualified to do business in the State of Wisconsin, and has legal authority to sell the business and assets herein contemplated. The owner of all the authorized and issued stock of the Seller are Joe Jones, Jim Jones, and Cougar Products, a Wisconsin corporation. Joe Jones represents and warrants that he is the owner of all the issued stock of Cougar Products. He further represents that his brother, Jim Jones, owns approximately four percent (4%) of the issued stock of the Seller.

(B) The execution and delivery to the Purchaser of this agreement, and the transactions contemplated hereby, have been duly authorized by the Seller's Board of Directors and all shareholders.

(C) The Seller is the owner of, and on the date of closing and subsequent inventory transfer date will convey to the Purchaser, good and marketable title to the business and assets sold hereunder, free and clear of all liens, security interests, charges or encumbrances of any kind.

(D) Machinery and equipment utilized by the Seller in its business are in good condition and repair and will be maintained in such condition and repair, reasonable wear and tear excepted, from the date hereof to the date of closing.

(E) The assets to be sold hereunder include part of the inventory and all of the machinery and equipment of the Seller used in the conduct of its business, excluding furniture, fixtures, and office equipment and vehicles.

(F) The Seller is in compliance with all laws, ordinances and regulations of government agencies applicable to its business and has all licenses and permits necessary for the conduct of its business.

(G) From the date of this agreement to the date of closing, there has been and will be no material adverse change in the financial condition, assets, liabilities, net worth, or business of the Seller, except such changes as do not affect the business and assets which are the subject of this agreement.

(H) There are no actions pending or threatened against the Seller for infringement of any trademarks or trade names and the Seller is not aware of any conflicting use or claim respecting any trademarks, trade names, copyrights or patents or similar intangible rights or assets used by the Seller in the conduct of its business, except to the extent such use by the Seller is limited by existing license or franchise agreements.

(I) The Seller is not in breach of or default under any outstanding lease, contract, agreement or other instrument to which it is a party or by which it is bound.

(J) Use or occupancy by the Seller of premises which it now occupies does not contravene any applicable law, zoning ordinance, administrative regulation, or restrictive covenant.

(K) The Seller has complied with all applicable federal and state laws relating to the employment of labor, including the provisions relating to wages, hours, conditions of employment, collective bargaining and the payment of social security taxes, and the Seller is not in and at the closing will not be liable for any arrears of wages or any tax or penalties for failure to comply with any of the foregoing, other than those of an immaterial or insubstantial nature. There are no controversies pending or threatened between the Seller and any of its employees, or any association or group of employees, and the Seller has not taken any action which would provide the basis for any such controversy.

(L) No representation or warranty made by the Seller or Stockholders in this agreement or in any Exhibit attached hereto or in any certificate, written data, or other paper furnished or to be furnished by or on behalf of the Seller or Stockholders under or pursuant to this agreement contains, or shall contain, any untrue statement of a material fact or omission of a material fact necessary to make this statement contained therein not misleading.

(M) The Seller has no knowledge or reason to know of any termination, cancellation, limitation, modification, or change in a business relationship of Seller with any customer of the business or group of customers whose purchases individually or in the aggregate consisted of more than five percent (5%) of the sales of the business for its year ending on December 31, 1983.

(N) The labor force of the Seller is not organized in any labor union or association and the Seller has no knowledge of any attempted organizational activities among its employees.

(O) Since the Balance Sheet data supplied to the Purchaser dated December 31, 1983, there has been no material adverse change in the Balance Sheet, condition of business as shown on the Balance Sheet, nor any other material adverse change in the condition of Seller's business, including its business organization, personnel, properties or relationships with suppliers, employees, customers or others.

(P) Seller has delivered to Purchaser copies of the following financial statements:

(i) Balance Sheet of the Seller for the years 1979 through 1983.

(ii) Statement for Profit and Loss of the business for those years.

(iii) Income tax returns for those years.

The financial statements are true, correct and complete. The Balance Sheet presents fairly the financial condition of the business as of the date shown and the Profit and Loss Statement presents fairly the result of operations of the business for the period shown. The financial statements have been prepared in conformity with general accepted accounting principles consistently applied.

(Q) Seller is not a party to any:

(i) Written contract for employment by or in connection with its business which may not be terminated on not more than thirty (30) days' notice to the Seller.

(ii) Continuing contract or agreement for the purchase or

sale of materials, services, machinery or equipment by or in connection with the business.

(iii) Lease or license of real or personal property used or otherwise relating to the business except as set forth herein on Exhibit "F".

(iv) Agreement for purchase or sale of equipment or machinery by or in connection with the business.

(v) Pension or profit sharing plan, retirement, bonus agreement or plan or any similar plan, formal or informal, covering one or more employees or former employees of the business.

(vi) Distributor's sales agency, franchise agreement or commission contract or license, relating to the business.

(vii) Any other contract arising from or in connection with the business involving payment by the Seller or to Seller of more than $1,000 or performance of which extends beyond ninety (90) days of the date of this agreement.

(R) All physical properties and assets of the business being sold are covered by insurance in reasonable amounts and Seller carries public liability, workmen's comp, product liability and other types of insurance in reasonable amounts and Seller will deliver to Purchaser, at closing, certificates of insurance showing such insurance to be in effect on the closing date.

(S) Seller's unemployment compensating rating and contribution is ________%. Seller has no knowledge of any proposed increase thereof and knows of no conditions or circumstances applicable to the business which might result in such increase.

21. *Representations and Warranties of the Purchaser.* The purchaser represents and warrants that:

(A) It is a corporation duly organized, validly existing and in good standing under the laws of the State of Wisconsin.

(B) It has legal authority to purchase the business and assets herein contemplated.

(C) The execution and delivery to the Seller of this agreement and all related documents, and the transactions contemplated thereby have been duly authorized by the Purchaser's Board of Directors.

22. *Accountants' Review.* Within five (5) days of the execution of this agreement, the Purchaser, at its own expense, will have its accountants commence a review of the books and records of the Seller. In the event that the accountants' review indicates any material distortions from the financial representations made by Seller and Seller's agents, either orally or in the financial records already supplied to the Purchaser, or in the event that in the accountants' opinion the books and records of the Seller as reflected in its

previously supplied do not properly represent either the financial position or the profit and loss for the appropriate period covered, Purchaser shall have the right within five (5) days after receiving said opinion to terminate this agreement and be relieved of any further obligation under the terms and conditions of the agreement and Seller will return the earnest money deposit.

IN WITNESS WHEREOF, the parties have duly executed this Agreement as of the date first above written.

SELLER:

SELL-RIGHT, INC.

BY: ______________________________
Joe Jones, President

PURCHASER:

WORLDWIDE FABRICATING, INC.

BY: ______________________________
Sam Smith, President

ACKNOWLEDGED AND APPROVED:

____

____

____

____

Being all the shareholders of Sell-Right, Inc.

____

____

____

____

Being all the directors of Sell-Right, Inc.

APPENDIX K

§253:3062 Security agreement—General form

SECURITY AGREEMENT

Agreement made __________, 19____, between __________, of __________ *[address]*, City of __________, County of __________, State of __________, herein referred to as debtor, and __________, of __________ *[address]*, City of __________, County of __________, State of __________, herein referred to as secured party.

In consideration of the mutual convenants and promises set forth herein, debtor and secured party agree:

SECTION ONE
CREATION OF SECURITY INTEREST

Debtor hereby grants to secured party a security interest in the collateral, described in Section Two, to secure the performance and payment of __________ *[describe obligation secured, such as:* debtor's note dated __________, 19____, in the amount of __________ Dollars ($__________) given to secured party and payable as to principal and interest as therein provided]: __________ *[if appropriate, add:* all expenditures by secured party for taxes, insurance, repairs to and maintenance of the collateral and all costs and expenses incurred by secured party in the collection and enforcement of the note and other indebtedness of debtor; future advances to be evidenced by like notes to be made by debtor to secured party at secured party's option; and all liabilities of debtor to secured party now existing or hereafter incurred, matured or unmatured, direct or contingent, and any renewals and extensions thereof and substitutions therefor].

SECTION TWO
DESCRIPTION OF COLLATERAL

The collateral subject to this security agreement, herein referred to as collateral, is the personal property of the following description: __________ *[list and describe property, including, in the case of crops growing or to be grown, oil, gas, or minerals to be extracted, or timber to be cut, a description of the land concerned]*, together with all equipment, parts, appliances, accessions, and appurtenances now or hereafter placed thereon, all of which shall be a component part of collateral.

SECTION THREE
OBLIGATIONS OF DEBTOR, GENERALLY

(a) Payment. Debtor shall pay to secured party the sum evidenced by the above mentioned note or any renewals or extensions thereof executed pursuant to this security agreement in accordance with the terms of such note ____________ *[if appropriate, add:* and any other obligations that now exist or may hereafter accrue from debtor to secured party, including all future advances that may be made at the option of secured party as provided herein].

(b) Warranties and representations. Debtor warrants and covenants that:

(1) Except for the security interest hereby granted, debtor has, or on acquisition will have, full fee simple title to collateral free from any lien, security interest, encumbrance, or claim, and debtor will, at debtor's cost and expense, defend any action that may affect secured party's security interest in, or debtor's title to, collateral.

(2) Collateral is used or is to be used primarily ____________ *[designate principal use, such as:* for personal or household purposes or for use in business, including a profession; however, the collateral is not to be purchased or held for lease or sale].

(3)____________ *[if appropriate, provide:* Collateral is being acquired by debtor with the proceeds of the loan evidenced by the above mentioned note].

(c) Performance of agreement. Debtor shall perform all covenants and agreements set forth in this security agreement.

SECTION FOUR
OBLIGATION OF SECURED PARTY

Secured party shall make the loan to debtor as agreed and as evidenced by the above mentioned date.

SECTION FIVE
PROCEEDS OF COLLATERAL

Debtor hereby grants to secured party a security interest in and to all proceeds of collateral, as defined by ____________ *[cite local enactment of UCC §9-306(1)]*. This provision shall not be construed to mean that debtor is authorized to sell, lease, or dispose of collateral without the consent of secured party.

SECTION SIX
DECREASE IN VALUE OF COLLATERAL

If in the judgment of secured party collateral has materially decreased in value, or if secured party shall at any time deem itself insecure, debtor shall either provide additional collateral sufficient to satisfy secured party or reduce the total indebtedness by an amount sufficient to satisfy secured party.

SECTION SEVEN
FINANCING STATEMENT

At the request of secured party, debtor will join in executing, or will execute as appropriate, all necessary financing statements in a form satisfactory to secured party, and will pay the cost of filing such statements. Debtor will execute all other instruments deemed necessary by secured party and pay the cost of filing such documents. Debtor warrants that no financing statement covering collateral or any part thereof or any proceeds thereof is presently on file in any public office.

SECTION EIGHT
LOCATION AND IDENTIFICATION OF COLLATERAL

Debtor will keep collateral separate and identifiable and at the address of debtor shown herein, and debtor will not remove collateral from such address without the written consent of secured party.

SECTION NINE
ALIENATION OF COLLATERAL

Debtor will not, without the written consent of secured party, sell, contract to sell, lease, encumber, or otherwise dispose of collateral or any interest therein until this security agreement and all debts secured thereby have been fully satisfied.

SECTION TEN
INSURANCE

Debtor shall insure collateral with companies acceptable to secured party against such casualties and in such amounts as secured party shall require. The insurance shall be for the benefit of debtor and secured party as their interests may appear. Secured party is hereby authorized to collect from the insurance company any amount that may become due under any of such insurance, and the secured party may apply the same to the obligations hereby secured.

SECTION ELEVEN
TAXES AND ASSESSMENTS

Debtor shall pay promptly when due all taxes and assessments levied on collateral or on its use and operation.

SECTION TWELVE
PROTECTION OF COLLATERAL

Debtor shall keep collateral in good order and repair; debtor shall not waste or destroy collateral or any part thereof; and debtor shall not use collateral in violation of any statute or ordinance. Secured party shall have the right to examine and inspect collateral at any reasonable time.

SECTION THIRTEEN
REIMBURSEMENT OF EXPENSES

Secured party may at its option and at any time discharge taxes, liens, or interest on collateral, perform or cause to be performed for and on behalf of debtor any actions and conditions, obligations, or covenants that debtor has failed or refused to perform, or pay for the repair, maintenance, and preservation of collateral. All sums so expended shall bear interest from the date of payment at the rate of __________ per cent (__________%) per year, shall be payable at the place designated in the above mentioned note, and shall be secured by this security agreement.

SECTION FOURTEEN
TIME OF PERFORMANCE

When performing any act under this security agreement and the note secured thereby, time shall be of the essence.

SECTION FIFTEEN
WAIVER

Failure of secured party to exercise any right or remedy, including but not limited to the acceptance of partial or delinquent payments, shall not be a waiver of any obligation of debtor or right of secured party or constitute a waiver of any other similar default subsequently occurring.

SECTION SIXTEEN
DEFAULT

If debtor fails to pay when due any amount payable on the above mentioned note or on any other indebtedness of debtor secured hereby, or shall fail to observe or perform any of the provisions of this agreement, debtor shall be in default.

SECTION SEVENTEEN
REMEDIES

On any default, and at any time thereafter:

(a) Secured party may declare all obligations secured hereby immediately due and payable and may proceed to enforce payment of the same and exercise any and all of the rights and remedies provided by ____________ *[cite local enactment of Part 5 of Article 9 of UCC]* as well as any and all other rights and remedies possessed by secured party.

(b) Secured party shall have the right to remove collateral from debtor's premises. Secured party may require debtor to assemble collateral and make it available to secured party at any place to be designated by secured party that is reasonably convenient to both parties. For purposes of removal and possession of collateral, secured party or its representatives may enter any premises of debtor without legal process, and debtor hereby waives and releases secured party of and from any and all claims in connection therewith or arising therefrom.

(c) Unless collateral is perishable or threatens to decline speedily in value or is of a type customarily sold on a recognized market, secured party shall give debtor reasonable notice of the time and place of any public sale thereof or of the time after which any private sale or any other intended disposition thereof is to be made. The requirements of reasonable notice shall be met if such notice is mailed, postage prepaid, to the address of debtor shown herein at least ____________ days before the time of the sale or disposition. Expenses of retaking, holding, preparing for sale, selling, or the like shall include reasonable attorneys' fees and legal expenses incurred by secured party.

SECTION EIGHTEEN
GOVERNING LAW

(a) This security agreement shall be construed according to ____________ *[cite local enactment of UCC]* and other applicable laws of the State of ____________, and all obligations of the parties created hereunder are to be performed in the State of ____________.

(b) All terms used herein that are defined in ____________ *[cite local enactment of UCC]* shall have the same meaning herein as therein defined.

In witness whereof, the parties have executed this agreement at ____________ *[designate place of execution]* the day and year first above written.

[Signatures]

Author's Commentary:

The 1972 revision of Article 9 omits the requirement that a security agreement describe the land when the security interest is created in oil, gas, or minerals, for the practical reason that an Article 9 security interest cannot exist in such property prior to extraction. 4 Anderson on the Uniform Commercial Code §9-203:5

The 1972 revision of Article 9 omits the provision of UCC §9-203(1)(b) as to the sufficiency of description of "proceeds" for the reason that every security agreement under the revision covers proceeds unless such coverage is expressly excluded. 4 Anderson on the Uniform Commercial Code §9-203:3

☑ Tax Notes:

Tax consequences of debt transactions, generally. FEDERAL TAX GUIDE TO LEGAL FORMS, Loan Agreements ¶3240 (1 et seq.).

SECTION THREE

Tax aspects of interest payments. FEDERAL TAX GUIDE TO LEGAL FORMS, Loan Agreements ¶3240 (30 et seq.).

☑ Notes on Use:

Text references: Formal requisites of security agreement. 15 AM JUR 2d, Commercial Code §55.

—General requirements of security agreement. 69 AM JUR 2d, Secured Transactions §§290 et seq.

Annotation: Construction and effect of UCC Art 9, dealing with secured transactions, with regard to security agreements and the rights of parties thereto. 30 ALR3d 9,42.

SECTION ONE

Text reference: Description, in security agreement, of obligation secured. 69 AM JUR 2d, Secured Transactions §§ 310 et seq.

SECTION TWO

Text reference: Description of collateral in security agreement. 69 AM JUR 2d, Secured Transactions §§ 291 et seq.

Annotation: Construction and effect of UCC, Art 9, dealing with secured transactions, with regard to sufficiency of description of collateral. 30 ALR3d 9,48.

SECTION SEVEN

Annotation: Construction and effect of UCC Art 9, dealing with secured transactions, with regard to filing of financing statement. 30 ALR3d 9,53.

SECTION NINE

Text reference: Requirement, in security agreement, of additional collateral. 69 AM JUR 2d, Secured Transactions § 327.

SECTION TWELVE

Text reference: Provisions, in security agreement, regarding care and use of collateral. 69 AM JUR 2d, Secured Transactions §§ 317 et seq.

SECTION EIGHTEEN

Annotation: Construction and effect of UCC Art 9, dealing with secured transactions, with regard to secured party's remedies on default. 30 ALR3d 9,74.

APPENDIX L

Wisconsin Legal Blank Co. Inc.
Milwaukee, Wis.

UCC-2
(For use after 1-1-78)

STATE OF WISCONSIN – STANDARD (OFFICIAL) FORM

FINANCING STATEMENT FOR FILING – SECRETARY OF STATE

(FILING INSTRUCTIONS ON REVERSE SIDE OF SECURED PARTY COPY)

Financing Statement for Secretary of State – Uniform Commercial Code

		For Filing Officer
1 Debtor(s) (Last Name First) and Address(es)	2 Secured Party and Address	
4 This Financing Statement covers the following types (or items) of Property (Collateral):		3 No. of Additional Sheets Presented:
Proceeds of collateral are covered. Products of collateral are covered unless checked ☐		5 Assignee of Secured Party and Address
6 "Continuing Business Relationship" under S.409.404(1)(c) Wis. Stats. exists if checked ☐		

7

SIGNATURE OF DEBTOR – TITLE

SIGNATURE OF DEBTOR – TITLE

SIGNATURE OF DEBTOR – TITLE

SIGNATURE OF DEBTOR – TITLE

8

SIGNATURE OF SECURED PARTY OR ASSIGNEE – TITLE

Signature of Secured Party permitted in lieu of Debtor's signature:

(1) Collateral is subject to a security interest in another jurisdiction, and ☒

☐ Collateral is brought into this state;
☐ Debtor's location was changed to this state.

(2) For other situations, see s.409.402(2), Wis. Stats.

(1) FILING OFFICER — Alphabetical

(5) Debtor copy ORIGINATOR—Remove this copy and forward balance of form including carbons intact for filing.

(6) Secured Party Copy ORIGINATOR—Remove this copy and forward balance of form including carbons intact for filing.

APPENDIX M

AGREEMENT NOT-TO-COMPETE

THIS AGREEMENT is made this 1st day of December, 19XX, by and between Widgets International, Inc., a Wisconsin corporation, hereinafter referred to as "Company," and Joseph Seller, hereinafter referred to as "Seller."

1. Seller agrees that neither any corporation of which he is an officer, director, or stockholder, nor he himself individually, will for a period of three (3) years from the date of this agreement, directly or indirectly engage in any of the services performed by the Company, as an owner, employee, partner, stockholder or otherwise in the area defined below; nor will he aid or assist anyone else in that territory except an employee of Company, nor will he let his name be used in such a business.

2. Seller and Company agree that the area to be covered in said covenant shall be limited to Outagamie, Waupaca, Winnebago, and Brown Counties, all located in the State of Wisconsin.

3. In consideration of paragraphs 1 and 2 above, the Company agrees to pay Seller the sum of $36,000. This amount shall be paid in equal installments of $1,000 each on the 1st day of January, 19XX, and on the 1st day of every month thereafter until fully paid.

4. In the event of the death or incapacity of Seller, the payments shall be made to the personal representative of his estate.

5. This agreement shall be binding on and shall inure to the benefit of the successors, assigns, personal representatives, heirs and legatees of the parties.

The parties have executed this Agreement on the day and year first above written.

____

Joseph Seller

WIDGETS INTERNATIONAL, INC.

BY: ____________________________

Paul Purchaser, President

NOTE: In addition to the terms set forth above, language could be inserted relative to the legal consequences in the event of competition by Joe. These provisions could either provide liquidated damages and/or injunction.

WARNING: In the event that the liquidated damages are deemed a penalty, the provisions may be legally unenforceable.

INDEX

-I-

-L-

-M-

-N-